British Civilization

ROUTLEDGE

LONDON AND NEW YORK

British Civilization

An introduction

THIRD EDITION

■ John Oakland

First published in 1989
by Routledge
11 New Fetter Lane
London EC4P 4EE

Simultaneously published in the USA
and Canada
by Routledge
29 West 35t Street, New York
NY 10001

Second edition 1991
Third edition 1995
Reprinted 1996

*Routledge is an International
Thomson Publishing company*

Third edition © 1995 John Oakland

Text design: Barker/Hilsdon

Typeset in Sabon and Futura by
Florencetype Ltd, Stoodleigh, Devon

Printed and bound in Great Britain by
Biddles Ltd, Guildford and King's
Lynn

*British Library Cataloguing in
Publication Data*

A catalogue record for this book is
available from the British Library

*Library of Congress Cataloguing in
Publication Data*

Oakland, John
British civilization: an introduction
/John Oakland. — 3rd ed.
p. cm.
Includes bibliographical references
and index.

1. Great Britain–Civilization. I. Title.
DA110.025 1995   94–36499

ISBN 0–415–12258–9

Contents

List of plates	xii
List of figures	xiv
List of tables	xv
Preface and acknowledgements	xvi

Introduction   1

1 The country   11

Physical features	13
Climate	21
Agriculture, fisheries and forestry	23
Energy resources	28
Transport	31
Communications	25
Attitudes to the environment	36
Exercises	39

CONTENTS

2 The people 41

Early settlement to AD 1066 42
Growth and immigration to the twentieth century 45
Immigration in the twentieth century 50
Population movements in the twentieth century 55
Attitudes to Britishness and national identity 58
Exercises 63

3 Political institutions 65

English political history 66
The constitutional framework 73
The monarchy 76
The Privy Council 79
Parliament 80
The parliamentary electoral system (general
   elections) 85
The party-political system 89
Parliamentary procedure and legislation 95
The government 100
Parliamentary control of government 104
Attitudes to politics and politicians 106
Exercises 107

4 Local government 109

English local government history 111
The functions of local government 119
Attitudes to local government 124
Exercises 125

5 International relations   127

Foreign policy and defence	128
The Commonwealth	133
The European Union (EU)	135
Eire and Northern Ireland	140
Exercises	145

6 The legal system   147

English legal history	149
Sources of contemporary English law	150
The court system in England and Wales	152
Civil and criminal procedure in England and Wales	161
Punishment and law enforcement	168
The legal profession in England and Wales	173
Attitudes to the legal system	176
Exercises	177

7 Economic and industrial institutions   179

The modern economy: policies, structure and performance	182
Economic policy and performance since 1979	189
Social class, the workforce and employment	190
Financial institutions	197
Industrial and commercial institutions	202
Consumer protection	208
Attitudes to the economy and economic structure	209
Exercises	211

8 Social security, health and housing 213

Welfare history	215
Changing family and demographic structures	217
Social security	221
The National Health Service (NHS)	223
The personal social services	228
Housing	231
Attitudes to social security, health and housing	235
Exercises	237

9 Education 239

English school history	240
The present state school system	246
The independent (or private fee-paying) school sector	249
School organization and examinations	251
Higher education	255
Further and adult education	260
Attitudes to education	261
Exercises	263

10 The media 265

The print media	266
The broadcasting media	278
Media ownership and freedom of expression	286
Attitudes to the media	291
Exercises	292

11 Religion 293

Religious history	294
The Christian tradition	299
The non-Christian tradition	308
Cooperation among the churches	311
Religion in schools	312
Religious membership and observance	313
Attitudes to religion and morality	314
Exercises	316

12 Leisure, sports and the arts 317

Leisure activities	318
Sports	322
The arts	328
Attitudes to leisure, sports and the arts	332
Exercises	333

Bibliography	335
Suggested further reading	337
Index	343

Plates

Frontispiece: At the races

1.1	Welsh countryside	19
1.2	Barley fields in Devon, England	24
1.3	Agricultural crops in Ireland	25
2.1	On the way to work: commuters	56
2.2	A female crowd	57
3.1	The Houses of Parliament	82
3.2	Inside the House of Commons	86
4.1	Islington town hall, London	114
4.2	Manchester town hall	116
4.3	Britain's first Asian mayor: Rabindara Pathak at Ealing town hall, London, 1987	120
5.1	The Foreign and Commonwealth Office, Whitehall, London	132
6.1	Magistrates' court building, Peterborough	153
6.2	Inside the magistrates' court	154
6.3	The Old Bailey	157
6.4	Inside the Old Bailey	158
6.5	Law Courts	160

7.1	The Bank of England	198
7.2	Coal miners' demonstration, 1992	205
8.1	Hospital nurse	226
8.2	Woman with walking frame in local authority home for the elderly	229
8.3	Homeless men	235
9.1	Pupils of Harrow public school preparing for cricket	250
9.2	A science class in a state comprehensive school	252
9.3	Children in an inner city comprehensive school	253
10.1	*Daily Mirror* newspaper building, Central London	270
10.2	*Guardian* newspaper building, Docklands, London	271
10.3	Press photography and coverage: Althorp wedding, 1989	273
10.4	Newspaper rack	275
11.1	Anglican village church, Northamptonshire	300
11.2	At prayer: Catholic mass	305
11.3	Regent's Park mosque, London	310
12.1	Working men's club	321
12.2	Crowd of people at football match	323
12.3	Football match: Derby County vs. Queen's Park Rangers	324
12.4	Cricket in the city, Kennington estate, London	325
12.5	Cricket in the country, Kent	326

Figures

1.1	The British Isles	14
1.2	Highland and lowland Britain	17
1.3	The British regions	30
3.1	Ballot paper	85
3.2	The House of Commons	94
3.3	From bill to Act of Parliament	99
4.1	The British counties and regions	118
5.1	The European Union (1994)	137
6.1	Civil and criminal courts	152
6.2	A typical magistrates' court in action	164
6.3	A typical crown court in action	165
6.4	Criminal procedure	167
7.1	Inflation rate, 1980–94	191
7.2	Unemployment rate, 1977–94	196
9.1	The 1944 organization of state schools	244
9.2	The current state school system	248
9.3	The independent school sector	249
10.1	The structure of British broadcasting	287
11.1	Contemporary religious groups	298

Tables

2.1   Early settlement to AD 1066   44

2.2   Populations of major British cities (1991)   58

3.1   British governments and Prime Ministers
since 1945   90

3.2   General elections results, 1992   93

5.1   European Union Parliament: election results
(Britain), 1994   139

10.1   The main national newspapers (average daily
sales), 1994   269

Preface and acknowledgements

This book mainly examines institutional features of British civilization, although introductory chapters on the country and the people provide a wider background. It gives information on recent developments in Britain, and combines factual, descriptive and analytical approaches within a historical context. Contrasting critical views and the people's attitudes on institutions are presented, which should allow students to develop their own responses to British life.

A book of this type is necessarily indebted to many sources for its facts and statistics, to which acknowledgement is gratefully made (see Bibliography and Suggested further reading). Particular thanks are due to *Britain: An Official Handbook* (the current edition of which contains the latest information); *British Social Attitudes*, and Market and Opinion Research International (MORI).

Introduction

MOST OF THE FOLLOWING CHAPTERS examine the historical development and contemporary roles of central British institutions. Institutions are organizations which have been gradually constructed over varying periods of time and reflect established values and practices. They take many different forms and sizes, operate on both state and local levels, and may be public or private in character.

The major elements, like Parliament, monarchy, law and government, are concerned with state business. They have been conditioned by the military power, economic strength and imperial status of Britain's past. But there are other institutional structures, such as sports, religious groups, families, local government, neighbourhoods and the theatre, which take more localized and individualistic forms.

The 'British way of life' is largely determined by how people function within and react to institutions, whether negatively or positively. Institutions

are not remote abstractions, but affect individuals directly in their daily lives. The large number and variety of such organizations mean that there are many different 'ways of life', and all contribute to the diversity of contemporary British society.

Institutions are adaptable, provide frameworks for new situations, and their present roles may be very different from their original functions. The larger state institutions, like those concerned with political, legal and economic matters, have evolved slowly and pragmatically over the past thousand years, and within a unified Britain from 1707. Similar processes have formed British society generally, and change has mainly occurred through compromise within the law, rather than by radical upheaval.

These evolutionary characteristics have often been attributed to the allegedly insular and conservative mentalities of the island peoples who comprise the British Isles, with their supposed preference for traditional habits and structures. Although some influences have come from abroad, the absence of any successful foreign military invasion of Britain since the Norman Conquest of AD 1066 has allowed institutions to develop internally in distinctive ways. The resulting institutional principles, like religious beliefs and parliamentary democracy, have frequently either been imitated by other countries, or exported abroad through the creation of a colonial empire and a commercial need to establish worldwide markets for domestic products.

The gradual development of the British state and its empire was aided by an increasing military and economic strength. By the nineteenth century Britain had become a dominant world power and a united kingdom consisting of England, Wales, Scotland and Ireland. But the country has undergone considerable changes since the earlier imperial period and from the mid-twentieth century. Today it is a complex society in which diversity has produced problems as well as advantages.

Britain gives a surface impression of homogeneous behaviour, which largely corresponds to an English norm centred on the widespread influence of London. But there is also considerable heterogeneity, such as the cultural distinctiveness and separate identities of Wales, Scotland and Northern Ireland; demands for greater local autonomy in the English regions; disparities between affluent and economically depressed areas of the country, including the decay of inner-city locations; continuing debates on the positions of women, minority groups and ethnic communities; and campaigns for a variety of individual and collective rights.

Such features illustrate some of the present divisions in British society. They may partly derive from a 'North–South Divide', which is said to split Britain economically, socially and politically between the relatively deprived north and the relatively prosperous south. These differences also suggest a decline in the traditional respect for and deference to established authority, consensus views and national institutions. They indicate that the people are now more nonconformist and individualistic than in the past.

Indeed, a 1980 MORI/*Sunday Times* public opinion poll reported that the British felt they had become more aggressive (86 per cent); more selfish (76); less tolerant (67); less kind (58); less moral (70); less honest (72); and less polite (80). Critics argue that such findings are today reflected in increasing anti-social behaviour. They maintain that the tolerant civic image (based on individual liberty and a sense of community), which foreigners and the British often have of the country (rightly or wrongly), has suffered.

Pressures are consequently placed on institutions to reflect and respond to current differences more adequately. The performances of state and local institutions are vigorously debated in Britain, and many of them have been found wanting. Questions are asked as to whether the existing structures can satisfactorily cope with the needs and demands of contemporary life, and whether (and how) they might be reformed in order to operate more efficiently and responsively. Such questioning is also linked to debates about the nature of British national identity, and to the retreat from a post-war consensus (or agreement) among the major political parties on how the country should be organized socially and economically.

This domestic situation has been influenced by external pressures. Since the Second World War (1939–45), Britain has had to adjust with considerable difficulty to the consequences of a withdrawal from empire; a reduction in world status; a series of global economic recessions; increased competition from abroad; and the growth of a different geo-political world order. Britain has been forced into a reluctant search for a new identity and direction. It has moved from empire and the Commonwealth towards an economic and political commitment to Europe, mainly through membership of the European Union (EU). This impetus will inevitably increase as the EU develops further integrated institutions and policies.

In recent centuries, Britain has rarely considered itself to be part of mainland Europe. It has sheltered behind the barrier of the English Channel, and its outlook has been westwards and worldwide. Today the psychological and physical isolation from Europe is slowly changing, as illustrated by increased cooperation between Britain and other European countries and by the opening in 1994 of a Channel rail tunnel between England and France. But the relationship between Britain and its European partners continues to be difficult, and the new associations have been forced by circumstances and events, rather than wholeheartedly sought.

Despite such developments and more internal social diversity, there is still a conservatism in many areas of British life which regards change with suspicion. This attitude can result in a tension between the often enforced need for reform and a nostalgia for an assumed ideal past. It can cause difficulties for national progress and the evolution of institutions. Historical fact demonstrates that the past in Britain was not as idyllic as is sometimes imagined. But the myth and traditional patterns of behaviour still hold considerable force and attraction for many people.

Fundamental change does not come easily to old cultures such as Britain, and institutions (or the human beings who operate them) are frequently resistant to major alteration. The countries that avoid decline are those which are capable of political progress, social innovation, economic development and institutional reform. Critics maintain that Britain since the 1950s has not shown itself willing to face such a large-scale reassessment. It has instead avoided hard decisions; continued the tradition of pragmatic evolution; lurched from one economic crisis to another; revealed mismanagement at all levels of society; complacently persisted with its ancient institutions and ways of doing things; and ignored lessons that could have been learned from abroad.

It is argued that a long-term relative economic decline since the late nineteenth century has been joined to a political constitution and national mentality which cannot cope with the reality or needs of the post-industrial and culturally diverse society that Britain has now become. Much of this decline can be explained by long-term and global events which are not reversible. But critics insist that the country still suffers from structural and institutional defects, which need to be remedied by radical rethinking.

Britain does have its problems, in spite of greater opportunities and prosperity for most of its people. There is evidence of instability, such as widespread unemployment; economic difficulties; a gap between rich and poor; fear of crime and increased violence against persons and property; industrial change; inadequacies in some social institutions; alleged lack of governmental vision; political volatility; and a decline in national confidence, cohesion and identity.

But, despite the often lurid picture painted by some commentators and the popular media, these features do not mean that the essential fabric of society is necessarily falling apart. Particular ideological perspectives and a British capacity for self-denigration and complaint can encourage unbalanced, sensational views, and incidents may be exaggerated beyond their national importance. However, the existing problems warn against undue complacency.

There have in fact been considerable changes in recent years, and old assumptions about British life have been questioned. Conservative governments since 1979 have tried to reform institutional structures and promote new attitudes.

The term 'Thatcherism' (after the former Conservative Prime Minister, Margaret Thatcher) has been used to describe such developments. They have included the attempted reduction of the role of the state in national affairs and its replacement by 'free-market forces'; the creation of jobs through the 'market'; the restoration of economic stability and growth by control of inflation; the encouragement of competition, business activity and investment: cuts in taxes and public spending; privatization programmes by which state concerns are transferred to the private sector of the national economy; the reduction of the influence of the trade unions and some of the monopolistic professions; the creation of greater choice, accountability and higher standards in the educational, health and social security systems; and the attack upon an alleged local government inefficiency and monopoly. Conservative governments have urged people to be more responsible for their own affairs without automatic reliance on the state for support (the 'dependency culture'), and tried to persuade them to adopt more individual competitiveness and efficiency (the 'enterprise culture').

But changes effected by these policies, although substantial, have been addressed largely to economic organization rather than cultural reform. It is an open question whether, when tested by time, they will be fundamental and durable enough to substantially alter the face of British civilization, or the national mentality.

There has in fact been considerable resistance to some of the Conservative reforms, and a public wish for more interventionist policies in social areas of national life. *British Social Attitudes: 1988–89* concluded that 'British public opinion has actually become more alienated from many of the goals of an enterprise culture. To the extent that attitudes have moved, they have become less sympathetic to these central tenets of the Thatcher Revolution' (p. 121). A 1990 MORI opinion poll supported these finding by showing that 54 per cent of interviewees regarded themselves as 'socialists'; 34 per cent as 'Thatcherists'; and 12 per cent did not know.

Such views, repeated in later polls, have probably been influenced by a severe economic recession and consequent high unemployment from 1989 to 1993. They suggest that many British people still look to the state for support and provision in crucial social areas. Nevertheless, the broad thrust of Thatcherite policies has continued under the Conservative Prime Minister John Major, and the future of such reforms depends upon the continuance of the Conservatives in office.

Opposition to some government programmes and acceptance of others demonstrate that institutional change can occur in various, often interconnected, ways. Some institutions wither away because they are no longer used. Others are reformed internally as new situations arise. Additional forces which contribute to change are opposition political parties parading their alternative programmes; interest or pressure groups exerting their influence upon formal decision-makers; grassroots movements protesting at some action or lack of action; campaigns by the media to promote reform or uncover scandals; and the weight of public opinion for or against official plans. However, government initiatives are the single most important factor in determining institutional change as governments implement their policies or respond to events. Such reforms directly affect ordinary people.

The British allow their governments a great deal of power in the running of the country. But there is a limit to their tolerance. Most politicians are sensitive to the views of the people, since their hold upon political power is dependent upon the electorate at each general election. Governments usually govern with at least one eye on public opinion, and generally attempt to gain acceptance for their policies. Even the Conservative government, which has won the last four general elections of 1979, 1983, 1987 and 1992, has sometimes had to move cautiously, and suffered setbacks in some of its programmes. But critics argue that there is now a gap between government policies and popular culture, and that the length of Conservative rule since 1979 has produced a staleness and lack of direction in current British life.

The British assume, rightly or wrongly, that they have an individual independence and liberty within the framework of the national institutions, and are quick to voice disapproval if their interests are threatened. Protest is a natural and traditional reaction, as well as being a safety valve against more serious social and political disruption. But dissension may be neutralized by the promise of reform, or ignored by the central government. Adequate responses may not come from the authorities, and there is always the danger of more serious conflict. However, peaceful evolution continues to characterize most of British life, and gradualist changes reflect the diverse nature of the society and its attitudes.

But the British do have a healthy cynicism about their institutions and political leaders. *British Social Attitudes: 1988–89* suggested that

> the British electorate is far from being compliant or deferential. For all Britain's political and social stability over the years, and despite the obvious pride its people have in the system of government, the British reveal an uncompromisingly irreverent and critical streak ... The public's trust in the pillars of the British establishment is at best highly qualified ... [they] seem intuitively to have discovered that the surest protection against disillusionment with their public figures and powerful institutions is to avoid developing illusions about them in the first place.
>
> (*British Social Attitudes: 1988–89*, pp. 121–2)

The British today are trying to cope with different cultural and economic realities than those of the past. But they appear to lack the traditional national certainties. They have also lost the benefits of their first industrial revolutions in the late eighteenth and nineteenth centuries, such as cheap raw materials, cheap labour and an uncompetitive world market. The old pragmatic methods of innovation, which illustrate the British tendency to muddle through difficulties without long-term planning or fundamental reform, may no longer be sufficient for a very different era. Yet, in the past, these evolutionary characteristics have revealed an instinct for survival on institutional, individual and national levels. They have also enabled institutions and the British people to adapt successfully to new conditions.

■ **Explain and examine the following terms:**

tolerance	insular	grassroots	pragmatic
deference	conservative	inner city	diversity
norm	recession	heterogeneous	ethnic
nostalgia	homogeneous	post-industrial	autonomy
myth	consensus	nonconformist	evolution

■ **Write short essays on the following questions:**

1 Try to define the term 'institutions', and examine its possible usages.

2 What are some of the characteristics that you would associate with the British people and their society? Why?

Chapter 1

The country

- Physical features   13
- Climate   21
- Agriculture, fisheries and forestry   23
- Energy resources   28
- Transport   31
- Communications   35
- *Attitudes to the environment*   36
- *Exercises*   39

T HE COUNTRY'S FULL TITLE for constitutional and political cal purposes is the United Kingdom of Great Britain and Northern Ireland, although the short terms 'UK' and 'Britain' are normally used for convenience. It is part of that group of islands, described geographically as the British Isles, which lie off the north-west coast of continental Europe. The mainlands of England, Scotland and Wales form the largest island, and are known politically as Great Britain. Northern Ireland shares the second-largest island with the Republic of Ireland (Ireland or Eire), which is politically independent and not part of the United Kingdom. Other smaller islands, such as Anglesey, the Orkneys, the Shetlands, the Hebrides, the Isle of Wight and the Isles of Scilly, lie off the coasts and are also included in the British political union.

But the Isle of Man in the Irish Sea and the Channel Islands off the French west coast are not part of the United Kingdom. They are self-governing Crown Dependencies which have a historical relationship with the British Crown, and possess their own independent legal systems, legislatures and administrative structures. However, the British government is responsible for their defence and foreign relations, and can interfere if good administration is not maintained.

Britain is often discussed and divided up according to 'regions'. This term can mean several things, such as political and geographical identification; assistance and development aid areas; and the provision of services like gas, water, electricity and health to specific places. It should not be confused with formal local government structures (except for Scotland where counties are called regions), and is often based, as in figure 1.3, on former economic planning regions. (See also figure 4.1 in chapter 4 for local government counties and regions.)

'Regionalism', as a cultural factor, is important in British life.

It illustrates a sense of local identity and community, which tends to become stronger with increasing distance from London. It may also reflect a reduction in the influence of central government on local populations, and a determination to assert individual liberty and choice.

Physical features

Historically, Britain's physical features have influenced human settlement, population movements, military conquest and political union. They have also conditioned the location and exploitation of industry, transport systems, agriculture, fisheries, woodlands, energy supplies and communications. Today they continue to influence such activities, and are tied to public concerns about pollution and the quality of the natural environment.

Britain's geographical position is marked by 0° longitude, which passes through the international time zone of Greenwich east of London; by latitude 50°N in south-west England; and by latitude 60°N across the Shetlands. Britain thus lies within only 10° of latitude, and has a relatively small and compact size when compared with some other European countries. Yet it also possesses a great diversity of rural landscape and contrasting physical features, which surprises those visitors who expect a mainly urban and industrialized country. The many beauty spots and recreation areas, such as the ten National Parks in England and Wales and areas of natural beauty in Scotland and Northern Ireland, may be easily reached without a great expenditure of time or effort.

Britain's physical area amounts to some 93,025 sq miles (240,842 sq km). Most of this is land, and the rest comprises inland water such as lakes and rivers. England has 50,052 sq miles (129,634 sq km), Wales has 7,968 (20,637), Scotland has 29,799 (77,179), and Northern Ireland has 5,206 (13,438). England is therefore much larger than the other countries and has a bigger population. These factors explain the English dominance in British history.

FIGURE 1.1 The British Isles

The distance from the south coast of England to the most northerly tip of the Scottish mainland is 600 miles (960 km), and the English east coast and the Welsh west coast are 300 miles (480 km) apart at their widest points. These relatively small distances have in recent centuries aided the development of political union and communications. They have also contributed to standardized social, economic and institutional norms. But, prior to the mid-eighteenth century, there were considerable obstacles to this progress, such as difficult terrain and inadequate transportation.

Britain's varied physical characteristics are the result of a long geological and climatic history. Over time, earth movements have caused mountain chains to rise from the sea-bed to form the oldest parts of Britain. Warmer, sub-tropical periods intervened between the earth movements, and large swamp forests covered most lowland zones. These, in their turn, were buried by sand, soil and mud, so that the forests' fossil remains became the coal deposits of modern Britain. Later, the climate alternated between warmth and sub-Arctic temperatures. During these latter Ice Age periods, ice-sheets or glaciers moved southwards over most of the British Isles, leaving only southern England free from their effects.

The raised land areas were gradually worn away by weathering agents such as wind, ice and water. This process rounded off the mountain peaks and moved waste materials into lowland zones, where they were pressed into new rocks and where the scenery became softer and less folded than the mountain areas. The geological and weathering changes shaped the details of valleys and plains, and dictated the siting of Britain's major rivers, such as the Clyde, Forth and Tweed in Scotland; the Tyne, Trent, Humber, Severn and Thames in England and Wales; and the Bann and Lagan in Northern Ireland.

Natural forces have also affected the coastlines as the seas have moved backwards and forwards over time. Parts of the coastal area have either sunk under the sea or risen above it. These processes continue today, particularly on the English east and south coasts. The sea's retreat has created chalk and limestone uplands, and sand beaches along the coasts, while erosion has resulted in the loss of land in some places.

Britain was originally part of the European mainland. But the melting of the glaciers in the last Ice Age caused the sea level to rise. The country was separated from the continent by the North Sea at its widest, and by the English Channel at its narrowest, points. The shortest stretch of water between the two land masses is now the Strait of Dover between Dover in southern England and Calais in France (20 miles, 32 km).

There are many bays, inlets, peninsulas and estuaries along the coasts, and most places in Britain are less than 75 miles (120 km) from some kind of tidal water. Tides on the coasts and in inland rivers can cause flooding in many parts of the country. Substantial financial resources are needed by water companies and local authorities, particularly on the English east and south coasts, to enable them to construct defences against this threat. For example, a London flood barrier was completed in 1984 across the river Thames.

The coastal seas are not deep and are often less than 300 feet (90 m) because the greater part of the British Isles lies on the Continental Shelf, or raised sea-bed adjacent to the mainland. The warm North Atlantic Current (Gulf Stream) heats the sea and air as it travels from the Atlantic Ocean across the Shelf. This gives the British Isles a more temperate climate than would otherwise be the case, considering their northerly position. It also influences the coastal waters, which are important fish breeding grounds, on which the national fishing industry is considerably dependent.

Britain's physical relief can be divided into highland and low-land Britain (see figure 1.2). The highest ground is mainly in the north and west. Most of the lowland zones, except for the Scottish Lowlands and central areas of Northern Ireland, are in the south and east of the country, where only a few points reach 1,000 feet (305 m) above sea level.

The north and west consist of the older, harder rocks created by the ancient earth movements, which are generally unsuitable for cultivation. The south and east comprise younger, softer materials formed by weathering processes, which have produced fertile soils and good agricultural conditions. Much of the lowland area, except for regions of urban settlement and industrial usage, has

1 North-West Highlands	3 Southern Uplands	5 Antrim Mountains	8 Pennines
2 Central Highlands (Grampians)	4 Sperrin Mountains	6 Mourne Mountains	9 Peak District
		7 Cumbrian Mountains	10 Welsh Massif (Cambrians)

FIGURE 1.2 Highland and lowland Britain

been cultivated and farmed. It is largely composed of fields, which are normally divided by fences or hedges. Animal grazing land in upland zones is separated either by moorland or stone walls.

England

England (population 48,208,000) consists largely of undulating or flat lowland countryside, with some upland areas in the north and south-west. But lower hill ranges also stretch over much of the country, such as the North Yorkshire Moors, the Cotswolds, the Kent and Sussex Downs and the Chiltern Hills. In the east of the country are the low-lying flat lands of the Norfolk Broads, the Suffolk Marshes, and the Lincolnshire and Cambridgeshire Fens.

The upland zones are marked by the Cheviot Hills (between England and Scotland); the north-western mountain region of the Lake District and the Cumbrian Mountains; the northern plateau belt of the Pennines forming a backbone across north-west England; the Peak District at the southern reaches of the Pennines; and the south-western plateau of Devon and Cornwall.

The heaviest population concentrations centre on the largest towns and cities, such as London and in south-east England generally; the West Midlands region around Birmingham; the Yorkshire cities of Leeds, Bradford and Sheffield; the north-western industrial area around Liverpool and Manchester; and the north-east region comprising Newcastle and Sunderland.

Wales

Wales (population 2,891,000) is mainly a highland country, with long stretches of moorland plateau, hills and mountains, which are often broken by deep valleys, such as those created by the rivers Dee, Wye and Severn. This upland mass, which contains the Cambrian Mountains and is sometimes known as the Welsh Massif, descends eastwards into the English counties of Shropshire and Hereford and Worcester. The highest mountains are in Snowdonia in the north-west, where the dominant peak is that of Snowdon (3,560 feet, 1,085 m).

PLATE 1.1   Welsh countryside *(Brenda Prince/Format)*

The lowland zones are restricted to the narrow coastal belts and to the lower parts of the river valleys in south Wales, where two-thirds of the Welsh population live. The chief urban concentrations of people and industry are around the bigger southern cities, such as the capital Cardiff, Swansea and Newport, and to a lesser extent in the north-east of the country. In the past, the highland nature of Wales has hindered conquest, agriculture and the settlement of people.

Scotland

Scotland (population 5,107,000) may be divided into three main areas. The first is the North-West and Central Highlands

(Grampians), together with a large number of islands off the west and north-east coasts. These areas are thinly populated, but comprise half the country's land mass. The second is the Central Lowlands, which contain one-fifth of the land area but three-quarters of the Scottish population, most of the industrial and commercial centres, and much of the cultivated land. The third is the Southern Uplands, which cover a number of hill ranges stretching towards the border with England.

The Highlands, with their inland lochs and fiord coastlines, and the Southern Uplands are now mainly smooth, rounded areas since the originally jagged mountains formed by earth movements have been worn down over time. The highest point in the Central Highlands is Ben Nevis (4,406 feet, 1,342 m), which is also the highest place in Britain.

The main population concentrations are around the administrative centre and capital of Edinburgh; the commercial and industrial area of Glasgow; and the regional centres of Aberdeen (an oil industry city) and Dundee. The climate, isolation and harsh physical conditions in much of Scotland have made conquest, settlement and agriculture difficult.

Northern Ireland

Northern Ireland (population 1,594,000) has a north-eastern tip which is only 13 miles (21 km) from the Scottish coast, a fact that has encouraged both Irish and Scottish migration in the past. Since the partition of Ireland in 1921, Northern Ireland has had a 303-mile (488-km) border in the south and west with the Republic of Ireland. It has a rocky coastline in the north, a south-central fertile plain, and mountainous areas in the west, north-east and south-east. The south-eastern Mourne Mountains include the highest peak, Slieve Donard, which is 2,796 feet high (853 m). Lough Neagh (147 sq miles, 381 sq km) is Britain's largest freshwater lake, and lies at the centre of the country.

Most of the large towns, like the capital Belfast, are situated in valleys which spread out from the Lough. Belfast is located at the mouth of the river Lagan, and has the biggest population concentration. But Northern Ireland generally has a sparse and scattered population, and is a largely rural country with good agricultural land in parts of the central plain.

Climate

Temperature

The relative smallness of the country and the widespread influences of a warm sea and westerly winds mean that there are no extreme contrasts in temperature throughout Britain. The climate is mainly temperate, but with variations between coolness and mildness. Altitude modifies temperatures, so that higher ground is colder than low-lying land. Much of Scotland and upland areas of Wales and England are therefore cool in summer and cold in winter compared with most of England.

Temperatures rarely reach 32°C (90°F) in the summer or fall below −10°C (14°F) in the winter. But there are differences between north and south. The average monthly temperature in the Shetlands ranges from 3°C (37°F) during the winter months to 11°C (52°F) in the summer months. The corresponding measurements for the Isle of Wight are 5°C (41°F) and 16°C (61°F). There may be exceptions to these average figures throughout the year and throughout the country.

Rainfall

The main factors affecting the amount of British rainfall are (1) the depressions, or low-pressure areas, which travel eastwards across the Atlantic Ocean; (2) the prevailing south-westerly winds throughout much of the year; (3) the exposure of the western coasts to the Atlantic Ocean; and (4) the fact that most of the highest ground lies in the west.

As a result, the heaviest annual rain falls in the west and north (over 60 inches, 1,600 mm), with an autumn or winter maximum. The high ground in the west protects the lowlands of the south and east, so that annual rainfall here is moderate (30 inches, 800 mm), with a slight summer maximum. The total national rainfall average is over 40 inches (1,100 mm) annually; March to June tend to be the driest months; September to January the wettest; and drought conditions are infrequent, although they do occur and can cause problems for farmers, the water companies and consumers.

Low-pressure systems may produce very variable weather. They normally pass over the northern British Isles, and south-westerly winds have a strong influence for much of the year. The result can be windy, wet and unstable conditions. But high-pressure systems, which also occur throughout the year, are relatively stable and move more slowly, producing light winds and generally settled weather. This pattern can result in fine and dry effects, both in winter and summer.

Sunshine

The amount of sunshine in Britain varies between regions. It decreases from south to north; inland from the coastal belts; and with altitude. In summer, the daily average sunshine varies from five hours in northern Scotland to eight hours on the Isle of Wight. In winter, it averages one hour in northern Scotland, and two hours on the English south coast.

These average statistics indicate that Britain is not a particularly sunny country, although there are periods of relief from the general greyness. The frequent cloud-cover over the British Isles is a complicating factor, so that even on a hot summer's day there may be little sunshine breaking through the clouds. This can give humid, sticky conditions.

Such climatic features give the British weather its changeability and what some regard as its stimulating variety. There are often discrepancies between weather forecasts and the actual results, and words such as 'changeable' and 'unsettled' are generously employed. The unpredictable weather is virtually a national institution, a topic of daily conversation, and for some a conditioning factor in the national character. The British tend to think that they live in a more temperate climate than is actually the case. But many escape abroad in both winter and summer.

Agriculture, fisheries and forestry

Agriculture

Britain has had a long agricultural history spread over a series of revolutions in farming methods. Today agriculture (including horticultural products such as apples, berries, flowers and vegetables) is an important industry, and covers much of the country. It is highly productive and efficient with mechanized and specialized farming, and technological advances have increased crop and animal yields.

Soils vary in quality from the thin, poor ones of highland Britain to the rich, fertile land of low-lying areas in eastern and southern England. The climate usually allows a long, productive growing season without undue drought or extreme cold. But weather conditions can create problems for farmers, because of droughts, or when there is too much rain and too little sunshine at ripening time.

There are some 242,000 farm units, varying in size from one-man farms to huge business concerns, and many of them are owner-occupied. They use some 77 per cent of the total land area, although farming land is being increasingly used for building and recreational purposes. Only some 500,000 people, some 2.3 per cent of the national workforce, are engaged in farming. But agriculture provides nearly two-thirds of Britain's food requirements, which reduces its reliance upon imports, and allows it to export a range of food products.

Half of the country's full-time farms specialize in dairy farming, beef cattle and sheep herds. Dairy herds and milk yields have increased, and about two-thirds of beef consumption now comes from national resources. The long-established tradition of sheep farming, on which Britain's economic prosperity was once based, also continues.

PLATE 1.2 Barley fields in Devon, England *(Ken Lambert/Barnaby)*

Some farms concentrate on pig production, particularly in eastern and northern England, and in Northern Ireland. The poultry meat and egg industries are also widespread, and have increased their production levels in recent years, due largely to intensive 'factory farming', so that Britain is now almost self-sufficient in these foodstuffs.

Most of the other farms tend to specialize in arable crops, and have increased their production, despite occasional bad harvests. Root crops, like potatoes, sugar beet and vegetables, are widely cultivated, but mainly in southern and eastern England and in eastern Scotland. Cereal or grain crops, such as wheat, barley, oats and oilseed rape, are grown in many areas, but chiefly in the eastern regions of England.

PLATE 1.3 Agricultural crops in Ireland *(Joanne O'Brien/Format)*

The agricultural industry is a well-organized interest group. But some farmers do have problems in surviving and making a profit because of high commodity prices, high rents for tenanted farms, increased costs, bad harvests and a lack of capital investment.

The Common Agricultural Policy (CAP) of the European Union (EU), which accounts for some 50 per cent of the EU's total budget, has also affected British farmers. The aims of the CAP are to increase agricultural productivity and efficiency; stabilize the market by ensuring regular supplies of essential foodstuffs; give farmers a reasonable standard of living and return for their work by providing them with subsidies; and to produce goods at fair prices. The CAP sets minimum guaranteed prices for food products, like wheat, beef, eggs and butter, by operating a price support system, and also standardizes the quality and size of produce.

The British attitude to the CAP has been negative. Critics argue that it is unwieldy, bureaucratic and open to fraud. It can result in surplus foodstuffs which have to be stored at great expense. British farming and consumers suffer because prices have risen to accommodate other EU farmers. Farmers have had to curb the production of certain goods under EU quota systems in order to become less competitive, at a time when the country could be aiming for self-sufficiency in cheap agricultural produce. The set-aside programme, whereby farmers are paid to divert their activities away from agricultural production, has also contributed to a decline in some farming in recent years.

British governments have kept up pressure on the EU to reform the CAP, with some success. The Conservatives argue that supply and demand should reflect the real needs of the market, rather than concentrating solely on production, and that budgetary discipline should be improved by cutting support levels and subsidies. High EU subsidies and farm prices have concerned agricultural nations outside the EU. Subsidies will now be reduced in an attempt to cut expense, reflect market forces, permit greater access to the EU by foreign countries, and protect the environment.

Fisheries

Britain is one of Europe's leading fishing nations, and operates in continental waters, the North Sea, the Irish Sea and the Atlantic. The fishing industry is important to the national economy, and has been centred on a number of ports around the British coasts.

However, employment in and income from fishing have declined substantially in recent years. This is due to the reduction in available fish stocks in European waters because of overfishing, and fluctuations in fish breeding patterns. Many fishermen have become unemployed, and traditional fishing towns, such as Grimsby and the Scottish ports, have suffered. But the fishing industry still accounts for some 55 per cent of Britain's fish consumption. The number of fishermen is now about 17,000, with some 5,000 occasionally employed and about three jobs in associated occupations for every one fisherman.

The fishing industry has also been affected by EU and British government policies. These insist on the need to conserve fish resources and prevent overfishing. Zones have been established in which fishermen may operate. EU countries and some non-members can fish in specified areas up to Britain's 6-mile (10-km) fishing limit. Quota systems are in force inside and beyond the zones in order to restrict fish catches to prescribed amounts. British government measures to limit the time fishing vessels spend at sea will further restrict employment. These EU and government policies have affected the fishermen's old freedom of choice and operation.

The conflicting interests of EU members and other nations have gradually been improved by fishing agreements. But there are continuing problems, and critics argue that British governments have not acted in the best interests of their own national fisheries. Fishermen have been angry with government policies, the EU quotas and fishing zones, and their resulting loss of livelihood. But without fish conservation, there will be reduced supplies in the future.

The most important British fish catches are cod, haddock, whiting, herring, mackerel, plaice, sole and various types of shell-fish. They are caught by the 11,000 registered vessels of the fishing fleet. The fish-farming industry, unlike the reduced fishing trade elsewhere, is a large and expanding business, particularly in Scotland, and is chiefly concerned with salmon, trout and shellfish. Fish meal and fish oil are important by-products of the fishing industry, and fish imports continue. But the import of whale products has been banned since 1982 in order to protect the whale population.

Forestry

Woodlands cover an estimated 5.8 million acres (2.4 million hectares) of Britain, and comprise 7.3 per cent of England, 14.6 per cent of Scotland, 11.9 per cent of Wales and 5.2 per cent of Northern Ireland. Some 40 per cent of productive national forests are managed by the state Forestry Commission or government departments, and the rest by private owners. Some 42,000 people are employed in the state and private forestry industries, and 10,000 are engaged in timber processing.

However, these activities contribute only 15 per cent to the national consumption of wood and associated timber products, which means that the country is heavily dependent upon wood imports. The government has encouraged tree-planting programmes, particularly in Scotland, and allowed the sale of state woodlands to private owners in order to reduce public expenditure and to encourage productivity. New plantings, controlled felling, the expansion of timber industries and a profitable private sector may reduce Britain's present dependence upon imports and benefit the environment.

Forestry policy is supposed to take environmental and conservation factors into account in the development of timber facilities. But such aims are not always achieved, and there is disquiet about government programmes. Environmentalists campaign to increase tree planting and to preserve the quality of the existing woodlands, which in recent years have been badly affected by disease, unreasonable felling and substantial storm damage in October 1987 and January 1990.

Energy resources

Britain is rich in current and reserve energy resources. The main primary sources of energy are oil, natural gas, nuclear power, coal and water power, and the most important secondary source is electricity. Some 470,000 people (2.2 per cent of the national workforce) are employed in the business. But there are problems associated with these energy sources, and concerns about pollution and environmental damage.

Since 1980, Britain has produced an increased amount of its own energy needs and is largely self-sufficient. This is due to the growth in offshore oil and gas supplies, which make a crucial contribution to the national economy. Multinational companies operate under government licence and extract these fuels from the

North Sea fields, and gas and oil distribution throughout Britain is in the private sector. But, because of the government's policy of high extraction, oil and gas are decreasing from their maxima, and will provide substantial amounts only into the early years of the twenty-first century.

The development of existing provisions and the search for alternative sources of energy are therefore crucial for Britain and its economy. As oil and gas decline, the positions of coal and nuclear power will continue to be debated, and further research will be necessary into renewable energy forms such as solar, wind, wave and tidal power.

Coal is the country's richest natural energy resource, and until recently was extracted by a nationalized, or state, industry (British Coal). Britain produces most of its own coal requirements, but some still has to be imported, mainly to service coal-burning electricity power stations. In recent years, Conservative governments have tried to develop a competitive coal industry by reducing the workforce and closing uneconomic pits. After a period of intense trade union opposition to these policies, the workforce has been cut and mines have been closed down, although productivity and profitability have improved. But British coal remains expensive and suffers from a lack of demand from big consumers, such as power stations, which have moved to fuels like gas and oil. More pit closures are planned as the government moves towards privatization of the coal industry, and the future of coal is uncertain.

Most electricity generation and distribution has been privatized, and is mainly provided by coal-, gas- and oil-fired power stations, in addition to a small amount of hydroelectricity. But 25 per cent of electricity is produced by some 14 state-owned nuclear power stations of various types. The Conservative government had originally encouraged the development of nuclear power to satisfy Britain's energy requirements. After a period of delay, it is now likely that an expansion and partial privatization of the nuclear industry will occur. But problems exist about the potential ownership and operation of privatized nuclear power stations.

Alternative forms of renewable energy are becoming more important, and their potential exploitation more urgent. Electricity

NORTH SEA
OIL
AND GAS

1 Scotland
2 North
3 North-west
4 Yorkshire and Humberside
5 East Midlands
6 West Midlands
7 Wales
8 East Anglia
9 Greater London
10 South-east
11 South-west
12 Northern Ireland

● Nuclear power stations
x Coal- or oil-fired power stations
 Active coalfields
o Hydro-electric power stations

FIGURE 1.3 The British regions

generation by wind power is already operative, although there is public opposition to wind farms in the countryside. The possibilities of extracting heat from underground rocks are being explored, and the potential use of tidal and wave power is being examined on the Severn (Bristol) and Mersey (Liverpool) estuaries. Some solar energy is already provided, with plans for more research. These, and other, forms of renewable energy are crucial for Britain's future energy needs, particularly as environmental concerns grow.

But critics argue that insufficient work and research money is being devoted to potential alternative supplies; that too much reliance has been placed on nuclear power; that oil and gas have been wasted rather than extracted more slowly; and that not enough effort and finance have been spent on the coal industry. British domestic and industrial energy users are extravagant when compared to other European countries. Nevertheless, energy consumption has shown a decline recently because of better building insulation and the relative success of government savings campaigns. However, the provision of cheap and environmentally suitable energy for both domestic and industrial use will continue to be a problem for Britain.

Transport

Transport facilities in Britain are divided between the public and the private sectors of the national economy. Roads, railways, shipping and civil aviation account for most of the country's transport infrastructure.

Central and local government are responsible for the *road network* in Britain. Various types of public roads make up most of the highway system. The rest are motorways and trunk roads, which nevertheless carry most of the passenger traffic and heavy goods vehicles. Critics argue that Britain's roads are in bad condition and unable to handle the number of vehicles on them, leading to congestion and traffic jams. The planned expansion, repair and modernization of roads may be inadequate to meet the estimated future number of vehicles.

There are 25 million licensed vehicles, of which 21 million are private cars and light goods vehicles; 2.7 million commercial lorries; 688,000 motor cycles, scooters and mopeds; and 108,000 passenger vehicles (buses, coaches and taxis). Car transport is most popular and accounts for some 82 per cent of passenger mileage, while buses and coaches take 6 per cent. Britain has one of the highest densities of road traffic in the world, but also a relatively good safety record.

Private road haulage has a dominant position in the movement of inland freight. It accounts for some 80 per cent of the market, and lorries have become larger and more efficient. Critics have long campaigned for the transfer of road haulage to the railways and the publicly owned inland waterways (or canals), but to relatively little effect. At present the waterways are used for only a small amount of freight transportation because of the expense, although they are popular for recreational purposes and boating holidays.

Passenger services have declined in Britain because of increased private car usage. The Conservative government has deregulated bus operations, and most local bus companies have now been privatized, although some services are still operated by local government authorities. There has been a considerable expansion in private long-distance express coach services, which have attracted increased numbers of passengers because they are cheaper than the railways.

The world's first public passenger steam *railway* was opened in 1825 between Stockton and Darlington in north-east England. After more than 100 years of private operation, the railways became a state concern in 1947. British Rail accounts for some 6 per cent of total passenger mileage, but is now being privatized through a complicated sale of routes, management structures and equipment. This is causing public concern about the quality and availability of future rail services.

Rail passenger structures consist of a fast intercity network, linking all the main British centres; local trains which supply regional needs; and commuter services in and around the large areas of population, particularly London and south-east England.

Increased electrification of lines, and the introduction of fast diesel trains such as the InterCity 125s travelling at a maximum speed of 125 mph (201 km/h), have improved rail journeys considerably. But such speeds and facilities are still inferior to those in other countries. Many railway lines and trains are old and need replacing, and more electrification is required. There is much criticism by passengers, particularly in south-east England, about fare increases, overcrowding, delays, cancellations, staffing problems and poor services. Similar complaints are also made about the London Underground system (the Tube), which covers 254 miles (408 km) of railway line in the capital.

Critics argue that the inadequate state of Britain's railways is due to lack of government investment; Conservative policy that the rail system should be run on commercial lines, rather than as a public service; cuts in government subsidies to British Rail; and a failure to realize that rail could be part of a modernized and properly funded integrated transport system catering for passengers and freight. This latter point would arguably ease road congestion, satisfy demand and improve the environment.

The rail *Channel Tunnel*, privately operated by a French/British company (Eurotunnel), opened for commercial use in 1994. It is meant to improve passenger and freight travel between Britain and mainland Europe, although there are doubts about its pricing policy and competitiveness. The system has two main tunnels and a smaller service tunnel. It provides a drive-on, drive-off shuttle service on specially designed trains for cars, coaches and freight vehicles as well as passenger trains. The two terminals, Folkestone and Coquelles, are 31 miles (50 km) apart. Improved rail services from Folkestone to London should have been provided, but there have been delays and confusion over cost and policy. A high-speed connection has yet to be constructed, and there are no adequate facilities which would allow freight from the rest of Britain to cross London to the Tunnel.

Although there are over 300 *ports* in Britain, most are small concerns which do not handle much cargo or passenger traffic. However, the bigger ports such as Clyde, Dover, Tees, London,

Southampton, Grimsby, Hull, Felixstowe, Liverpool, Cardiff and Swansea service most of the country's trade and travel requirements. But there has been a big decline in work and labour since the great days of the ports in the past. The British shipping fleet has been greatly reduced from its peak year in 1975, owing to increased competition and a world shipping recession. The cargo market is now dominated by a small number of large private sector groups. But 77 per cent of Britain's overseas trade is still carried by sea, although passenger mileage has been much reduced. Both may decline further because of competition with the Channel Tunnel.

Britain's *civil aviation* system accounts for some 1 per cent of passenger mileage, and is in the private sector following the privatization of the former state airline, British Airways, in 1987. But there are other carriers, such as British Midland, Britannia Airways and Virgin Atlantic, which run scheduled and charter passenger services on domestic and international routes. All are controlled by the Civil Aviation Authority (CAA), an independent body which regulates the industry, including air traffic control, and which the government may privatize. The airlines also provide air cargo and freight services.

There are 137 licensed civil aerodromes in Britain, varying considerably in size. Heathrow and Gatwick Airports outside London are the largest. These airports, together with Stansted in south-east England, and Glasgow, Edinburgh and Aberdeen in Scotland, are owned and managed by the private sector British Airports Authority (BAA). They handle about 73 per cent of air passengers and 84 per cent of air cargo in Britain. Most of the other larger regional airports, such as Manchester, Birmingham, Luton, Belfast, Newcastle and East Midlands, are controlled by local authorities, and cater for the country's remaining passenger and cargo requirements.

Expansion of existing airports (particularly regional facilities), and the provision of new ones, will be necessary if Britain is to cope with increased consumer demand and competition from Europe. But such projects are very expensive and controversial because of environmental problems, such as construction work, noise and traffic. Some disquiet also exists about plane congestion in the skies over Britain, the efficiency of the air traffic system, and safety generally.

There is much public concern about the adequacy of Britain's transport systems and the lack of an integrated infrastructure of roads, railways and airlines. Improvements and expansion involve considerable expense, and Britain invests less in transport than any other European country. Government initiatives and investment are ideally needed to remedy the existing problems, not only domestically but also in terms of European trade and competition. Otherwise Britain could lose its important transport role, particularly in the air. But the Conservatives are reluctant to spend public money on transport, and are considering more private ownership and charges for road usage in order to cut costs.

Communications

Communications systems in Britain are also divided between the public and the private sectors. The main suppliers are the private British Telecom (BT) and the public Post Office.

British Telecom was privatized in 1984, and provides telephone and telecommunications systems domestically and internationally. There are 20 million domestic and 6 million business telephone subscribers. British Telecom is responsible for these as well as public payphones, telephone exchanges, telex connections and a range of other telecommunications services. Following privatization, there was considerable disquiet about British Telecom's performance. But most of the initial problems have now been solved and it is operating efficiently and profitably. The private company, Mercury, competes fiercely with British Telecom in the provision of telecommunications facilities, and the Conservative government plans to allow other competitors, such as cable networks.

The *Post Office*, founded in 1635, is still a state industry, following the failure of plans to privatize it in late 1994. It is responsible for collecting, handling and delivering some 61 million letters and parcels every day. It has sorting offices throughout the country with handling equipment, based on the postcodes which every address in Britain has. Local post offices throughout the country provide postal and other services, but there are fears that possible future privatization will reduce rural facilities and increase costs.

ATTITUDES

Attitudes to the environment

The physical face of Britain has become dirtier in both urban and rural areas. Such a small and densely populated country quickly feels the effects of environmental damage, and there are worries about pollution, the quality of the natural habitat, the use of energy resources and the safety of agricultural products. Opinion polls show that the state of the environment is high on Britons' list of concerns. But, while a majority of interviewees feel that protection of the environment should rate higher than economic growth, this does not lead to environmentally sensitive behaviour in all cases.

Awareness of these issues coincided with the rise of the Green movement in the 1980s, and the political parties adopted 'green' policies. The government has introduced Environmental Protection Acts and other measures to safeguard the environment, reduce pollution levels and penalize polluters. European Union legislation also makes very stringent demands.

But critics argue that government action is insufficient and often ineffective. Controls and protection are not strict enough; polluters can evade regulations, or suffer only minor fines; insufficient pressure is put on companies to modernize their facilities; tension exists between local and central government in environmental matters; and there is a conflict between the cost of protection and the government's privatization policies (like water, coal and electricity).

Air pollution in Britain is a considerable threat to people's health, particularly asthmatics and those suffering from respiratory problems. Although much pollution was reduced by Clean Air Acts in the 1950s and 1960s, poor air quality continues in much of the country. Factories and power stations discharge pollutants into the air, and these can also cause acid rain in Britain and abroad. Emissions from cars, buses and lorries seriously affect urban centres, despite the introduction of unleaded petrol and catalytic converters in new cars. More cars and road-building will make the situation worse unless there are stricter regulations, and the deterioration of public transport services will encourage more people to use private vehicles.

Increased freight and private transport has resulted in traffic congestion, noise, and damage to roads and property. Pressures upon the road system will increase as competition among road users grows, car ownership increases, and the European Union's internal market develops. The Channel Tunnel and its rail links have also attracted opposition from environmentalists, although landscaping and noise suppression have alleviated some damage. Fears have also been raised about safety and diseases such as rabies in the Tunnel.

Sea and beach pollution is partly caused by untreated sewage and toxic industrial waste being pumped directly into the sea by commercial companies, particularly the North Sea. Britain is committed to reducing such discharge levels, but pollution levels on a number of beaches still exceed European Union safety levels. Some rivers are seriously polluted by industrial waste, toxic agricultural fertilizers, pesticides and farm silage. This has caused public concern about the safety of drinking water, and the water companies have been pressurized to raise the quality. Many polluted rivers, lakes and estuaries have now been cleaned up, and more stringent controls of the oil and shipping industries in the North Sea have also been instituted to prevent pollution.

Problems have been experienced with the exploitation of energy resources, such as expense, capacity and availability, as well as environmental concerns about the burning of fossil fuels (coal, oil and gas), and the damage to the countryside caused by new developments. Nuclear expansion was halted briefly because of public opposition to nuclear facilities, the danger of radioactive leaks, the reprocessing of nuclear waste at the Thorp and Sellafield plants in north-west England, and the dumping of radioactive waste. There is still much debate about the future of nuclear power.

Considerable public worry surrounds the agricultural industry because of its widespread use of fertilizers and pesticides, its methods of animal feeding, and the effects of intensive farming on the environment. Much hedgerow, which is important for many forms of animal and vegetable life, has been lost in recent years as fields have become bigger and farming more mechanized. The quality and standards of food products, particularly those concerned with intensive farming techniques, are of concern. This has led in some cases to a drop in demand and consequent hardship for farmers. Yet the impact upon consumers of organic farming in Britain has been relatively small, largely because of the high cost of such goods.

■ **Explain and examine the following terms:**

Britain	Heathrow	InterCity 125	Post Office
weathering	Highland Britain	Lough Neagh	Ben Nevis
cereal	Welsh Massif	horticulture	tidal
CAP	earth movements	the Tube	drought
Eire	British Telecom	postcodes	Greenwich

■ **Write short essays on the following questions:**

1   Does Britain have an energy crisis? If so, why?

2   Examine the impact of Britain's membership of the European Union upon its agricultural and fisheries industries.

3   What are the reasons for environmental concerns in Britain?

Chapter 2

The people

■ Early settlement to AD 1066   42

■ Growth and immigration
  to the twentieth century   45

■ Immigration in the
  twentieth century   50

■ Population movements
  in the twentieth century   55

■ *Attitudes to Britishness
  and national identity*   58

■ *Exercises*   63

THE BRITISH ISLES have attracted settlers and immigrants throughout most of their history. The contemporary British are consequently composed of people from worldwide origins. They are mainly divided into the English, Scots, Welsh and Irish, who have national identities derived from early settlement and invasion movements into the country. But there are also immigrant minorities with their own cultures who have come to Britain over the centuries. Even the English language, which binds most of these people together linguistically, is a mixture of Germanic, Romance and other world languages. This historical development has created a contemporary society with multinational and multiracial characteristics. But it also raises questions about the meaning of 'Britishness'.

Early settlement to AD 1066

There is no accurate picture of what the early settlement of Britain was actually like. Historians and archaeologists are constantly revising traditional theories about the gradual growth of the country as new evidence comes to light.

The earliest human bones found (1994) in Britain are 500,000 years old. The first people were Palaeolithic (Old Stone Age) nomads from mainland Europe, who were characterized by their primitive use of stone implements. They travelled to Britain by land and sea, especially at those times when the country was joined to the European land mass.

Later settlers, who had more sophisticated talents in stone carving, came from Europe and the Mediterranean region in the Mesolithic and Neolithic (New Stone Age) periods between 8300 and 2000 BC. Some historians argue that Neolithic groups from the Iberian area, who populated south-west England, Ireland, Wales, the Isle of Man and western Scotland, are the oldest large sections of British society, whose descendants live today in the same western parts. Relatives of these peoples came from north-central Europe, and settled in eastern Britain. The Neolithic groups built large stone and wood monuments, such as Stonehenge, and later arrivals introduced a Bronze Age culture into the country.

Between 800 and 200 BC there was a movement of Celtic peoples into Britain from mainland Europe, who brought an Iron Age civilization with them. This Celtic population was then overcome by Belgic tribes (also of Celtic origin) around 200 BC when the first major armed invasions of Britain took place. The Belgic tribes (or Britons) were in their turn subjected to a series of Roman military attacks from 55 BC.

The effective Roman occupation of much of Britain, which lasted for 367 years from AD 43, was broken by the arrival of Germanic Angles and Saxons from north-central Europe in AD 410. They pushed the existing population westwards, and the British Isles became divided into mainly Anglo-Saxon zones in England, with Celtic areas in Wales, Scotland and Ireland. All these regions were to suffer from the Scandinavian military invasions of the eighth and ninth centuries AD.

This early history was completed when the Anglo-Saxons were defeated by French-Norman invaders at the Battle of Hastings in AD 1066, and England was subjected to Norman rule. The Norman Conquest was an important watershed in English history; greatly influenced the English people and their language; marked the last successful foreign military invasion of the country; and initiated many of the social and institutional frameworks, like a feudal system, which were to characterize future British society. However, Celtic civilizations continued in Wales, Scotland and Ireland.

People have entered the British Isles from the south-west, the east and the north. But settlement was often hindered by climatic and geographical obstacles, particularly in the north and west, so that many newcomers tended to concentrate initially in southern England, and habitation patterns were not uniform over all of Britain at the same time. Despite some intermixture between the various settlers, there were racial differences between the English and the people of Ireland, Wales and Scotland, as well as varying identities between groups in the English regions. It is this mixture, increased by later immigration, which has produced the present racial and national diversity in Britain.

The early settlement and invasion movements substantially affected the developing fabric of British life, and formed the first foundations of the modern state. The newcomers often imposed their cultures on the existing society, as well as adopting some of the native characteristics. Today there are few British towns which lack any physical evidence of the successive changes. They also profoundly influenced social, legal, economic, political, agricultural and administrative institutions, and contributed to the evolving language.

TABLE 2.1 Early settlement to AD 1066

500,000–8300 BC	Palaeolithic (Old Stone Age)
8300 BC	Mesolithic
4000 BC	Neolithic (New Stone Age)
2000 BC	Beaker Folk (Bronze Age)
800 BC	Celts (Iron Age)
200 BC	Belgic tribes
55 BC	The Romans
AD 410	The Anglo-Saxons
8th and 9th centuries	The Scandinavians
AD 1066	The Norman Conquest

There are no realistic population figures for early Britain. However, archaeological evidence suggests that the nomadic life of groups of up to 20 people gradually ceased, and was replaced by more permanent settlements of up to a few hundred inhabitants. It has been estimated that the English population during the Roman

occupation was about 1 million. By the Norman period, the eleventh-century Domesday Book showed an increase to 2 million. The Domesday Book was the first systematic attempt to evaluate England's wealth and population, mainly for taxation purposes.

Growth and immigration to the twentieth century

Britain grew gradually to statehood after 1066, largely through the political unification of England, Wales, Ireland and Scotland under the English Crown. This process was accompanied by fierce and bloody conflicts between the four nations, which resulted in lasting tensions and bitterness.

But immigration from abroad also continued over the centuries due to factors such as religious and political persecution, trade, business and employment prospects. Immigrants have had a significant impact on British society. They have contributed to financial institutions, commerce, industry and agriculture, and influenced artistic, cultural and political developments. However, immigrant activity and success have also provoked jealousy, discrimination and violence from the native population.

Britain's growth was conditioned by two major events: first, a series of agricultural changes, and second, a number of later industrial revolutions. Agricultural expansion started with the Saxons who cleared the forests, cultivated crops and introduced inventions and equipment which remained in use for centuries. Their open-field system of farming (one field being unproductive in alternate years) slowly gave way to widespread sheep-herding and wool production. Finally, in the period between 1760 and 1845, most agricultural land was enclosed (divided up into hedged fields for cultivation), leaving room for animals to graze in other areas.

Britain was expanding as an agricultural and commercial nation from the eleventh century, as well as developing a manufacturing base. Immigration was characterized by agricultural, financial and commercial skills. Jewish money-lenders entered Britain with the Norman Conquest, and their financial talents later passed to Lombard bankers from northern Italy. The Lombard connection is today commemorated in Lombard Street in the City of London. This financial expertise helped to create greater wealth, and Britain's trade and commerce were influenced by the merchants of the mainly German Hansa League, who set up their trading posts in London and on the east coast of England. Around 1330, Dutch and Flemish weavers arrived, and by the end of the fifteenth century had helped to transform England into a major nation of sheep farmers, cloth producers and textile exporters. Further immigration in the fourteenth century introduced specialized knowledge in a variety of manufacturing trades.

Some immigrants stayed only for short periods. Others remained and adapted themselves to British society, while preserving their own cultural and ethnic identities. Newcomers were often encouraged to settle in Britain, and the policy of using immigrant expertise continued in later centuries. But foreign workers had no legal rights, and early immigrants, such as Jews and the Hansa merchants, could be frequently and summarily expelled from the country.

Agricultural and commercial developments were reflected in changing population concentrations. From Saxon times to around 1800, Britain had an agriculturally based economy, and some 80 per cent of the people lived in villages in the countryside. Settlement was mainly concentrated in the south and east of England, where the rich agricultural regions of East Anglia and Lincolnshire had the greatest population densities. During the fourteenth century, however, the steady increase of people was halted by a series of plagues, and numbers did not start to increase again for another 100 years.

As agricultural production moved into sheep farming and its associated clothing manufactures, larger numbers of people settled around woollen ports, such as Bristol on the west coast and coastal towns in East Anglia. Others moved to inland cloth-producing areas in the West Country, the Cotswolds and East Anglia, and contributed to the growth of market towns. The south midland and eastern English counties had the greatest densities of people, and the population at the end of the seventeenth century has been estimated at 5.5 million for England and Wales, and 1 million for Scotland.

Meanwhile, political and military attempts had long been made by England to unite Wales, Scotland and Ireland under the English Crown. English monarchs tried to conquer or ally themselves with these other countries as a protection against threats from within the British Isles and from continental Europe, as well as for increased power and possessions.

Ireland was attacked in the twelfth century. The later colonization and partial control of Ireland by the English became a source of hatred between the two countries. But it also led to Irish settlements in London and west-coast ports such as Liverpool. Ireland became part of the United Kingdom in 1801 but, after unrest in the nineteenth and twentieth centuries, was divided in 1921 into the two political units of the independent Republic of Ireland and Northern Ireland (which remains part of the UK).

Wales lost its independence in 1285 after years of bloody conflict with the English and, apart from a period of freedom in 1402–7, was eventually united with England by an Act of Union in 1536.

The English also tried to conquer Scotland by military force, but were repulsed at the Battle of Bannockburn in 1314. Scotland was then to remain independent until the political union between the two countries in 1707, when the creation of Great Britain (England, Wales and Scotland) took place. However, Scotland and England had shared a common king since 1603 when James VI of Scotland became James I of England.

England, Wales and Scotland had meanwhile become predominantly Protestant in religion as a result of the European Reformation. But Ireland remained Catholic, and tried to distance itself from England, thus adding religion to colonialism as a foundation for future problems.

Britain therefore is not a single, culturally homogeneous country, but rather a recent and potentially unstable union of four old nations. The political entity called Great Britain is only slightly older than the United States of America, and the United Kingdom (1801) is younger. Nor did the political unions appreciably alter the relationships between the four nations. The English often treated their Celtic neighbours as colonial subjects rather than equal partners, and Englishness became a dominant strand in concepts of Britishness, because of the role that the English have played in the formation of Britain.

However, despite the tensions and bitterness between the four nations, there was a steady internal migration between them. This mainly involved movements of Irish, Welsh and Scottish people into England. Relatively few English emigrated to Wales and Scotland, although there was English and Scottish settlement in Ireland over the centuries.

Other newcomers continued to arrive from overseas, including gypsies, blacks (associated with the slave trade), and a further wave of Jews, who in 1655 created the first permanent Jewish community. In the sixteenth and seventeenth centuries, the country attracted a large number of refugees, such as Dutch Protestants and French Huguenots, who were driven from Europe by warfare, political and religious persecution, and employment needs. This talented and urbanized immigration contributed considerably to the national economy, and added a new dimension to a largely agricultural population. But, from around 1700, there was to be no more large immigration into the country for the next 200 years. Britain was now exporting more people than it received, mainly to North America and the expanding colonies worldwide.

A second important development in British history was a number of industrial revolutions in the eighteenth and nineteenth centuries. These transformed Britain from an agricultural economy into an industrial and manufacturing country. Processes based on steam power and the use of coal for generating steam were discovered and exploited. Factories and factory towns were needed to mass-produce new manufactured goods. Villages in the coalfields and industrial areas grew rapidly into manufacturing centres, while rural industries and localities declined. A drift of population away from the countryside began in the late eighteenth century, as people sought work in mines and factories to escape from rural poverty and unemployment. They moved, for example, to textile mills in Lancashire and Yorkshire, and to heavy industries and pottery factories in the West Midlands.

The earlier agricultural population changed radically in the nineteenth century into an industrialized workforce. The census of 1801, which is the first reliable modern measurement of population, gave figures of 9 million for England and Wales, and 1.5 million for Scotland. But, between 1801 and 1901, the population of England and Wales trebled to 30 million. The numbers in Scotland increased less rapidly, owing to emigration, but in Ireland the population was halved from 8 to 4 million because of famine, deaths and emigration. The greatest concentrations of people were now in London and in the industrial areas of the Midlands, south Lancashire, Merseyside, Clydeside, Tyneside, Yorkshire and South Wales.

The industrial revolution reached its height during the first quarter of the nineteenth century. It did not require foreign labour because there were enough skilled British workers and a ready supply of unskilled labourers from Wales, Scotland, Ireland and the English countryside. Welshmen from North Wales went to the Lancashire textile mills; Highland Scots travelled to the Lowland Clydeside industries; and Irishmen flocked to both England and Scotland to work in the manual trades of the industrial infrastructure constructing roads, railways and canals.

Industrialization in nineteenth-century Britain resulted in an expanded commercial market. This attracted new immigrants who often provided important business and financial skills to exploit the industrial wealth. Some newcomers joined City of London financial institutions and the import/export trades, to which they contributed their international connections. Other settlers were involved in a wide range of occupations and trades. Immigration to Britain might have been greater in the nineteenth century had it not been for the attraction of North America, which was receiving large numbers of newcomers from all over the world, including Britain.

By the end of the nineteenth century, Britain was the world's leading industrial nation and one of the richest. But it gradually lost its world lead in manufacturing industry, most of which was in native British hands. However, its position in international finance, some of which was under immigrant control, was retained into the twentieth century.

Immigration in the twentieth century

Immigrants had always been allowed relatively free access to Britain. But they could be easily expelled; had no legal rights to protect them; and increasing restrictions were imposed upon them in the eighteenth and nineteenth centuries. At the 1871 census, the number of people in Britain born outside the British Empire was only 157,000 out of a population of some 31.5 million.

Irrespective of these low figures, immigration became a topic of public and political concern, which continued through the twentieth century. In the early years of the century, Jews and Poles escaped persecution in Eastern Europe and settled in the East End of London, which has been a traditional area of immigrant concentration. Public demands for immigration control grew, and an anti-foreigner feeling spread, increased by the nationalism and spy mania caused by the First World War (1914–18). But laws (like the Aliens Act of 1905), which were designed to curtail foreign entry, proved ineffective. By 1911 the number of people in Britain born outside the empire was 428,000, or 1 per cent of the population.

Despite legal controls, and partly as a result of the 1930s world recession and the Second World War, refugees from Nazi-occupied Europe and other immigrants entered Britain. After the war, Poles, Latvians, Ukrainians and other nationalities chose to stay in Britain. Later in the twentieth century, political and economic refugees arrived, such as Hungarians, Czechs, Chileans, Libyans, East African Asians, Iranians and Vietnamese, in addition to other immigrants. Many of these groups today form sizeable communities, and are scattered throughout the country. Such newcomers have often suffered from discrimination, some more than others, since racism is not a new phenomenon in Britain.

But public and political concern later turned to the issues of race and colour, which were to dominate the immigration debate. The focus of attention became non-white Commonwealth immigration. Before the Second World War, most Commonwealth immigrants to Britain came from the largely white Old Commonwealth countries of Canada, Australia and New Zealand,

and from South Africa. All Commonwealth citizens were allowed free access and were not treated as aliens.

But in the late 1940s people from the non-white New Commonwealth nations of India, Pakistan and the West Indies came to Britain (sometimes at the invitation of government agencies) to fill the vacant manual and lower-paid jobs of a growing national economy. By the 1960s, West Indians had found positions in public transport, catering, the Health Service and manual trades in London, Birmingham and other large cities. Indians and Pakistanis later arrived to work in the textile and iron industries of Leeds, Bradford and Leicester. By the 1970s, non-white people had become a familiar sight in other British cities such as Glasgow, Sheffield, Bristol, Huddersfield, Manchester, Liverpool, Coventry and Nottingham. There was a considerable dispersal of such immigrants throughout Britain, although many did tend to settle in the central areas of industrial cities.

These non-white communities have now increased and are involved in a broad range of occupations. Some, particularly Asians and black Africans, have been relatively successful in economic and professional terms. Others have experienced considerable problems such as low-paid jobs, unemployment, educational disadvantage, decaying housing in the inner cities and racial discrimination. Some critics argue that Britain possesses a deep-rooted racism based on the legacy of empire and notions of racial superiority, which continues to manifest itself and has limited the practical integration of the non-white population into the larger society. Many young non-whites who have been born in Britain feel particularly bitter at their experiences, and at their relative lack of educational and employment possibilities and advancement.

So many New Commonwealth immigrants were coming to Britain that from 1962 successive governments have passed legislation to enforce a two-strand policy on immigration. This has consisted, first, of Immigration Acts to restrict the number of immigrants entering the country and, second, of Race Relations Acts to protect the rights of those immigrants who are already settled in Britain. Eventually all Commonwealth citizens were treated as aliens. But those Commonwealth people who are either born in Britain or have a parent or grandparent born in Britain (patriality) have the right to apply for a British passport, claim British citizenship and live permanently in Britain. This patrial rule in practice meant that New Commonwealth people were barred from automatic entry, and led critics to condemn the Immigration Acts as racist.

Successive Race Relations Acts have made it unlawful to discriminate against another person on grounds of racial, ethnic or national origin. They cover such areas as education, housing, employment, services and advertising. Complainants who have suffered alleged discrimination can appeal to special Race Relations Tribunals. Official bodies to deal with racial discrimination have also been established, culminating with the Commission for Racial Equality in 1976. This organization, which has been relatively successful, supports Community Relations Councils that have been set up in areas of ethnic concentration, and it works for the elimination of discrimination and the promotion of equality of opportunity.

There has been much criticism of the immigration laws and the race-relations organizations. Some people argue that one cannot legislate satisfactorily against discrimination, and others would like stricter controls. Immigration and the issues of race continue to be problems in contemporary Britain, and have been increased by unemployment and cuts in public services. The concerns of the white population have been made worse by racialist speeches; by the growth of extreme nationalist parties such as the National Front and the British National Party; and by alleged racially inspired violence in the cities. Non-white citizens, on the other hand, often feel that they too easily and unfairly become the scapegoats for any problems that arise. Some become alienated from British society, and reject institutions such as the police, the legal system and the political structures. Government policies since the 1940s have not always helped to lessen either white or non-white anxieties.

The immigration and race debates are complex matters, and are frequently exploited for political purposes, from both the right and the left. It is easy to exaggerate the issues and to overdramatize them. Many non-white immigrants and their British-born children have slowly adapted to the larger society, while still being able to retain their cultural identities. This relative optimism, however, does not hide the fact that there are serious and continuing problems in these areas, and tensions do persist. But Britain today does have a relatively stable diversity of cultures, which should not be obscured by undue reference to racial concerns. Outbreaks of racial tension and harassment do occur, but they can be exaggerated by the popular media.

The number of people in Britain in 1967–8 of non-white origin or descent was estimated at 1,087,000, or 2.2 per cent of the population. In later years the numbers increased, as did the percentage of those born in Britain. The 1991 census showed that 94.5 per cent of the population were classified as white, while 5.5 per cent (3 million people) described themselves as belonging to a non-white group, and 46 per cent of these were born in Britain. Indians are the largest non-white group, followed by West Indians (Afro-Caribbeans), Pakistanis, black Africans, Bangladeshis and Chinese.

The non-white population in the past was largely composed of immigrant families, single people or the head of the family. But this structure has changed as more dependants join settled immigrants and as British-born non-whites develop their own family organizations. The term 'immigrant' has now lost some of its earlier significance and the emphasis has switched to debates about what constitutes a 'multicultural society', particularly in education and employment.

Apart from a few categories of people who have a right of abode in Britain and who are not subject to immigration control, virtually all others require either entry clearance or permission to enter and remain. Generally speaking, such newcomers (apart from short-term visitors) need a work permit and the promise of a guaranteed job if they hope to stay in the country for longer periods of time. But dependants of immigrants already settled in Britain may be granted the right of entry and permanent settlement.

Immigration into Britain from the Republic of Ireland

continues; the Irish have historically been the largest immigrant group; and there are some 800,000 people of Irish descent. Movement from the Old Commonwealth countries has declined, while that of other Commonwealth citizens has dropped following entry restrictions. There has been an increase in immigrants from European Union countries, who have the right to seek work and settle in Britain, with sizeable immigration from the USA and the Middle East.

The 1992 official figures show that 53,000 people were accepted for permanent settlement that year, and 20 per cent were from New Commonwealth countries. Such statistics reveal that a significant permanent immigration into Britain still continues, despite more restrictive legislation. Opinion polls suggest that race relations, immigrants and immigration are a source of concern for British people. Many admit to being racially prejudiced, and a majority are opposed not only to further non-white immigration, but also to immigration from the European Union and the Old Commonwealth.

However, acceptance for settlement does not mean automatic citizenship. Naturalization only occurs when certain requirements have been fulfilled, together with a period of residence. New conditions for naturalization and redefinitions of British citizenship are contained in the Nationality Act of 1981. This Act has been criticized by some who have seen it as providing further restrictions on immigration procedures.

In view of the often emotional arguments about race and immigration, it is important that the relevance of emigration from Britain is considered if the debate is to be kept in perspective. Historically, there has usually been a consistent pattern of movement, and a resulting balance of migration. This means that emigration has traditionally cancelled out immigration in real terms. But there have been periods of high emigration. For example, groups left England and Scotland in the sixteenth and seventeenth centuries to become settlers and colonists in Ireland and North America. Millions in the nineteenth and early twentieth centuries emigrated to New Zealand, Australia, South Africa, Canada, other colonies and the USA. In 1992, there was again a net loss to the population as more people left the country than entered.

Population movements in the twentieth century

There have been considerable shifts of population distribution in the twentieth century, which have been mainly due to economic and employment changes.

There was a drift of people away from Tyneside and South Wales during the trade depression of the 1930s, when coal production, steel manufacture and other heavy industries were badly affected. Since the 1950s there has been little increase in population in industrial areas of the Central Lowlands of Scotland, Tyneside, Merseyside, West Yorkshire and South Wales, which have seen a rundown in traditional industries, and substantial rises in unemployment.

Instead, there was a movement of people away from these regions, first to the English Midlands with their more diversified industries, and then to London and the south-east where employment opportunities and affluence have been greater. But the English Midlands have also suffered economically in recent years, and southern England experienced increased unemployment in the 1980s and 1990s.

The reduction of the rural population and the expansion of urban centres continued into the twentieth century. But, by the middle of the century, there was a movement of people away from the centres of big cities such as London, Manchester, Liverpool, Birmingham and Leeds. This was due to bomb damage during the Second World War, slum clearance and the need to use inner-city land for shops, offices, warehouses and transport utilities. New Towns in rural areas and council housing estates outside the inner cities were specifically created to accommodate the displaced population. Road systems were built with motorways and bypasses to avoid congested areas, and rural locations around some cities were designated as Green Belts, in which no building was permitted.

Many people choose to live some distance from their workplaces, often in a city's suburbs or neighbouring towns (commuter towns). These features have contributed to the decline of the inner-city populations, although not of the total urban statistics. It is estimated that some 89 per cent of the British people now live in towns and cities. Densities are highest in Greater London and in south-east England, and lowest in the rural regions of northern Scotland, the Lake District, Wales and Northern Ireland. But the latest figures suggest an increasing movement of people to rural areas and to East Anglia and south-west England. This has been accompanied by population losses in and company relocations from large cities, particularly London.

In 1991 the population of the United Kingdom was some 57,800,000, which consisted of England with 48,208,000, Wales

PLATE 2.1 On the way to work: commuters *(Joanne O'Brien/Format)*

PLATE 2.2 A female crowd *(Joanne O'Brien/Format)*

with 2,891,000, Scotland with 5,107,000 and Northern Ireland with 1,594,000. These figures give a population density for the United Kingdom of some 600 persons per sq mile (234 per sq km), well above the European Union average. England has an average density of some 930 persons per sq mile (364 per sq km), and this average does not reveal the even higher densities in some areas of the country, such as parts of the south-east. Within Europe, only the Netherlands has a higher population density than England.

The British population grew by only 0.3 per cent between 1971 and 1978, which gave it one of the lowest increases in Western Europe. A similarly low growth rate is forecast into the twenty-first century, with the population expected to be some 59.4 million in the year 2011. It is also estimated that the counties of southern and central England will have the highest population growth up to 2001, and that the heaviest population losses will occur on Tyneside and Merseyside.

TABLE 2.2   Populations of major British cities (1991)

Greater London	6,889,900	Bradford	475,400
Birmingham	1,006,500	Edinburgh	439,700
Leeds	717,400	Manchester	438,500
Glasgow	688,600	Bristol	397,000
Sheffield	529,300	Cardiff	293,600
Liverpool	480,700	Belfast	287,100

ATTITUDES

Attitudes to Britishness and national identity

Immigrants have historically been seen by some people as a threat to British moral, social and cultural values, whose presence would radically change the society. However, this view ignores the difficulty of defining what is meant by British norms at specific times in history. Immigrants have obviously changed the composition of British society to some degree, and contributed to changing attitudes. But the British Isles have always been culturally diverse. There are many differences between the four nations of England, Wales, Scotland and Ireland, as well as diverse ways of life within each country's boundaries. Such distinctive nationalities and the presence of immigrant communities raise questions about the meaning of contemporary 'Britishness'.

'Britishness' since the 1707 political union has been largely identified with the stability and distinctiveness of centralized state institutions, as well as focusing on national myths. But the history of the British Isles before the eighteenth century is not about a single British identity or political entity. It is about the four different nations and their peoples, who have often been hostile towards one another.

Important cultural and national identities have been

retained by the peoples who comprise the present United
Kingdom population. Political terms such as 'British' and
'Britain' can therefore seem very artificial to many of them.
Foreigners often call all British people 'English', and sometimes have difficulties in appreciating the distinctions,
or the annoyance of the non-English population at such
labelling.

The Scots, Welsh and Northern Irish are largely Celtic
peoples, while the English are mainly Anglo-Saxon in origin.
Critics consequently maintain that the contemporary 'British'
do not have a strong sense of a 'British' identity, and suggest
that many of them no longer know who they are as Britons.
It is argued that there needs to be a radical rethinking of
what it means to be British in the contexts of a multinational,
multiracial state and a changing Europe.

But there has obviously been some racial and cultural
intermixture over the centuries, which has accompanied
adaptation by immigrant groups and an internal migration
between the four nations. Social, political and institutional
standardization, and a British awareness, have been established. However, the British identification is often equated
with English norms because political unification occurred
under the English Crown, state power is concentrated in
London and southern England, the English predominate
numerically, and because of England's historical role.

English nationalism is arguably, therefore, the most
potent of the four nationalisms, and the English have no real
problems with the dual national role, although most would
no doubt respond primarily to their Englishness. The Scots,
Irish and Welsh have always been more aware of the duality
between their nationalism and Britishness; resent the English
dominance and influence; see themselves as very different to
the English; and regard their nationalist feelings as crucial.
Their sense of identity is conditioned by the tension between
their own distinctive histories and centralized government
from London. Yet the English also have strong local identities and react against London influences.

National identifications have until recently been largely cultural, and the British political union was generally accepted in the four nations, except for some people in the minority Catholic population of Northern Ireland. However, political nationalism increased in the 1960s and 1970s in Scotland and Wales. Today it seems that calls for independence from England in these two nations have died down, except for political groups such as the Scottish National Party (SNP). But there are still demands for greater powers of self-government at local and regional levels within the United Kingdom (devolution) from the Liberal Democrats, the Labour Party, Plaid Cymru (the Welsh National Party) and the SNP, following the rejection by the Scottish and Welsh people of devolution proposals in referendums in 1979.

Demands for decentralized autonomy within England reflect regional differences there. Since the English themselves are a relatively mixed people, their customs, accents and behaviour vary considerably, and local identification is still strong. The Cornish, for example, see themselves as a distinctive cultural element in English society, and have an affinity with Celtic and other similar racial groups in Britain and Europe. The northern English have often regarded themselves as superior to the southern English, and vice versa. English county, regional and local community loyalties are still maintained, and may be demonstrated in sports, politics, competitions, cultural activities, or a specific way of life.

In Wales, there are also cultural and political differences between the industrial south (with its Labour Party support) and the rest of the mainly rural country; between Welsh-speaking Wales in the west (which supports Plaid Cymru) and English-influenced Wales in the east and southwest (which still provide some Conservative Party support).

Yet Welsh people generally are very conscious of their differences from the English. Their national and cultural identity is grounded in their history, literature, the Welsh language (actively spoken by 19 per cent of the population), sport (such as rugby football), and festivals such as the

National Eisteddfod (with its Welsh poetry competitions, dancing and music). It is also echoed in close-knit industrial and agricultural communities, and in a tradition of social, political and religious dissent from English norms. Today, many Welsh people feel that they are struggling for their national identity against political power in London, and the erosion of their culture and language by English institutions.

Similarly, the Scottish people generally unite in defence of their national identity and distinctiveness because of historical reactions to the English. Scots are conscious of their traditions, which are reflected in cultural festivals and in different legal, religious and educational systems to those of England. There is resentment against the centralization of political power in London and the alleged economic neglect of Scotland (although the British government provides greater economic subsidies per head of population to Scotland and Wales than to England). Political nationalism has grown in Scotland, and the goal of independence is held by some 30 per cent of the people.

But Scots are divided by two languages (Gaelic and Scots, the former being spoken by 1.5 per cent of the Scottish population, or 70,000 people), different religions, prejudices and regionalisms. Cultural differences separate Lowlanders and Highlanders, and deep rivalries exist between the two major cities of Edinburgh and Glasgow.

In Northern Ireland, the social, cultural, political and economic differences between Roman Catholics and Protestants have long been evident, and today are often reflected in geographical ghettos. Sizeable groups in both communities feel frustration with the English and hostility towards the British government in London. The Protestant Unionists, or Loyalists, do not regard themselves as English, although they wish to continue the union with Britain. Many Catholic Nationalists feel Irish and would prefer to be united with the Republic of Ireland. On both sides there is a general interest in local culture, music and the preservation of the Irish language.

These features suggest that the contemporary British are a very diverse people, particularly when original settlement has been added to by centuries of later immigration. It is consequently as difficult, if not impossible, to find a typical English, Welsh, Scottish or Irish person who conforms to all or even some of the assumed national stereotypes as it is to find a typical Briton.

Foreigners often have either specific notions of what they think the British are like or, in desperation, seek a unified picture of national character, based sometimes upon quaint traditions, or theme-park and tourist views of Britain. The emphasis in this search should perhaps be more upon an examination of diversity in British life.

Sometimes, however, the four nations do employ national stereotypes. The English might like to see themselves as calm, reasonable, patient and commonsensical people, who should be distinguished from the excitable, romantic and impulsive Celts. The Celts, on the other hand, may consider the English to be arrogant, patronizing and cold, and themselves as having all the virtues. The English, and sometimes the British as a whole, are often thought of as restrained, reserved, unemotional, private and independent individuals, with a respect for the amateur and the eccentric. Underlying all, there is supposed to be a dry sense of humour which specializes in understatement, irony, self-deprecation and an enjoyment in using the language in very flexible ways. Such qualities may be offset by a certain aggressiveness, stubbornness and lack of cooperation. The British appear to have a relaxed attitude towards work and economic production, and have often been characterized as tolerant and somewhat lazy, with a happy-go-lucky attitude to life. These stereotypes may have some limited value, but cannot be taken to represent the whole truth about the four nations, Britain, or individuals.

■ **Explain and examine the following terms:**

nomads	bypass	Anglo-Saxon	industrialization
Neolithic	East End	Hansa	National Front
density	Celtic	devolution	Hastings
Merseyside	Domesday Book	immigrant	naturalization
racism	Britishness	Anglo-Saxon	discrimination
census	emigration	Huguenots	Green Belt

■ **Write short essays on the following questions:**

1 Describe in outline the history of settlement and immigration in Britain.

2 Examine the changing patterns of population distribution in Britain.

3 Is it correct to describe contemporary Britain as a 'multiracial' and 'multinational' society? If so, why?

Chapter 3

Political institutions

■ English political history 66

■ The constitutional framework 73

■ The monarchy 76

■ The Privy Council 79

■ Parliament 80

■ The parliamentary electoral system
(general elections) 85

■ The party-political system 89

■ Parliamentary procedure and
legislation 95

■ The government 100

■ Parliamentary control of government 104

■ *Attitudes to politics and politicians* 106

■ *Exercises* 107

THE POLITICAL HISTORY OF THE BRITISH ISLES (especially that of England) over the past 800 years has been largely one of reducing the power of the monarchy, and transferring authority to Parliament as the sovereign legislative body. It has also involved the growth of political parties and campaigns for the extension of the vote to all adults. These struggles have produced governmental, social and religious conflicts, as well as evolving political institutions. The original structures were monarchical, aristocratic and non-democratic. But they have been gradually adapted to changing social conditions, parliamentary democracy and a mass franchise.

The roles of the political structures are still vigorously debated in contemporary Britain. Governments are accused of being too secretive, too centralized, too party-political and insufficiently responsive to the wider needs of the country. It is argued that Parliament has lost its controlling influence over the Cabinet-led government, and that political power has shifted to executive bodies and the Prime Minister. Critics maintain that the political system needs to be fundamentally reformed in order to make it more adaptable to modern needs, and to reduce the gap which allegedly exists between the London government and the diverse peoples of the United Kingdom.

English political history

English political and military expansionism within the British Isles over the centuries has resulted in a united country. English systems were adopted in many areas of society after the 1536–43 Acts of Union uniting England and Wales, the 1707 Act of Union between England and Scotland, and the 1801 Act of Union joining Great Britain and Ireland as the United Kingdom.

Decline of monarchy and
the rise of Parliament

Early English monarchs had considerable power, but generally accepted advice and some limitations on their authority. However, later kings, such as King John (1199–1216), often ignored these restrictions, and the powerful French-Norman barons opposed John's dictatorial rule by forcing him to sign Magna Carta in 1215. This document protected the aristocracy rather than the ordinary citizen. But it came to be regarded as a cornerstone of British liberties. It restricted the monarch's powers; forced him to take advice; increased the influence of the aristocracy; and stipulated that no citizen could be punished or kept in prison without a fair trial.

Such developments encouraged the establishment of parliamentary structures. In 1265 Simon de Montfort called commoners to the existing Parliament, which was based on the nobility. This initiative was followed in 1295 by the Model Parliament of Edward I (1272–1307), which was the first representative English Parliament and an example for future structures. Its two sections consisted of the Lords and Bishops, who were chosen by the monarch, and the Commons, which comprised male commoners.

However, the combined Parliament of aristocrats and commoners was too large to rule the country effectively. A Privy Council was created, which was an expansion of the small circle of advisers at the royal court. This body became the dominant royal government outside Parliament, until it lost power to the present parliamentary structures in the late eighteenth and early nineteenth centuries.

But, although Parliament now had some limited powers against the monarch, there was a return to royal dominance in Tudor England from 1485. The nobility had been weakened by wars and internal conflicts, and monarchs chose landed gentry as members of their Privy Councils, which made them dependent upon royal patronage. Monarchs controlled Parliament and summoned it only when they needed to raise money.

Parliament showed more resistance to royal rule under the

Stuart monarchy from 1603 by using its gradually acquired weapon of financial control. It was influenced by the gentry, who had now become more independent of the Crown, and had a majority in the House of Commons. Parliament began to refuse royal requests for money. It forced Charles I to sign the Petition of Rights in 1628, which further restricted the monarch's powers and prevented him from raising taxes without Parliament's consent. Charles tried to ignore these political developments, until he was obliged to summon Parliament for finance. Parliament again refused the request.

Realizing that he could not control Parliament, Charles next attempted to arrest parliamentary leaders in the House of Commons itself. His failure to do so meant that the monarch was in future prohibited from entering the Commons. Today Black Rod (a royal appointment) is a reminder of these constitutional changes. He knocks on the door of the Commons after it has been closed against him, in order to summon members of the Commons to the State Opening of Parliament. This is normally performed each autumn by the monarch in the House of Lords. Members of the Commons do not enter the main body of the Lords, but listen from the entrance.

Charles's rejection of parliamentary ideals and his belief in the monarch's supreme authority to rule without opposition provoked anger against the Crown, and a Civil War broke out in 1642. The Protestant Parliamentarians under Oliver Cromwell won the military struggle against the Catholic Royalists. Charles I was beheaded in 1649; the monarchy was abolished; England was ruled under a Protectorate by Cromwell and his son Richard (1649–60); and Parliament comprised only the House of Commons, which met every three years.

However, Cromwell's Protectorate was harsh and unpopular, and most people wanted the restoration of the monarchy. The two Houses of Parliament were re-established, and in 1660 they restored the Stuart Charles II to the throne. Initially Charles cooperated with Parliament, but his financial needs, belief in royal authority and support of the Catholic cause lost him popular and parliamentary backing. Parliament ended his expensive wars;

forced him to sign the Test Act of 1673, which excluded Catholics and Protestant dissenters from holding public office; and passed the Habeas Corpus Act in 1679, which stipulated that no citizen could be imprisoned without a fair and speedy trial.

The growth of political parties and constitutional structures

The growing power of Parliament against the monarch in the seventeenth century was reflected in the development of more organized political parties. These derived largely from the ideological and religious conflicts of the Civil War. Two groups (Tories and Whigs) became dominant, and this feature was to characterize future British two-party politics, in which political power has shifted between two main parties. The Whigs were mainly Cromwellian Protestants and gentry, who did not accept the Catholic James II as successor to Charles II, and who wanted religious freedom for all Protestants. The Tories generally supported Royalist beliefs, and helped Charles II to secure James's right to succeed him.

But James's behaviour caused a further reduction of royal influence. He attempted to rule without Parliament, ignored its laws and tried to repeal the Test Act. His manipulations forced the Tories to join the Whigs in inviting the Protestant William of Orange to intervene. William arrived in England in 1688, James fled to France, and William succeeded to the throne as England's first constitutional monarch. Since no force was involved, this event is called the Bloodless or Glorious Revolution. Although critics differ in their interpretation of the 1688–9 changes, the English constitution and politics were affected. The monarch's powers were restricted and it was practically impossible for future monarchs to reign without the consent of Parliament.

A series of Acts laid the foundations for constitutional developments. The Declaration of Rights (1689) created basic civil liberties, and prevented the monarch from making laws or raising an army without Parliament's approval. The Act of Settlement (1701) gave religious freedom to all Protestants, and stipulated that all future English monarchs had to be Protestant. A Triennial Act established that Parliament was to be called every three years.

The Glorious Revolution effectively created a division of powers between an executive branch (the monarch through the government of the Privy Council); a legislative branch (both Houses of Parliament and formally the monarch); and the judiciary (a legal body independent of monarch and Parliament). This structure, in which the legislature was supposed to control the executive, evolved slowly into its modern counterparts.

Parliamentary power continued to grow in the early eighteenth century, initially because the German-born George I lacked interest in English affairs of state. He mistrusted the Tories with their Catholic sympathies, and appointed Whigs such as Robert Walpole to his Privy Council. Walpole became Chief Minister, Leader of the Whig Party and head of the Whig majority in the House of Commons, which now mainly comprised wealthy land- and property owners. Walpole's political power enabled him to increase parliamentary influence, and he has been called Britain's first Prime Minister. But parliamentary authority was not absolute, and later monarchs tried to restore royal power. However, George III lost much of his authority after the loss of the American colonies in 1776. He was obliged to appoint William Pitt the Younger as his Tory Chief Minister, and it was under Pitt that the office of Prime Minister really developed.

The expansion of voting rights

But although parliamentary control continued to grow in the late eighteenth and early nineteenth centuries, there was still no widespread democracy in Britain. Political authority was in the hands of landowners, merchants and aristocrats in Parliament, and most people did not possess the vote. Bribery and corruption were common, with the buying of those votes which did exist and the giving away or sale of public offices.

The Tories were against electoral reform, as were the Whigs initially. But the country was now rapidly increasing its population and developing industrially and economically. Pressures for political reform became irresistible. The Whigs extended voting rights to the expanding middle class in the First Reform Act of 1832. The Tory Disraeli later gave the vote to men with property and a certain income. However, the majority of the working class had no votes and were unrepresented in Parliament. It was only in 1884 that the Whig Gladstone gave the franchise to all male adults.

Women had to wait until 1928 for the full franchise to be established in Britain. Previously, only women over 30 had achieved political rights, and for centuries wives and their property had been the legal possessions of their husbands. The traditional role of women of all classes had been confined to that of mother in the home, although some found employment in home industries and factories, or as domestic servants, teachers and governesses.

The position of women in society became marginally better towards the end of the nineteenth century. Elementary education for all was established and a few institutions of higher education began to admit women in restricted numbers. Some women's organizations had been founded in the mid-nineteenth century to press for greater political, employment and social rights. But the most famous suffragette movement was that of the Pankhursts in 1903. Their Women's Social and Political Union campaigned for the women's vote and an increased female role in society. However, some critics argue that a substantial change in women's status in the twentieth century occurred largely because of a recognition of the essential work that they performed during the two World Wars.

The growth of governmental structures

The elements of modern government developed haphazardly in the eighteenth and nineteenth centuries. Government ministers were generally members of the Commons, which gradually achieved dominance over the House of Lords. They became responsible to the House of Commons rather than to the monarch, and shared a collective responsibility for the policies and acts of government, in addition to the individual responsibility owed to Parliament for their own ministries. The prime ministership developed from the monarch's Chief Minister to 'first among equals' and eventually to the leadership of all ministers. The central force of government became the parliamentary Cabinet of senior ministers, which had grown out of the Privy Council. The government was formed from the majority party in the House of Commons. The largest minority party became the Official Opposition, which attempted through its policies to become the next government chosen by the people.

The nineteenth century also saw the growth of more organized political parties. These were conditioned by changing social and economic factors, and reflected the modern struggle between opposing ideologies. The Tories, who became known as the Conservatives around 1830, had been a dominant force in British politics since the eighteenth century. They believed in established values and the preservation of traditions; supported business and commerce; had strong links with the Church of England and the professions; and were opposed to radical ideas. The Whigs, however, were becoming a more progressive force, and wanted social reform and economic freedom without government restrictions. They gradually developed into the Liberal Party, which promoted enlightened policies in the late nineteenth and early twentieth centuries.

But the Liberal Party declined after 1918. The new Labour Party, established in its present form in 1906, became the main opposition party to the Conservatives, and continued the traditional two-party system in British politics. It was supported by the trade unions, the working class and some middle-class voters. The first Labour government was formed in 1924 under Ramsay MacDonald. But it only achieved majority power in 1945 under Clement Attlee, when it embarked on radical programmes of social and economic reform, which laid the foundations of the modern corporate and welfare state.

Historically, the House of Commons has gained power from both the monarch and the House of Lords, and become the dominant element in the parliamentary system. Reforms, such as the Parliament Acts of 1911 and 1949, were later made to the House of Lords and removed much of its political authority. Subsequent Acts have created non-hereditary titles (life peers) which supplement the old arrangement in which most peerages were hereditary. The Lords now has only delaying and amending power over parliamentary bills, and cannot interfere with financial legislation. These changes demonstrated that political and taxation matters are decided by the members of the Commons as elected representatives of the people.

The constitutional framework

There have been no radical upheavals in the English system of government over the centuries, despite the Civil War and the 1688 changes. Rather, existing institutions have been pragmatically adapted to new conditions. Britain today, unlike most countries, has no written constitution contained in any one document. Instead, the constitutional system consists of statute law (Acts of Parliament); common law (judge-made law); conventions (or principles and practices of government which are not legally binding, but have the force of law): some ancient documents such as Magna Carta; and European Union law.

These elements are said to be flexible enough to respond quickly to new conditions. National law and institutions can be created or changed by Acts of Parliament. The common law can be extended by the judges, and conventions can be altered, formed or abolished by general agreement.

The governmental model that operates in Britain today is a constitutional monarchy, or parliamentary system, and is divided into legislative, executive and judicial branches. The monarch is still head of state and has a role to play on some executive and legislative levels. But it is Parliament or the legislature (consisting collectively of the House of Lords, the House of Commons and formally the monarch) which possesses supreme legislative power (except for some EU law).

The executive government of the day governs by passing its political policies through Parliament in the form of Acts of Parliament. It operates through ministries or departments headed by Ministers or Secretaries of State.

The judiciary is composed of the judges of the higher courts, who determine the common law and interpret Acts of Parliament and EU law. The judges are independent of the legislative and executive branches of government.

These branches of the governmental system, although distinguishable from each other, are not entirely separate. For example, the monarch is formally head of the executive, the legislature and the judiciary. A Member of Parliament (MP) in the House of Commons and a member of the House of Lords may both be in the government of the day. A Law Lord in the House of Lords also serves that House as the highest appeal court.

The correct constitutional title of Parliament is the 'Queen-in-Parliament', and all state and governmental business is carried out in the name of the monarch by the politicians and officials of the system. But the Crown is sovereign only by the will of Parliament. In constitutional theory, the British people, although subjects of the Crown, hold the political sovereignty to choose their government, while Parliament, consisting partly of their elected representatives in the Commons, possesses the legal sovereignty to make laws and is the focus of national sovereignty.

But a new challenge to parliamentary sovereignty and the political tradition in Britain has arisen as a result of membership of the European Union (1973). Parliament is no longer the sole legislative and sovereign body in Britain since EU law is now superior to British national law in certain areas, and British courts must give it precedence. This means that EU law has been added to, and coexists with, Acts of Parliament as part of the British constitution.

Criticisms of the constitutional system

The British system, which is largely dependent upon conventions and observing the rules of the game, has been admired in the past. It combined stability and adaptability, so that a balance of authority and toleration was achieved. Most British governments tended to govern pragmatically when in power, in spite of ideological party manifestos at election time. The emphasis was on whether a particular policy worked and was generally acceptable.

Governments were conscious of how far they could go before displeasing their own followers and the electorate, to whom they were accountable at the next general election. From a basis in the two-party system, the combination of Cabinet government and party discipline in the Commons seemed to provide a balance between efficient government and public accountability.

But this system has been increasingly criticized. Governments have become more radical in their policies, and have been able to implement them because of strong majorities in the Commons. There has been concern at the apparent absence of constitutional safeguards for the individual citizen against state power, especially since there are few legal definitions of civil liberties in Britain. There are also few effective parliamentary restraints upon a strong government which is intent upon carrying out its policies.

These features have been seen as potentially dangerous, particularly when governments and their administrative bodies have a reputation for being too secretive. Government secrecy has become a widely discussed issue, with critics arguing that Britain is ruled by a largely hidden system of executive agencies. There have consequently been campaigns for more open government and more effective civil protection in the forms of a bill of rights (to safeguard individual liberties); a written constitution (to define and limit the powers of Parliament and government); greater judicial scrutiny of the merit of parliamentary legislation; a Freedom of Information Act (to allow the public to examine official documents); and the incorporation of the European Convention on Human Rights into British domestic law (allowing British citizens to pursue legal claims in Britain rather than having to go through the European Court of Human Rights). But none of these suggested reforms has been achieved, and there is considerable opposition to the proposals.

Critics claim that the British political system no longer works satisfactorily. They maintain that it has become too centralized, and that the traditional bases are no longer adequate for the organization of a complex society. It is felt that political policies have become too conditioned by party politics at the expense of consensus; that government is too removed from popular and regional concerns; and that national programmes lack a demo-cratic and representative basis. It is argued that there must be a fundamental reform of the existing political institutions if they are to reflect a contemporary diversity. However, changes are occasionally made to the present apparatus, and the old evolu-tionary principles may be successfully adapted to new demands and conditions.

The monarchy

The continuity of the English monarchy has been interrupted only by Cromwellian rule from 1649 to 1660, although there have been different lines of descent. The Crown is one of the oldest secular institutions in Britain and there is automatic hereditary succession to the throne, but only for Protestants.

Since 1689 the monarch's executive powers have been limited. But the monarch still has a number of formal constitutional roles, and serves as head of state, head of the executive, judiciary and legislature, commander-in-chief of the armed forces, and 'supreme governor' of the Church of England. Ministers and officials of the central government are the monarch's servants, and judges, military officers, peers and bishops of the Church of England swear allegiance to the Crown. In holding these positions, the monarch personifies the British state and is a symbol of national unity.

The monarch is expected to be politically neutral, and is sup-posed to reign but not rule. But there are difficulties in defining the precise powers of the monarch. Proposals have often been made to create rules which would establish the real powers of the office, clarify the uncertain elements in the monarch's position, and avoid the dangers of involving the Crown in political and constitutional controversy.

However, for all practical purposes the monarch acts only on the advice of political ministers, which cannot be ignored. The monarch cannot make laws, impose taxes, spend public money or act unilaterally. Contemporary Britain is therefore governed by Her Majesty's Government in the name of the Queen.

But the monarch still performs some important executive and legislative duties. These include the summoning, opening, proroguing (or adjourning) and dissolving of Parliament; giving the Royal Assent (or signature) to bills which have been passed by both Houses of Parliament; appointing government ministers and other public figures; granting honours; leading proceedings of the Privy Council; and fulfilling international duties as head of state. In practice, these functions are performed by the monarch on the advice of the Prime Minister or other ministers.

A central power still possessed by the monarch is the choice and appointment of the Prime Minister. By convention, this person is normally the leader of the political party which has a majority in the House of Commons. However, if there is no clear majority or if the political situation is unclear, the monarch could in theory make a free choice. In practice, advice is given by royal advisers and leading politicians in order to present an acceptable candidate.

Constitutionally, the monarch has the right to be informed of, and advised on, all aspects of national life by receiving government documents and meeting regularly with the Prime Minister. The monarch also has the right to encourage, warn and advise ministers. This role could be a source of potential power not only in Britain, but also in the Commonwealth of which the monarch is head. It is difficult to evaluate the influence of monarchical advice on formal and informal levels, although critics suggest that it could be substantial. This raises questions about whether such authority should be held by an unelected, non-democratic figure who could potentially either support or undermine political leaders.

The monarch is a permanent fixture in the British political system, unlike temporary politicians, and often has a greater knowledge of domestic and international politics. The monarchy still has a considerable part to play in the operation of government at various levels. Its practical and constitutional importance is illustrated by provisions for the appointment of counsellors of state (or a regent in exceptional cases) to perform royal duties, should the monarch be absent from Britain or unable to carry out public tasks.

Much of the cost of the royal family's official duties is met from public funds. This finance is granted from the Civil List (money which previously had to be debated and approved by Parliament each year, but which from 1990 was frozen at inflation-indexed levels for a ten-year period). Following public concern over expense, the Civil List has now been reduced to some members of the immediate royal family. The monarch's private expenses as sovereign come from the Privy Purse (finance which is gathered from the revenues of some royal estates). The Crown now also finances the official expenses of members of the royal family outside the immediate circle. These and any other costs incurred by the monarch as a private individual must come from the Crown's own resources, which are very considerable.

Critics who are against the monarchy as a continuing institution in British life maintain that it is out-of-date, non-democratic, too expensive, too exclusive, too closely associated with aristocratic privilege and establishment thinking, and too closely identified with an English rather than a British role. It is argued that the monarchy's aloofness from ordinary life contributes to class divisions in society and sustains a hierarchical structure. It is also suggested that, if the monarch's functions today are merely ceremonial and lack power, it would be more rational and democratic to abolish the office and replace it with a cheaper non-executive presidency.

Critics who are in favour of the monarchy argue that it is popular, has developed and adapted to modern requirements, and is not remote. It serves as a personification of the state; demonstrates stability and continuity; has a higher prestige than politicians; is not subject to political manipulations; plays a worthwhile role in national institutions; possesses a neutrality with which people can feel secure; and performs an important ambassadorial function in Britain and overseas. The monarchy also has a certain glamour (some would say soap-opera quality) about it, which is attractive to many people.

The British public show considerable affection for the royal family beyond its representative role. But the behaviour of some of its younger members, and the role of monarchy itself, have attracted considerable criticism in recent years. Public opinion polls demonstrate majority support for the monarchy as against a republican alternative, although the possibility of a republic in the future is not discounted. But the polls also suggest that the monarchy should adapt more to changes in society; that less public money should be spent on it; and that its income should be subject to income tax (which the monarch has now agreed to pay on some investment income).

Traditionalists fear that a modernized monarchy would lose that aura of detachment which has been described as its main strength. It would then be associated with change rather than the preservation of existing values. At present, it balances between tradition and modernizing trends.

The Privy Council

The Privy Council developed historically from a small group of royal advisers into the main executive branch of the monarch's government. But its powerful position was weakened in the eighteenth and nineteenth centuries as functions were gradually transferred to a parliamentary Cabinet. Its work was later taken over by newly created ministries, which were needed to cope with a rapidly changing society.

Today its main role is to advise the monarch on a range of constitutional matters, such as the approval of Orders in Council, which grant Royal Charters to public bodies such as universities. Its members may be appointed to advisory and problem-solving committees and it can be influential.

Cabinet ministers automatically become members on taking government office. Life membership is also granted by the monarch, on the recommendation of the Prime Minister, to eminent people in Britain and in independent monarchical countries of the Commonwealth. There are about 400 Privy Councillors at present, but the body works mostly through small groups or committees. A full council is usually only summoned on the death of a monarch and the accession of a new one; when there are serious constitutional issues at stake; or when a monarch plans to marry. Should the monarch be indisposed, counsellors of state or an appointed regent would work partly through the Privy Council.

Apart from its practical duties and its role as a constitutional forum, the most important task of the Privy Council today is performed by its Judicial Committee. This is the final court of appeal for some Commonwealth countries and the remaining dependencies. It may also be used as an arbiter for a wide range of courts and committees in Britain and overseas, and its rulings can be influential.

Parliament

Parliament, also known as 'Westminster' because it is housed in the Palace of Westminster in London, is the supreme legislative authority in Britain. Since it is not controlled by a written constitution, it has legal sovereignty in all matters, subject only to some European Union law. This means that it can create, abolish or amend laws for all or any part(s) of Britain on any topic. In this sense, Parliament is the sovereign power in the state. Its main functions are to pass laws; vote on financial bills so that government can carry on its legitimate business; examine government policies and administration; scrutinize European Union legislation; and debate important political issues.

In pursuing these absolute powers, Parliament is supposed to legislate according to the rule of law, precedent and tradition. Politicians are generally sensitive to these conventions and to public opinion. Formal and informal checks and balances, such as party discipline, the Official Opposition, public reaction and pressure groups, normally ensure that Parliament legislates according to its legal responsibilities. But critics argue that parliamentary programmes may not reflect the will of the people.

Parliament comprises the House of Lords, the House of Commons and formally the monarch. It gathers as a unified body only on ceremonial occasions, like the State Opening of Parliament by the monarch in the House of Lords. Here it listens to the monarch's speech from the throne, which outlines the government's forthcoming legislative programme. All three parts of Parliament must normally pass a bill before it can become an Act of Parliament and therefore law. Historically, a correctly created Act could not be challenged in the law courts on its merits. However, the courts can now rule on British domestic law to see whether or not it is compatible with European Union law in those areas to which the latter is applicable. This means that EU law exists side by side with domestic law in Britain, and the former takes precedence over the latter in certain areas.

A Parliament has a maximum duration of five years, but it is often dissolved and a general election called before the end of this term. The maximum has sometimes been prolonged by special parliamentary legislation in emergency situations like the two World Wars. Each Parliament is divided into annual sessions, running normally from one October to the next, with a long recess from July to October. A dissolution of Parliament and the issue of writs for the ensuing general election are ordered by the monarch on the advice of the Prime Minister. If an individual MP dies, resigns or is given a peerage, a by-election is called only for that member's seat, and Parliament as a whole is not dissolved.

The contemporary *House of Lords* consists of the Lords Temporal and the Lords Spiritual. The Lords Spiritual are the Archbishops of York and Canterbury, and 24 senior bishops of the Church of England. The Lords Temporal consist of (1) some 760 hereditary peers and peeresses who have kept their titles; (2) about 380 life peers and peeresses, who have usually been created by political parties; and (3) the Lords of Appeal (Law Lords), who become life peers on their judicial appointments. The latter serve the House of Lords as the ultimate court of appeal for most purposes from most parts of Britain. This court does not consist of the whole House of Lords, but only nine Law Lords who have held senior judicial office, who are under the chairmanship of the Lord Chancellor, and who form a quorum of three to five when they hear appeal cases.

The active daily attendance varies from a handful to a few hundred. Peers receive no salary for their parliamentary work, but

are eligible for attendance and travelling expenses. The House is presided over by the Lord Chancellor, who is a political appointee of the sitting government, and who sits on the Woolsack (or stuffed woollen sofa) to control the procedure and meetings of the House.

There are frequent demands that the unrepresentative, unelected House of Lords should be abolished and replaced by a second democratically elected chamber. The problem consists of which alternative model to adopt. An elected second chamber could threaten the constitutional powers of the House of Commons, and might result in conflict between the two.

Meanwhile, the House of Lords does its job well as an experienced and less partisan corrective to the House of Commons. It retains an important revising, amending and delaying function. This may be used either to block government legislation for up to one year, or to persuade governments to have a second look at bills. It is a safeguard against over-hasty legislation by the Commons, and plays a considerable constitutional role at times when governments may be very powerful. This is possible because members of the Lords tend to be more independently minded than MPs in the Commons, and do not suffer such rigid party discipline. The House has a large number of crossbenchers (or Independents sitting across the back of the chamber) who do not belong to any political party. Although there is a Conservative majority in the total membership, Conservative governments cannot automatically count on this support. The House of Lords is an anachronism in many ways. But it does take a substantial legislative and administrative burden from the Commons.

The *House of Commons* comprises 651 MPs, who are elected by the adult suffrage of the British people; who represent the citizens in Parliament; and of whom only 60 are women. Women face problems in being selected as parliamentary candidates and winning seats in the Commons. There are 524 parliamentary seats for England, 38 for Wales, 72 for Scotland and 17 for Northern

---

PLATE 3.1 The Houses of Parliament *(Maggie Murray/Format)*

Ireland. MPs are paid expenses and a salary which, at about twice the average national wage, is low in international and domestic terms.

The parliamentary electoral system (general elections)

Britain is divided for parliamentary electoral purposes into 651 constituencies (geographical areas of the country), each containing about 66,000 voters. Each returns one elected MP to the House of Commons at a general election. The constituencies are supposed to be periodically adjusted by Boundary Commissioners in order to ensure fair representation and to reflect population movements. But such aims are not always successfully achieved.

General elections for parliamentary seats are by secret ballot, but voting is not compulsory. British, Commonwealth and Irish Republic citizens may vote in the elections provided they are

1	**BROWN** James Edward Brown, 42 Spinney Road, Upton, Northshire **Labour**	
2	**SMITH** Frederick Alistair Smith, The Hut, Peasants' Row, Upton, Northshire **Conservative**	
3	**JONES** Gertrude Mary Jones 15 Lavender Crescent, Upton, Northshire **Liberal Democrat**	

FIGURE 3.1 Ballot paper

resident in Britain, included on the annual register of voters for the constituency, aged 18 or over, and not subject to any disqualification. People not entitled to vote include members of the House of Lords, mentally ill patients who are detained in hospital or prison, and persons who have been convicted of corrupt or illegal election practices.

Each elector casts one vote, normally in person, at a polling station set up on election day in the constituency. He or she will make a cross on a ballot paper against the name of the party candidate for whom the vote is cast. However, there are provisions for those who are unable to vote in person in their local constituency to register postal or proxy votes. There are also certain voting rights for expatriate Britons.

The turnout of voters is over 70 per cent at general elections out of an electorate of some 42 million people. The candidate who wins the most votes in a constituency is elected MP for that area. This system is known as the simple majority or the 'first past the post' system. There is no voting by proportional representation (PR), except for local and EU Parliament elections in Northern Ireland.

There has been much debate about the British electoral system. Many see it as undemocratic and unfair to the smaller parties. Campaigns continue for some form of PR, which would create a wider selection of parties in the House of Commons and cater for minority political interests. But the two major parties (Conservative and Labour) have preferred the existing system. It gives them a greater chance of achieving power, and they have not been prepared to legislate for change. The Labour Party is now more sympathetic, and may implement a form of PR if returned to government.

It is argued that the British people prefer the stronger and more certain government which can result from the present arrangements. Defenders of the current system point to the assumed weaknesses of coalition or minority government, such as frequent breakdown, a lack of firm policies, power-bargaining

---

PLATE 3.2   Inside the House of Commons *(COI)*

between different parties in order to achieve government status, and tension afterwards. But weak and small-majority government can also result from the British system.

The party-political system

The electoral structure depends upon the party-political system, which has existed since the seventeenth century. Political parties present their policies in the form of manifestos to the electorate for consideration during the intensive few weeks of canvassing and campaigning before General Election Day. A party candidate (chosen by a specific party) in a constituency is elected to Parliament on a combination of election manifesto, the personality of the candidate and the attraction of the national party. But party activity continues outside the election period itself, as the politicians battle for power and the ears of the electorate.

Since 1945 there have been six Labour and seven Conservative governments in Britain. Some have had large majorities in the House of Commons, while others have had small ones. Some, like the Labour governments in the 1970s, had to rely on the support of smaller parties, such as the Liberals and nationalist parties, in order to remain in power. The present Conservative government must submit itself to a general election by 1997.

The great majority of the MPs in the House of Commons belong to either the Conservative or the Labour Party, which are the largest political parties. This division continues the traditional two-party system in British politics, in which power has alternated between two major parties.

The Labour Party is a left-of-centre party with its own internal right and left wings. It has historically emphasized social justice, equality of opportunity, economic planning, and the state ownership of big industries and services. It is supported by the trade unions (who have been influential in the party's policy development), the working class and some middle-class backing. Its electoral strongholds are in South Wales, Scotland, and the Midland and northern English industrial cities.

TABLE 3.1   British governments and Prime Ministers since 1945

Date	Government	Prime Minister
1945–51	Labour	Clement Attlee
1951–5	Conservative	Winston Churchill
1955–9	Conservative	Anthony Eden (1955–7)
		Harold Macmillan (1957–9)
1959–64	Conservative	Harold Macmillan (1959–63)
		Alec Douglas-Home (1963–4)
1964–6	Labour	Harold Wilson
1966–70	Labour	Harold Wilson
1970–4	Conservative	Edward Heath
1974 (Feb.)	Labour	Harold Wilson
1974 (Oct.)	Labour	Harold Wilson
1974–9	Labour	Harold Wilson (1974–6)
		James Callaghan (1976–9)
1979–83	Conservative	Margaret Thatcher
1983–7	Conservative	Margaret Thatcher
1987–92	Conservative	Margaret Thatcher (1987–90)
		John Major (1990–2)
1992–	Conservative	John Major

But, although the 1992 general election continued to reflect this national division, previous patterns of support are altering as social and job mobility change. In recent years the Labour Party has embarked on wide-ranging reviews of its policies in order to broaden its appeal, take account of changing economic and social conditions, and remain a major force in British politics. Its present leader, Tony Blair, is continuing this modernizing trend, and the party is moving to the centre ground, despite left-wing opposition.

The Conservative Party is a right-of-centre party, which also has its right- and left-wing sections. It regards itself as a national party, and appeals to people across the class barriers. It emphasizes personal, social and economic freedom, the individual ownership of property and shares, and the importance of law and order.

Although it has often criticized what it sees as the dogmatic and ideological fervour of the Labour Party, the Conservatives have also become more radical in recent years, and have departed from what used to be regarded as the consensus view of British politics.

The party's support comes mainly from business interests and the middle and upper classes, but a sizeable number of skilled workers and women vote Conservative. The party's strongholds tend to be in southern England, with scattered support elsewhere in the country, although it has recently suffered setbacks in Scotland and southern England.

The Social and Liberal Democratic Party (SLD, or Liberal Democrats for short) was formed in 1988 when the old Liberal Party and the Social Democratic Party (formed in 1981) merged into one party. The Liberal Democrats, under their present leader Paddy Ashdown, see themselves as an alternative political force to the Conservative and Labour Parties, based on the centre or centre–left of British politics.

They are strong in south-west England and have recently gained support from Conservative voters in southern England and Labour voters in northern England. But they suffer from the lack of a clearly separate identity from the Labour Party, particularly as Labour moves to the centre ground and improves its standing. The Liberal Democrats have won some dramatic by-elections, and achieved considerable success in local government elections. But they have not made a comparable breakthrough into the House of Commons or the EU Parliament.

Smaller political parties may also have some representation in the House of Commons. Among these are the Scottish National Party; Plaid Cymru (the Welsh National Party); the Protestant Northern Irish parties of the Official Unionists, the Democratic Unionists and the Ulster Popular Unionists; the Social Democratic and Labour Party (moderate Roman Catholic Northern Irish party); and Sinn Fein (Republican Northern Irish party). Other small parties such as the Greens, and publicity-seeking fringe groups, may also contest a general election. Candidates who do not achieve a certain number of votes in the election lose their deposits (the sum paid when candidates register to fight an election). Social class used to be the determining factor in voting behaviour. But this has been replaced by property, employment, share-owning and other considerations, which represent a decline in voting according to class loyalties. There is now a much more volatile political situation as voters switch between Labour, Conservatives and Liberal Democrats, and employ 'tactical voting' in constituencies to prevent specific party candidates from being elected. The changing character of the electorate may propel the political parties increasingly to the centre ground, and persuade them to adopt policies which are more representative of people's wishes and needs.

The party which wins most parliamentary seats in the House of Commons at a general election usually forms the new government, even though it has not obtained a majority of the popular vote. It is able to carry out its policies (the mandate theory) because it has achieved a majority of the seats in the House of Commons. A party will generally have to gather more than 33 per cent of the popular vote before winning a substantial number of seats, and nearly 40 per cent in order to expand that representation and have a chance of forming a government with an overall majority (a majority over all the other parties counted together).

These figures also depend on whether support is concentrated in specific geographical areas, for a party gains seats by its local strength. Smaller parties, which do not approach these percentages, will not gain many seats in the Commons. It is this system of representation that proponents of PR wish to change, in order to reflect more accurately the popular vote and the appeal of minority parties.

The situation may be illustrated by the 1992 general election results (see table 3.2). The Conservatives became the government with 41.9 per cent of the popular vote, while the opposition parties together obtained 58.1 per cent. The Conservatives gained 336 seats with their share of the popular vote, the Labour Party received 271 seats with 34.5 per cent, while the Liberal Democrats with 17.9 per cent received only 20 seats. The Conservatives thus had a 21-seat overall majority. The main reasons for this result are

TABLE 3.2   General election results, 1992

Party	Popular vote (%)	Members elected
Conservative	41.9	336
Labour	34.5	271
Liberal Democrat	17.9	20
Scottish National		3
Plaid Cymru		4
Official Unionists	5.7	9
Democratic Unionists		3
Social Democratic and Labour		4
Ulster Popular Unionists		1
Total	100	651

the 'first past the post' system itself; the Liberal Democrats' popular support is spread widely (and therefore thinly) over the country; and the Labour and Conservative Parties have specific geographical areas in which their votes are concentrated.

But the result of a general election may be a 'hung Parliament', where no one party has an overall majority. A minority or coalition government would have to be formed, in which the largest party would be able to govern only by relying on the support of smaller parties in the Commons.

In most cases, however, the largest minority party becomes the Official Opposition with its own leader and 'shadow government'. It plays an important constitutional role in the parliamentary system, which is based on adversarial and confrontational politics and the two-party tradition of government. The seating arrangements in the House of Commons reflect this system, since leaders of the government and opposition parties sit on facing 'front benches', with their supporting MPs, or 'backbenchers', sitting behind them. The effectiveness of parliamentary democracy is supposed to rest on the relationship between the government and opposition parties, and the observance of procedural conventions.

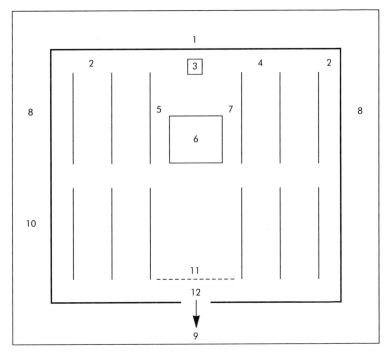

1	Press gallery	5	Government front	8	Galleries for MPs
2	Voting lobbies		bench	9	Public gallery
3	Speaker's chair	6	Dispatch box	10	VIP gallery
4	Civil servants	7	Opposition front	11	Bar of House
			bench	12	House of Lords

FIGURE 3.2 The House of Commons

The opposition parties may try to overthrow the government by defeating it on a 'vote of no confidence' or a 'vote of censure'. In general these techniques are not successful if the government has a comfortable majority and can count on the support of its MPs. The opposition parties consequently attempt to influence the formation of national policies by their criticism of pending legislation; by trying to obtain concessions on bills by proposing amendments to them; and by striving to increase support for their performance and policies inside and outside the Commons. They take advantage of any publicity and opportunity which might improve their chances at the next general election.

Inside Parliament, party discipline rests with the Whips, who are chosen from party MPs by the party leaders, and who are under the direction of a Chief Whip. Their duties include informing members of forthcoming parliamentary business, and maintaining the party's voting strength in the Commons by seeing that their members attend all important debates or are 'paired' with the opposition (agreed matching numbers so that MPs need not be present in the House on all occasions). MPs will receive notice from the Whips' office of how important a particular vote is, and the information will be underlined up to three times. A 'three-line whip' signifies a crucial vote, and failure to attend or comply with party instructions is regarded as a revolt against the party's policy.

The Whips also convey backbench opinion to the party leadership. This is important if rebellion and disquiet are to be avoided. Party discipline is very strong in the Commons and less so in the Lords. But in both Houses it is essential to the smooth operation of party politics. A government with a large majority should not become complacent, nor antagonize its backbenchers. If it does so, a successful rebellion against the government or abstention from voting by its own side may destroy the majority and the party's policy.

Outside Parliament, party control rests with the national and local party organizations, which can be very influential. They promote the party at every opportunity, but especially at election time, when local constituencies select the party candidates, and are in charge of canvassing the public and electioneering on behalf of their party.

Parliamentary procedure and legislation

Parliamentary procedure in both Houses of Parliament is based on custom, convention, precedent and detailed rules (standing orders). The House of Commons normally meets every weekday afternoon and sits until about 10.30 p.m., although business can continue beyond midnight. On Fridays it sits from 9.30 a.m. until 3 p.m., after which MPs normally travel to their constituencies for the weekend to attend to business there.

The organization of the Commons has been criticized. It is felt that the number of hours spent in the House should be reduced, pay and resources should be improved, and MPs should become more full-time representatives than they are at present. But attempts at reform have not been very successful, and there is opposition to MPs becoming professional politicians, since many combine their parliamentary duties with other jobs.

The Speaker (currently Betty Boothroyd, the first woman to hold the position) is the chief officer of the House of Commons; is chosen by MPs; has authority to interpret the rules of the House; and is assisted by three deputy speakers. The Speaker is an elected MP who, on election to the Speaker's chair, ceases to be a political representative and becomes a neutral official.

The Speaker protects the House against any abuse of procedure; may curtail debate so that a matter can be voted on; can adjourn the House to a later time: may suspend a sitting; controls the voting system; and announces the final result. Where there is a tied result, the Speaker has the casting vote, but must exercise this choice so that it reflects established conventions. The Speaker is important for the orderly running of the House. MPs can be very combative and often unruly, so that the Speaker is sometimes forced to dismiss or suspend a member from the House.

Debates in Parliament usually begin with a motion (or proposal) which is then debated by the whole House. The matter is eventually decided by a simple majority vote after a division, which is called at the end of the discussion. MPs enter either the 'Yes' or 'No' lobbies (corridors running alongside the Commons chamber) to record their vote, but they may also abstain from voting.

The proceedings of both Houses of Parliament are open to the public, and may be viewed from the public and visitors' galleries. The transactions are published daily in *Hansard* (the parliamentary 'newspaper'); debates in both Houses are now televised; and radio broadcasts may be in live or recorded form. This exposure to greater public scrutiny has increased interest in the parliamentary process, although negative comments are made about low attendance in both Houses and the behaviour of MPs in the Commons.

Legislative proceedings

The creation of new domestic law and changes to existing law are the responsibility of Parliament. In practice this means the implementation of the sitting government's policies. But it can also cover wider non-party matters, and responses to European Union rulings and law.

A government will usually issue certain documents before the parliamentary law-making process commences. A Green Paper is a consultative document which allows interested parties to state their case before a bill is introduced into Parliament. A White Paper is not normally consultative, but is a preliminary document which details prospective legislation.

A draft law is usually drawn up by parliamentary or government civil servants, and takes the form of a bill. The principal bills are 'public' because they involve state business, and are introduced in either House of Parliament by the government. Other bills may be 'private' because they relate to specific matters such as local government issues, while some are 'private members' bills' introduced by MPs in their personal or private capacity. These latter bills are on a topic of interest to MPs, but are normally defeated for lack of parliamentary time or support. However, some important private members' bills concerning homosexuality, abortion and sexual offences have survived the obstacles and become law.

Normally, politically contentious public bills go through the Commons first, but some of an uncontroversial nature may be initiated in the Lords. Whichever procedure is used, the bill must have passed through both Houses at some stage.

The Commons is normally the most important step in this process. A bill will receive a formal first reading when it is introduced into the Commons by the government. The bill is later given its second reading following a debate on its general principles, after which it usually passes to a standing committee for detailed discussion and amendment. This stage is followed by the report stage, during which further amendments to the bill are possible. The third reading of the bill considers it in its final form, usually on a purely formal basis. However, debate is still possible if demanded by at least six MPs. This delaying tactic may sometimes be used by the opposition parties to hold up the passage of a bill. But the government, in its turn, can introduce a 'guillotine motion' which cuts off further debate.

After the third reading, a Commons bill will be sent to the House of Lords. It will then go through broadly the same stages again. The Lords can delay a non-financial bill for one session, or roughly one year. It can also propose amendments, and if amended the bill goes back to the Commons for further consideration. This amending function is an important power, and has been frequently used in recent years. But the Lords' role today is to act as a forum for revision, rather than as a rival to the elected Commons. In practice, the Lords' amendments can sometimes lead to the acceptance of changes by the government, or even a withdrawal of the bill.

When the bill has eventually passed through the Lords, it is sent to the monarch for the Royal Assent (or signature), which has not been refused since the eighteenth century. After this, the bill becomes an Act of Parliament and enters the statute-book as representing the law of the land at that time.

This process from bill to Act may appear unduly drawn out. But it does normally avoid the dangers of hasty legislation, and ensures that the bill is discussed at all levels. It also allows the opposition parties to join in the legislative process, either by carrying amendments or sometimes by voting down a bill with the help of smaller parties and disaffected members of the government party.

Delegated legislation

Delegated legislation is a procedure which is designed to save parliamentary time. Once an Act has been passed by Parliament, provisions in it allow ministers, civil servants and other authorities to draft the administrative details applicable to the Act. These

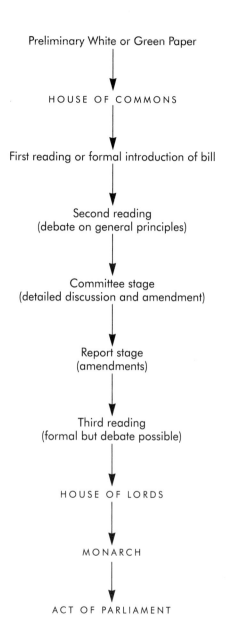

Preliminary White or Green Paper

HOUSE OF COMMONS

First reading or formal introduction of bill

Second reading
(debate on general principles)

Committee stage
(detailed discussion and amendment)

Report stage
(amendments)

Third reading
(formal but debate possible)

HOUSE OF LORDS

MONARCH

ACT OF PARLIAMENT

FIGURE 3.3 From bill to Act of Parliament

are necessary for the carrying out of the Act's intentions, and such powers are normally delegated to bodies which are directly responsible to Parliament.

However, despite the safeguards that are built into this system, there is concern that unelected officials might create provisions which have not been closely scrutinized by Parliament itself. Delegated legislation also weakens the legislative supremacy of Parliament. But demands on parliamentary time are great, and Parliament today can usually only be concerned with the broad outlines of legislation.

The government

The government is mainly centred on Whitehall in London where its ministries and the Prime Minister's official residence (10 Downing Street) are located. It consists of about a hundred ministers and other officials who can be chosen from both Houses of Parliament, and who are appointed by the monarch on the advice of the Prime Minister. They belong to the party which forms the majority in the Commons, from which they derive their authority, and are collectively responsible for the administration of national affairs. The composition of the government can vary in the number of ministers and ministries established by the Prime Minister.

The *Prime Minister* is appointed by the monarch and is normally the leader of the majority party in the Commons. His or her power stems from majority support in Parliament; the authority to choose and dismiss ministers; the leadership of the party in the country; and a control over policy-making. The Prime Minister usually sits in the Commons, as do most of the ministers, where they may be questioned and held accountable for government actions and decisions. The Prime Minister was historically the connection between the monarch and parliamentary government. This convention continues today in the weekly audience with the monarch, at which the policies and business of the government are discussed.

The Prime Minister consequently has great power within the British system of government, and it is suggested that the office has become like an all-powerful executive presidency. But there are considerable checks on this power, inside and outside the party and Parliament, which make the analogy less than accurate. However, there is a greater emphasis upon prime ministerial government today, rather than the traditional constitutional notions of Cabinet government.

The *Cabinet* is an executive body within the government, and usually comprises some 20 senior ministers, who are chosen and presided over by the Prime Minister. Examples are the Chancellor of the Exchequer (Finance Minister), the Foreign Secretary, the Home Secretary, the Minister of Defence, the Secretary of State for Education, and the Secretary of State for Trade and Industry. The Cabinet originated historically in meetings that the monarch had with ministers in a royal Cabinet or committee of the Privy Council. As the monarch gradually ceased to play a part in active politics because of the growth of parliamentary government and party politics, the royal Cabinet developed into a parliamentary body.

Constitutional theory has traditionally argued that the Cabinet collectively initiates and decides government policy at its weekly meetings in 10 Downing Street. It has control of the government apparatus and ministries because it is composed of members of the majority party in the Commons. But the convention that government rule is Cabinet rule has become weaker. Since the Prime Minister is responsible for Cabinet agendas and control of Cabinet proceedings, the Cabinet itself can become a 'rubberstamp' to policies which have already been decided upon by the Prime Minister, or by smaller groups. Cabinet government consequently appears to have lost some of its original impetus.

Much depends upon the personality of Prime Ministers in this situation, and the way in which they avoid potential Cabinet friction and tension. Some are strong and like to take the lead. Others give the impression of working within the Cabinet structure, allowing ministers to exercise responsibility within their own ministerial fields. Much of our information about the operation of the Cabinet comes from 'leaks', or information divulged by Cabinet ministers. Although the Cabinet meets in private and its discussions are meant to be secret, the public is usually and reliably informed of Cabinet deliberations by the media.

The mass and complexity of government business, and the fact that ministers are very busy with their own departments, suggest that full debate in Cabinet on every issue is impossible. But it is widely felt that the broad outlines of policy should be more vigorously debated. The present system arguably concentrates too much power in the hands of the Prime Minister; overloads ministers with work; allows too many crucial decisions to be taken outside the Cabinet; and consequently reduces the notion of collective responsibility.

Ministerial responsibility is an important constitutional concept. Collective responsibility is that which all ministers, but mainly those in the Cabinet, share for government actions and policy. All must support a government decision in public, even though some may oppose it during private deliberations. If a minister cannot do this, he or she may feel obliged to resign. Some Cabinet ministers have resigned in recent years because they cannot accept government policies.

A minister also has an individual responsibility for the work of his or her government department. This means that the minister is answerable for any mistakes, wrongdoing or bad administration which occur, whether personally responsible for them or not. In such cases, the minister may resign, although this is not as common today as in the past. This also enables Parliament to maintain some control over executive actions because the minister is answerable to Parliament.

Government departments (or *ministries*) are mainly centred in London and are the chief instruments by which central government implements its policy. A change of government does not necessarily alter the number or functions of departments. Examples of government departments are the Foreign Office, the Ministry of Defence, the Home Office, the Department of Education and the Treasury (of which the Chancellor of the Exchequer is head).

Government departments are staffed by the *Civil Service*,

which consists of career administrators. Civil servants are employed by central government in London and throughout the country, and are involved in a wide range of government activities. They are responsible to the minister in whose department they work for the implementation of government policies. A change of minister or government does not require a change of civil servants, since they are expected to be politically neutral and to serve the sitting government impartially. Restrictions on political activities and publication are consequently imposed upon them in order to ensure neutrality.

There are some 550,000 civil servants in Britain today. Nearly half of these are women, but few of them are appointed to top ranks in the service. Some aspects of departmental work have now been transferred to independent agencies in London and elsewhere, which have administrative rather than policy-making roles, such as the Driver and Vehicle Licensing Agency (DVLA) in Swansea, Wales.

The heart of the Civil Service is the Cabinet Office, whose Secretary is the head of the Civil Service. The latter is responsible for the organization of the whole Civil Service, organizes Cabinet business and coordinates high-level policy. In each ministry or department the senior official (Permanent Secretary) and his or her assistants are responsible for assisting their minister in the implementation of government policy.

There have been frequent accusations about the efficiency and effectiveness of the Civil Service, and civil servants do not have a good public image. The Conservative government plans to make the Civil Service respond to the demands of efficient administration in a cost-effective manner, and to allow a wider category of applicants than the traditional entry of Oxbridge-dominated university graduates. It is reducing numbers in the Service, departments are being broken down into executive agencies, and posts are being advertised in order to attract older people from industry, commerce and the professions.

It is often alleged that the Civil Service imposes a certain mentality upon its members and upon the implementation of government policies, which ministers are unable to combat. There is supposed to be a Civil Service way of doing things and a bias towards the status quo, which could be dangerous. But much depends upon the strength of individual ministers, and the manner in which they manage their departments. There may be some areas of concern. But the stereotyped image of a typical civil servant is not reflected in many who do an independent job of serving their political masters, and work with ministers for common departmental interests. The Civil Service is also highly regarded in other countries for its efficiency and impartiality.

Parliamentary control of government

Constitutional theory suggests that Parliament should control the executive government. But today, unless there is a small-majority government, rebellion by government MPs or widespread public protest, a strong government with an overall majority in the Commons should be able to carry its policies through Parliament, irrespective of what Parliament as a collective body can do to restrain it.

The opposition parties can only oppose in Parliament in the hope of persuading the electorate to dismiss the sitting government at the next general election. Critics argue for stronger parliamentary control over the executive, which has been described as an elective dictatorship. But, given the existing electoral system and present organization of Parliament, there seems little chance of this without fundamental reform.

Formal devices such as votes of censure and no confidence, as well as amendment motions, are normally inadequate when confronting a government with a large majority in the Commons. Even rebellious government MPs will usually rally round the party on such occasions, both out of a self-interested desire to preserve their jobs and a need to prevent the collapse of the government.

Examinations of government programmes can be employed at Question Time in the Commons, when the Prime Minister and other ministers are subjected to oral and written questions from MPs. But the government can prevaricate in its answers to written questions and, while reputations can be made and lost at oral Question Time, it is a rhetorical and political occasion rather than an opportunity for in-depth analysis of government policy. However, these Question Times do have a function in holding the executive's performance up to public scrutiny. The opposition parties can also choose their own topics for debate on a limited number of days each session, which can be used to attack the government.

A 1967 innovation in restraining the executive was the creation of the Parliamentary Commissioner for Administration, who can investigate alleged bad administration by ministers and civil servants. But the office does not have the wide-ranging powers of Ombudsmen in other countries and the public have no direct access to it. It has proved to be something of a disappointment as a watchdog over executive behaviour, although its very existence does serve as a warning. But there have been no attempts to strengthen it, nor to define it more closely for greater effectiveness.

In an attempt to improve the situation, a number of parliamentary committees have been established. Standing committees of MPs in the Commons examine bills during the procedural stages until they become law, and others may consider specific bills. Such committees generally have little influence on actual policy. But in 1979 a new select committee system was created, which now consists of 14 committees. These are composed of MPs from different parties who monitor the expenditure, administration and policy of the main government departments, and closely investigate the government's programmes, record and proposed legislation. MPs previously had problems in scrutinizing government activity adequately, and party discipline made it difficult for them to act independently of party policy.

It is often argued that the real work of the House and parliamentary control of the executive is done in the committees. Their members are now proving to be more independent in questioning civil servants and ministers who are called to give evidence before them. Select committees can be very effective in examining proposed legislation and expenditure, and their reports can be very damaging to a government's reputation. Although opinions differ about their role, it does seem that they have in practice strengthened Parliament's authority against government. Nevertheless, although parliamentary scrutiny is important, it should also be remembered that under the mandate system a government is elected to carry out its declared policies.

ATTITUDES

Attitudes to politics and politicians

Public opinion polls consistently show that British politicians, government ministers, political parties and Parliament rate very low in people's esteem. They are regularly criticized, and heavily satirized in magazines, the press, and on radio and television.

However, the public's attitudes are volatile, and the statistics can be confusing since they are conditioned by biases towards particular political parties and policies. The electorate clearly holds political views which are reflected in its voting behaviour. But its reactions to government programmes may be dependent upon the current economic climate, national issues and personal situations.

None of the political parties, in spite of their frequent drifts to the centre ground, individually encompasses the diversity of views represented by the people, who may vary between egalitarian economic views and authoritarian social and moral positions. 'Conservatives are anti-egalitarian [economically] but traditionalist in morals, while Labour is egalitarian [economically] but liberal on moral questions, and the [then] Social Democrat–Liberal Alliance is vaguely in the middle' (*The Times*, 30 October 1987).

Political parties cannot satisfy everyone. But the British people appear to be looking for a political party and society which would more adequately reflect their mixture of authoritarian and egalitarian values, their desire for state interventionist policies in some social areas, and also their sense of contemporary reality. The division of the popular vote in general elections, the abstention rate, political volatility and tactical voting reflect a wide diversity of opinion in the electorate.

■ **Explain and examine the following terms:**

Whigs	executive	'three-line whip'
constitution	minister	Black Rod
Cabinet	manifesto	Oliver Cromwell
Magna Carta	conventions	Question Time
civil servant	secret ballot	backbenchers
Lords Spiritual	Tories	constitutional monarchy
the Speaker	legislature	'hung Parliament'

■ **Write short essays on the following questions:**

1 Describe what is meant by the 'two-party system', and comment upon its effectiveness.

2 Does Britain have an adequate parliamentary electoral system? If not, why not?

3 Critically examine the role of the Prime Minister.

4 Discuss the position and powers of the monarch in the British constitution.

Chapter 4

Local government

- English local government history   111
- The functions of local government   119
- *Attitudes to local government*   124
- *Exercises*   125

B RITAIN HAS A UNITARY POLITICAL SYSTEM, based on the central government in London, to deal with national matters. But many essential public services, such as education, law and order, sanitation, personal social services, housing and transport, are provided by elected councils throughout the country in cooperation with central government departments. These functions are important to, and directly affect, local people.

The present local government structure has been created by Acts of Parliament since the nineteenth century. These have defined the duties and powers which exist between local and central government, and between different units at the local level. This statutory framework means that the central government, through Parliament, has considerable control over local government. It can and does intervene in local affairs, and specifies the services that must be available at the local level. It can change, increase or abolish the powers and structures of local government. Regulations or by-laws can be introduced by local councils to control specific small-scale services and activities in their areas, but generally only with government approval.

However, local authorities have a considerable autonomy within this parliamentary framework, and some discretion as to how they prioritize and organize their services to the public. This situation is said to combine the efficiency of knowing what is most suitable for a local area with the democratic right of local people to organize their own affairs. It implies a sense of community and liberty outside the restraints of central government.

But, because central government provides over 80 per cent of the money spent by local authorities on their services, there is political and financial friction between the two levels. Local councils can incline strongly to a particular political line or prioritize certain services, which may result in policies that are not acceptable to the electorate or the central government. Some councils have been accused of using public money to fund prestige projects, political programmes and minority concerns, which are not in the best interests of the community as a whole.

Although central government has not traditionally exercised detailed supervision over local activities, governments have increasingly intervened in policy and financial matters. Ultimately, central government does have the responsibility to maintain financial stability in local government, and has the power to demand national uniformity in the provision and standard of local services.

The Conservative government since 1979 has been trying to control local authorities more tightly by introducing reforms and more competitive considerations into their organization. Local government, on the other hand, has attempted to retain its traditional powers and freedom of operation. The conflicts and problems of local government are consequently central to life in contemporary Britain. They raise questions about the nature of local autonomy and the power of central government to intervene in local affairs in the national interest.

This chapter deals mainly with local government in England. But the English structures and reform processes have also been reflected in Wales, Scotland and Northern Ireland. These three countries each have a minister in the central government who is responsible for the organization of their affairs. The main links between local authorities and central government in England are the Environment, Health and Education Departments, and the Home Office.

English local government history

Early attempts to divide England up into smaller areas for the purpose of more efficient administration occurred in Saxon times. The main units of local government gradually became the parish, the borough and the county (or shire). Before the nineteenth century, boroughs and counties were organized on behalf of the central government by local civil officials.

The *parish* was, and still is, the smallest unit of local government. It was centred on the churches, which were built after England had been converted to Christianity in AD 596–7. The parish was gradually granted some civil functions in later centuries, which allowed it to provide for the welfare of the poor and the maintenance of public roads and buildings in its area. Today the inhabitants of rural parishes still elect councils, which have some limited duties in local government. But urban parishes have lost all their civil functions and serve only as church units.

The next largest local government entity was the *borough*. From Norman times until relatively recently, the status of borough was granted to large towns or areas by the monarch. This gave the new borough independence to organize its own local government services. It had its own courts of law, by-laws, agricultural markets and the privilege of sending representatives to Parliament. In addition, some towns were given the special title of 'city' because of their size, economic importance or roles as cathedral centres. Today British cities and towns vary considerably in size and population, but some have retained their own separate local government status, ancient titles and civic responsibilities.

The *county* has generally been the most important and largest unit of local government (now called regions in Scotland). The physical outlines of English counties have not altered much over the centuries, although there have been amalgamations of some of them in the twentieth century. But their population sizes have varied considerably over time, and have reflected demographic, social and economic changes.

The English population increased rapidly during the nineteenth century under the impetus of the industrial revolutions. Large manufacturing towns developed and the countryside was progressively depopulated. Demand grew in both urban and rural areas for basic public services, such as sanitation, education, housing, health facilities and transport, which could be placed under the control of elected local councils. The development of modern local government on a nationally planned basis was begun in the nineteenth century, in response to these needs.

The Municipal Corporations Act of 1835 established a council system of councillors and aldermen in the boroughs, who were elected by local ratepayers (property owners who paid taxes on their property). As urban areas expanded in the 1880s, larger towns were given a new independent status as county boroughs, and functioned separately from the geographical counties in which they were located.

Similar changes affected the counties in the 1880s. Local Government Acts gave administrative duties to county councils, which consisted of councillors who were elected by borough ratepayers. Later in the nineteenth century, each county was divided into urban and rural districts. The county councils were mainly responsible for large-scale functions in their area and for overall policy-making. The urban and district councils were concerned with more local duties and the implementation of county programmes.

This complicated system of local government continued into the twentieth century. It had to provide for further population increases, the growth of towns and the demands of the new welfare state. But the system became increasingly unsatisfactory as towns expanded their suburbs into rural areas and beyond the existing administrative boundaries. This development was particularly severe in the conurbations (large areas of dense population around the major cities, such as Birmingham, London, Manchester and Liverpool). Rural areas now included urban and suburban components, and the distinction between town and countryside was being lost in an 'urban sprawl'. Planning programmes, policy implementation and provision of services became more difficult and uncoordinated because of competing interests.

The local government system required radical reorganization, and a series of reform proposals was made in the 1960s, accompanied by much controversy and bitter debate. Most attempts before the 1960s to change local government structures had provoked fierce resistance from groups with community pride or vested interests. However, substantial alterations did take place in the 1960s and 1970s. They were intended to make local government more efficient, more representative and more suitable to the needs and complexity of contemporary society. Apart from

London, where reorganization had started in the 1960s, most of the present local government structures in England, Wales, Scotland and Northern Ireland date from changes in the early 1970s.

The London reforms

Local government in London was the first to be altered in the 1960s, because population growth in the old County of London had resulted in most people living outside the county limits. The London Government Act of 1963 created a new County of London ('Greater London'), which contained some 8 million people, 3 million of whom lived within the old county boundaries, or 'Inner London'. Today Greater London includes parts of the counties of Hertfordshire, Surrey, Essex and Kent, together with the whole of the old county of Middlesex.

PLATE 4.1 Islington town hall, London *(Melanie Friend/Format)*

But the new London population and its size of 610 sq miles (1,580 sq km) were too large for effective unified supervision by any one body. Greater London was therefore divided up into 32 boroughs, each with about 250,000 people. Local services were organized by elected councils in these boroughs, and the large-scale policy and planning functions rested with an elected Greater London Council (GLC).

The Greater London Council was the object of bitter political battles in the early 1980s, as it fought for its survival and policies against central government. But the Conservative government abolished the GLC in 1986, and transferred its powers and functions to the 32 boroughs or joint authorities. The abolition battle was controversial. Critics argued that the government was interfering politically in the running of a Labour-controlled authority. The government considered the GLC to be too large, inefficient, and given to overspending on dubious policies and causes. The exercise may be seen either as the restoration of functions to smaller, more accountable local government units in the boroughs, or as a governmental attempt to centralize power. Critics argue that London should have its own independent, elected council, and the Labour Party intends to restore a structure like the GLC if it is returned to power.

The ancient City of London, which covers 1 sq mile (2.6 sq km), was not part of the London reorganization and is a separate unit of local government within Greater London. The City is a commercial, banking, legal and financial centre with few public services and permanent inhabitants, although property developments such as the Barbican have encouraged more people to live there. The annually elected Lord Mayor of London is the chief official of the City. This office is largely ceremonial, but is important for fund-raising, public relations and chairing many of the City's institutions.

Reforms outside London

The Local Government Reorganization Act of 1972 simplified the local government system outside London and reduced the number of councils. England remained divided into counties, some of which, like Cleveland, Cumbria and Avon, were new, while others, like Westmorland and Rutland, disappeared. In some cases boundaries were changed and ancient counties were amalgamated, albeit in the face of strong local opposition. The remaining counties were mostly based on the existing geographical units, together with their county capitals.

Elected county councils today are responsible for overall planning policies and large-scale services in their areas, such as the police, education, fire brigades, libraries and social services. The counties are divided into elected district councils, which attend to items such as housing and sanitation, environmental health and the implementation of county programmes.

PLATE 4.2   Manchester town hall *(COI)*

The 1972 Act also established six metropolitan county councils to serve the needs of large conurbations with heavy population densities in the Midlands and the north (see figure 4.1). These councils contained 36 metropolitan district councils, which were responsible for many local services under the direction of the metropolitan county councils. However, the Conservative government abolished the metropolitan county councils in 1986, arguing that they were too large, inefficient, remote and financially wasteful. Today the metropolitan district councils or joint authorities have the powers which were enjoyed by the metropolitan counties.

Consequently England now has 39 non-metropolitan county councils, which are subdivided into 296 non-metropolitan district councils. Additionally there are the 36 metropolitan district councils, which cover the old metropolitan county council areas, and the 32 London boroughs and the City, which cover the old Greater London Council area. To add to the confusion, there are still some remnants of the old borough system, and a few cities have preserved their own city councils and ancient titles. But these areas are, in practice, district councils.

Similar changes in the rest of Britain were also being made. In Wales, the counties were reduced from 13 to eight and subdivided into 37 district councils; some new counties were created; and community councils, which function similarly to parish councils, were retained. Scotland was divided into nine regions with subdivisions into 53 districts, together with authorities having responsibility for the Orkneys, the Shetlands and the Western Isles. Northern Ireland had six counties which were divided into 26 districts.

These changes in local government structures were controversial, difficult and expensive. They were confusing to local citizens, and often seen as an affront to community pride and identity. The decrease in the number of local councils resulted in fewer elected councillors, and a corresponding reduction in local representation. Critics argue that, while the local government reforms introduced some rationalization and economic sense, they lacked any real discussion of how local democracy could best be served.

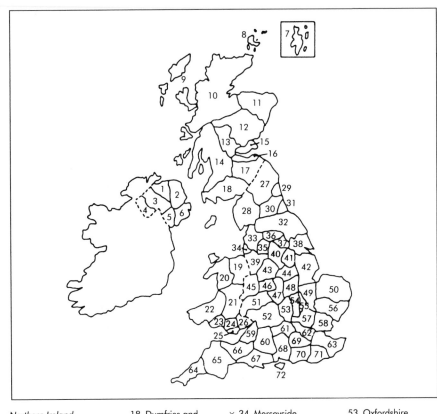

Northern Ireland	18 Dumfries and	× 34 Merseyside	53 Oxfordshire
1 Londonderry	Galloway	× 35 Manchester	54 Buckinghamshire
2 Antrin	*Wales*	× 36 West Yorkshire	55 Bedfordshire
3 Tyrone	19 Clwyd	× 37 South Yorkshire	56 Suffolk
4 Fermanagh	20 Gwynedd	38 Humberside	57 Hertfordshire
5 Armagh	21 Powys	39 Cheshire	58 Essex
6 Down	22 Dyfed	40 Derbyshire	59 Avon
	23 West Glamorgan	41 Nottinghamshire	60 Wiltshire
Scotland	24 Mid Glamorgan	42 Lincolnshire	61 Berkshire
7 Shetland	25 South Glamorgan	43 Staffordshire	O 62 London
8 Orkney	26 Gwent	44 Leicestershire	63 Kent
9 Western Isles		45 Shropshire	64 Cornwall
10 Highland	*England*	× 46 West Midlands	65 Devonshire
11 Grampian	27 Northumberland	47 Warwickshire	66 Somerset
12 Tayside	28 Cumbria	48 Northamptonshire	67 Dorset
13 Central	× 29 Tyne and Wear	49 Cambridgeshire	68 Hampshire
14 Strathclyde	30 Durham	50 Norfolk	69 Surrey
15 Fife	31 Cleveland	51 Hereford and	70 West Sussex
16 Lothian	32 North Yorkshire	Worcester	71 East Sussex
17 Borders	33 Lancashire	52 Gloucestershire	72 Isle of Wight

× Old Metropolitan County Councils   O Old Greater London Council

FIGURE 4.1   The British counties and regions

There had also been proposals in the 1960s and 1970s to give more devolved self-government to Wales and Scotland, and suggestions that regional assemblies should be established in England. But these attempts to bring about greater local self-determination failed due to the rejection of referendums in Scotland and Wales in 1979. Britain remains a unitary state with centralized power in London, rather than a federal one.

In 1992, the Conservative government appointed a Commission to review local government structures in England. It is likely that the Commission's work will result in a number of unitary or single-tier authorities in the English counties, although the existing two-tier structure of counties and districts may remain in some places. The unitary authorities will handle all local matters in their areas, and effectively remove the ancient county structure. There has been considerable tension between the Commission and central government over the plans, and controversy over suggested changes at local level. Critics argue that the exercise is further evidence of the Conservative government's attempts to centralize power and control smaller local government units. Similar changes are also planned for Scotland and Wales.

The functions of local government

Counties and districts in England have their own councils, which are elected by the adult population of the area. The number of councillors elected depends on population size. Most of the county councils have between 40 and 100, and district councils between 30 and 50. Elections are staggered, but in effect take place every four years, and councillors hold office for four years. They are elected by the 'first past the post' system in most parts of Britain (except Northern Ireland where PR operates). Public interest in local elections is small, unless there are pressing or controversial issues at stake, with less than 30 per cent of the electorate voting in many areas.

Councillors are not paid for their council work, thus continuing the amateur, part-time tradition of local government. But they may receive attendance and expense allowances for performing their duties. They decide policy for their local area, and come from a broad cross-section of society, such as industrial workers, teachers, business people, academics, trade unionists and housewives.

Their reasons for serving may derive from a sense of public duty, notions of prestige or a desire for political power. Councillors may gain some indirect personal benefit from their positions. But standards of honesty and integrity are generally high, although occasional cases of fraud and corruption are reported. Nevertheless, councillors do devote a considerable amount of time and energy to their duties, without which local government would collapse.

Councils have a chairman or woman who is chosen by the council members to preside over council meetings, and who usually holds office for one year. These chairmen or women have other formal duties, since they are the official representatives of their areas. In a borough, they may have the ancient title of Mayor, and in some large cities that of Lord Mayor. In Scottish towns, the equivalent titles are Provost and Lord Provost.

Local politics was once run partly on non-party lines, and many 'Independent' or non-party councillors were elected. Today, local government is dominated by the national political parties.

PLATE 4.3 Britain's first Asian mayor: Rabindara Pathak at Ealing town hall, London, 1987 *(Brenda Prince/Format)*

They try to achieve power bases in the regions, which will solidify their national position, and local government often serves as a training ground for potential Westminster politicians. Labour, Conservative and Liberal Democrat candidates fight each other for control of the councils. A council may be controlled by one of the parties if it wins a majority of the seats at the election. But a minority party may hold the balance of power if no other party has an overall majority, and can influence policy-making. Critics argue that the participation of national parties in, and the disappearance of Independents from, local government have affected local democracy and made it an aspect of national politics.

Local elections have increasingly been seen as an important indication of how the electorate in the country is responding to the current central government. The public may demonstrate disapproval of government policy by its voting patterns in local elections, to such an extent that the planning of a general election can in part depend upon local results. At the local elections in May 1994 the Conservatives performed very badly, losing many seats and control of local councils; the Labour Party capitalized on the Conservative government's unpopularity by substantially gaining seats and council control; and the Liberal Democrats also strengthened their position. Governments have become very sensitive to these barometers of popular feeling, and other parties also judge their national positions by such results.

The work of local government is onerous and must be shared out, rather than being dealt with by all the councillors in the full council. Most councils therefore operate through committees, which usually represent one main aspect of the council's work, such as education or housing. They consist of elected councillors, with the different parties represented proportionally to their strength on the full council. But, normally, important issues and matters of policy are decided by the full council, to which the individual committees can make recommendations. In most cases all the meetings, reports, minutes and papers of the council are now open to the public in the interests of greater freedom of information and official accountability.

Councillors and their committees are serviced by permanent

professional staff. These function similarly to civil servants in central government, and are expected to be neutral in carrying out the policies of the council. While they are essential to the operation of local government, critics argue that they have increased bureaucracy and inefficiency, as well as distancing elected representatives from their constituents. As more work is devolved to unelected officials, there is a potential danger of the further professionalization and remoteness of a system which was initially intended to provide citizen self-government.

Local government in Britain employs some 3 million people in professional, technical and administrative capacities (one-tenth of the national workforce). In addition to the professional administrators, these include teachers (who form half the number), firemen, manual workers, social services staff and the police. Conservative governments have tried to reduce public spending in these areas by financial restrictions and by encouraging greater competition, such as tendering contracts for local services to the private sector. Its policies regarding public housing ('right-to-buy') and state schools ('opting-out') have also limited local authority spending and control (see chapters 8 and 9). Nevertheless, the cost of local government still amounts to some one-quarter of total central government expenditure.

The councils need finance in order to pay for their services. In Britain there is no income tax paid directly by local inhabitants to the council. Local government finance comes mainly from central government grants (56 per cent), and non-domestic rates charged on commercial properties throughout Britain (28 per cent) which is redistributed by central government to local government. The main direct local government revenue derives from the new council tax (16 per cent), which replaced the controversial community charge, or 'poll tax' in 1993. Further finance may be raised by council borrowing and the rent from council houses and flats (public housing let usually to low-income groups). But the proceeds of the sale of such housing under the 'right-to-buy' policy (sitting tenants purchasing their rented property) go to central government and cannot be spent by local government.

The council tax is determined by the local council and is payable by every householder in the area. It is based on the value of domestic property (divided into eight price bands depending upon market value) and a personal element (based upon two adult people occupying a property). Rebates from the tax are given to the needy, low-income groups and single-occupancy properties. While the council tax model is not as controversial as its predecessors, some critics argue that it is not a great improvement.

The central government therefore makes substantial grants to local councils, amounting to over 80 per cent of local income. These come from the national tax revenues and provide finance, without which local government would be unable to implement its policies or services. The grants vary in amount because of disparities in wealth between different parts of the country, and because of different needs for specific services. However, the government can alter or withhold (cap) its grants to those councils which set excessive budgets, and this may lead to a reduction in local services.

Such policies have been seen by critics as financial and political interference in local affairs by central government. Local councillors maintain their right to set appropriate budgets in order to provide the services for which they were elected. The situation has resulted in a continuing battle between the two levels of government. Central government is now involving itself in local government to a greater extent than in the past, and over a wider area. Educational and housing reforms, privatization measures and pressures on central government grants have all meant a reduction in the traditional areas of local autonomy.

The problems of local government in Britain might be solved by more satisfactory local structures, in which councils have increased powers to promote their own legislation and raise local income tax directly from their constituents. But central government is loath to give up its powers and to devolve authority. There is consequently a widespread feeling that the twentieth-century reforms of local government have been inadequate.

Meanwhile, the Liberal Democrats want regional or federal

government throughout Britain. The Welsh and Scottish National Parties may again campaign for devolved powers (or even independence) for Wales and Scotland. The Labour Party would also restore greater authority to the regions. The Conservative government, however, has increased its political and economic control over local government, and, although the outcome of its review into local government in England is uncertain, the centralizing trend seems likely to continue.

ATTITUDES

Attitudes to local government

Public opinion polls reveal that local government and its services (particularly the council tax, housing, education and the social services) are a source of concern for British people. But while some are dissatisfied with their local councillors (particularly in London), others seem to be reasonably content and feel that officials are not as faceless as they are sometimes assumed to be. Attitudes differ in different parts of the country, and may depend upon the commitment and input of local political parties.

However, critics argue that low turnouts for local elections indicate that people feel local government is unimportant, or that it is too remote and party-based to respond effectively to their needs. But local inhabitants still count on council services, which are often essential to their daily lives, and can react to community issues.

■ Explain and examine the following terms:

by-laws	Provost	council tax	Inner London
district	Mayor	councillors	urban sprawl
borough	county	conurbation	regions
GLC	parish	'Independent'	council houses

■ Write short essays on the following questions:

1 How is local government finance raised, and what does it consist of?

2 Is the system of English local government satisfactory? If not, suggest alternatives.

3 What is the role of central government in English local government?

Chapter 5

International relations

- Foreign policy and defence   128
- The Commonwealth   133
- The European Union (EU)   135
- Eire and Northern Ireland   140
- *Exercises*   145

B RITAIN'S INTERNATIONAL POSITION as a colonial, economic and political power was already in relative decline by the early years of the twentieth century. Some large colonies had achieved self-governing status, and the growth of nationalism in African and Asian nations later persuaded Britain to decolonize further. The effects of global industrial competition, two World Wars, and domestic economic and social problems gradually forced Britain to recognize its reduced status, and to establish different priorities. Some of the previous international links continue in altered form, while other relationships are new. But, in spite of these changes, Britain still experiences uncertainties and dilemmas about its influence and appropriate role on the world stage.

Foreign policy and defence

Britain's international position today is that of a medium-sized country which is dwarfed economically by Germany, Japan and the Pacific economies, and the USA. Yet some of its leaders still seem to believe that it can have international influence and a global role. Critics argue that Britain's foreign policy and national self-image do not reflect the reality of its world position and conflict with its domestic interests. Although it is reducing its defence and overseas commitments, the expenditure currently involved might be directed more profitably to internal problems.

Nevertheless, Britain's foreign and defence policies reflect its traditional position as a major trading nation and its self-interested concern to maintain stable economic and political conditions through global cooperation. Although its manufacturing base has declined, international commercial activities continue to be important and Britain has maintained its position as a world finance centre. Its exports of goods and services account for over a quarter of its gross national product. It has substantial overseas investments and a range of international activities, and imports a third of its food and over half its raw-material requirements. Britain is therefore dependent upon maintaining its global connections, even though it is becoming increasingly committed to Europe.

Britain's major *defence* alliance is with the North Atlantic Treaty Organization (NATO), comprising Belgium, Canada, Denmark, France, Iceland, Italy, Luxembourg, the Netherlands, Norway, Spain, Portugal, Britain, the USA, Greece, Turkey and Germany. The original justification for NATO was that it provided its members with greater security than any could achieve individually, and was a deterrent against aggression.

All the major British political parties are in favour of retaining the NATO link and, according to opinion polls, the public would not support any party which tried to take Britain out of the alliance. Membership of NATO also allows Britain to operate militarily on the international stage. Its defence policy is based on NATO strategies, and it assigns most of its armed forces and defence budget to the organization.

Despite changes in Eastern Europe and proposals to transform NATO into a reduced and more flexible military association, the British government takes such developments cautiously and is concerned to maintain military defence with both conventional and nuclear forces. This position is due to fears of European instability and the risk to its own security if it were substantially to reduce its armed defences.

However, with the growth of European Union defence and foreign policies, it is likely that European countries will take on a larger share of their own defence and international security outside the NATO alliance. The vehicle for this development may be the Western European Union (WEU), of which Britain is a member. It is intended that the WEU will become a bridge between NATO defence structures and the security policies of European Union member states.

The British government plans considerable cuts in its defence budgets in the 1990s, with reductions in the number of the armed forces, ships, aircraft and equipment. It will in future depend on leaner, more flexible forces, although there have been strenuous objections to these policies from the military. Britain's defence expenditure remains a considerable proportion of its gross domestic product (4.1 per cent in 1992, with planned reduction to 3.2 per cent by 1995–6). The primary objectives of defence policy are to ensure the country's security and the NATO commitment. However, defence spending is still higher than in other European countries, and raises questions as to whether the money could be better spent in other areas of national life.

Nuclear weapons, which account for a large part of the defence budget, continue to be fiercely debated. Britain's independent nuclear deterrent consists mainly of long-range American-built Trident missiles carried by a fleet of four submarines. Successive governments have committed themselves to upgrading nuclear weapons at great expense. Critics would like to see cheaper alternatives provided, or the cancellation of the nuclear system. However, even with recent changes in Eastern Europe, it seems that the British nuclear strategy will continue. All the major political parties are now multilateralist (keeping nuclear weapons until they can be abolished on a global basis), although there are some variations in actual policy.

Britain is also able to operate militarily outside the NATO and European area, although this capacity is becoming increasingly expensive and limited. Military garrisons are stationed in Brunei, Cyprus, the Far and Middle East, the Falkland Islands, Gibraltar and Hong Kong. The 1982 Falklands War and the 1991 Gulf War showed that Britain was eventually able to respond effectively to challenges outside the NATO area, although the operations did draw attention to defects and problems in such commitments.

The total strength of the armed forces, which are now all volunteer following the abolition of conscription in 1960, was 271,000 in 1993. This was made up of 58,500 in the Royal Navy and Royal Marines, 133,000 in the Army and 79,300 in the Royal Air Force. Women personnel in the Army, Navy and Air Force amount to some 18,000 and are integral parts of the armed services. They were previously confined to support roles but, since 1989–90, Navy and Air Force women may now be employed in front-line military activities. Reserve and auxiliary forces support the regular professional forces, such as the Territorial Army, which reinforces NATO ground troops and helps to maintain security in Britain.

Britain's *civil defence*, which was mainly concerned with the threat of nuclear war, has been criticized for its unpreparedness, lack of resources and inefficiency. It is mainly based on the existing peacetime elements of government departments, local authorities and emergency services. Civil defence regulations require these institutions to prepare a range of essential functions in the event of war or emergencies, to arrange training courses for civil defence staff and to provide suitable emergency centres. However, although more money has been spent on these services, civil defence exercises still reveal limitations.

Britain's *foreign policy* and membership of international organizations are based on the notion that overseas objectives can be best attained by cooperation with other nations on a regional or global basis. The imperial days of unilateral action are now largely past, although Britain did take such action in the 1982 Falklands War. But British foreign policy can reflect particular biases, with support for one country outweighing that for another. The USA has been Britain's closest ally in recent years, and it has often been considered, rightly or wrongly, that a 'special relationship' exists between the two. However, this association varies according to circumstances, although Britain is concerned to maintain the American military presence in Europe and NATO.

Public opinion polls reveal that people feel the USA is now of less importance to Britain than Europe. Britain's membership of the European Union means that it is to some extent dependent upon common EU foreign policy. But, although the EU is moving to more unified policies, the member states do sometimes have conflicting interests.

Britain also has diplomatic relations with over 160 nations, and is a member of some 120 international organizations, ranging from bodies for economic cooperation to the United Nations (UN).

PLATE 5.1 The Foreign and Commonwealth Office, Whitehall, London *(COI)*

Support for the UN and the principles of its charter has been part of British foreign policy since 1945, although there has sometimes been scepticism about its effectiveness as a practical body.

However, as a permanent member of the UN Security Council, Britain has a vested interest in supporting the UN. It sees a strong UN as a necessary framework for achieving many of its own foreign policy objectives, such as the peaceful resolution of conflict, arms control, disarmament and the protection of human rights. UN agencies also provide important forums for discussing issues in which Britain is involved, such as disaster relief, the use of the sea-bed, terrorism, the environment, energy development and world resources. Yet Britain, like other nations worldwide, is ready to ignore the UN when it sees its own interests challenged.

The Commonwealth

The British Empire was built up over several centuries. It began with the internal domination of the British Isles by the English, and was followed by trading activities and colonization in North and South America. Emigrants from Britain then settled in countries such as Australia, South Africa and New Zealand. Parts of Africa, Asia and the West Indies were also exploited for trading purposes and became colonies. By the nineteenth century, British political rule and possessions embraced a quarter of the world's population.

The Empire developed into the British Empire and Commonwealth in the late nineteenth and early twentieth centuries when Canada, Australia, New Zealand and South Africa became self-governing dominions and achieved independence. Many of their people were descendants of those settlers who had emigrated from Britain in earlier centuries. They regarded Britain as the mother country, and preserved the values of a shared kinship. But this relationship has changed considerably as national identities have become more firmly established.

In the mid-twentieth century, the British Empire and Commonwealth became the British Commonwealth as British governments granted independence to other colonies. India and Pakistan became independent in 1947, followed by African territories in the 1950s and 1960s, and later most of the islands of the West Indies. The British Commonwealth then developed into the Commonwealth of Nations, as almost all the remaining British colonies became independent. They could choose whether they wanted to break all connections with the colonial past or remain within the Commonwealth as independent nations. Most of them decided to stay in the Commonwealth for various reasons. Only a few small British colonies, dependencies and protectorates now remain, and are scattered widely, such as the Falklands, Gibraltar and Hong Kong.

The present Commonwealth is a free and flexible association of some 50 independent states (including Britain). It does not have written laws, an elected Parliament or one political ruler. There is evidence of colonial rule in many of the countries, such as educational and legal systems modelled on British patterns. But few have kept the British form of parliamentary government. Some have adapted it to their own needs, while others are one-party states or have constitutions based on a wide variety of models, with varying records on civil and democratic rights.

The Commonwealth has nearly a quarter of the world's population, and comprises peoples of different religions, races and nationalities, who share a history of struggles for independence from colonialism. The Commonwealth is sometimes described, perhaps in an over-sentimental way, as a family of nations. However, despite occasional wars, tensions and quarrels between these family members, it can operate as a worthwhile organization.

The British monarch is its non-political head and has varying constitutional roles in different countries, depending on whether they are separate kingdoms or republics. The monarch is a focal point of identification and has an important unifying and symbolic function, which has often kept the Commonwealth together in times of crisis and conflict.

The Prime Ministers, or heads of state, in Commonwealth countries meet every two years under the auspices of the monarch for Commonwealth Conferences in different parts of the world. Common problems are discussed and sometimes settled, although there seem to have been more arguments than agreements in recent years, with Britain having a minority position on some issues.

There is a Commonwealth Secretariat in London which coordinates policy for the Commonwealth, in addition to many Commonwealth societies, institutes, libraries, professional associations and university exchange programmes. Commonwealth citizens still travel to Britain as immigrants, students and visitors, while British emigration to Commonwealth countries continues in reduced amounts. English in its many varieties remains the common language of the Commonwealth, and the Commonwealth Games are held every four years. There are many joint

British/Commonwealth programmes on both official and voluntary levels in agriculture, engineering, health and education, in which some vestiges of the old relationship between Britain and the Commonwealth are still apparent.

But doubts have been raised in Britain as to whether the Commonwealth any longer has an effective and influential voice in world affairs. Arguably, there is no longer the traditional sense of Commonwealth solidarity and purpose, and Britain has little in common with some Commonwealth nations. Critics argue that unless member countries feel there are valid reasons for continuing an association which represents historical accident rather than common purpose, the long-term future of the Commonwealth must be in doubt. Indeed, successive British governments have been moving closer to Europe and distancing themselves from the Commonwealth, and public opinion polls reveal that Europe is now more important for British people than the Commonwealth.

Britain had preferential trading arrangements with the Commonwealth before it joined the European Union in 1973, and the Commonwealth question formed part of the debate on membership. EU entry was seen as ending the relationship between Britain and the Commonwealth. But trading between the two has continued, although Britain has a declining share of this market, and its economic priorities are now more with the European Union and other world partners.

The European Union (EU)

The ideal of a united Europe, strong in economic and political institutions, became increasingly attractive to European statesmen after the Second World War. There was a desire to create a peaceful and prosperous Europe after the destruction of two World Wars, and after centuries of antagonism and mutual distrust between the European powers.

The foundations for a more integrated Europe were established in 1957 when six countries signed the Treaty of Rome and formed the European Economic Community (EEC). Britain did not join, but instead helped to create the European Free Trade Association (EFTA) in 1959, together with Sweden, Norway, Austria, Denmark, Portugal and Switzerland. Britain distanced itself from closer European connections in the 1950s, and saw its future in the trading patterns of the Commonwealth and an assumed 'special relationship' with the USA. It regarded itself as a commercial power, and did not wish to be restricted by European relationships. An ancient suspicion of Europe also caused many British people to shrink from membership of a European organization, which they thought might result in the loss of their identity and independence.

However, a European commitment was growing among influential sections of British society in the 1960s. But attempts by Britain to join the EEC were vetoed by the French President, Charles de Gaulle. He was critical of Britain's relationship with the USA (particularly on nuclear weapons policies), queried the extent of British commitment to Europe, and arguably did not want Britain as a potential rival for the leadership of the EEC.

De Gaulle resigned from the French presidency in 1969, and new British negotiations on membership began in 1970 under the pro-European Conservative Prime Minister, Edward Heath. In 1972, the British Parliament voted in favour of entry, despite widespread doubts and the strong opposition of a politically diverse group of interests among the British people. Britain, together with Denmark and the Irish Republic, formally joined the EEC on 1 January 1973, having left EFTA in 1972.

However, in 1974, a new Labour government under Harold Wilson was committed to giving the British people a referendum on continued membership. After further renegotiations of the terms of entry, the referendum was held in 1975, the first in British political history. The pro-marketeers won by a margin of two to one (67.2 per cent in favour, 32.8 per cent against).

Other nations later joined the EEC, and there are now 12 members with a total population of some 345 million people (Britain, Denmark, Germany, Greece, Belgium, the Republic of Ireland, Luxembourg, the Netherlands, France, Italy, Spain and Portugal). The EEC was based initially on economic concerns,

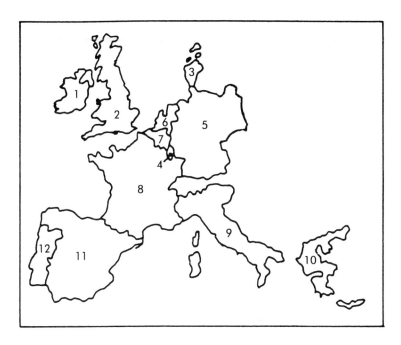

1	Irish Republic	5	Germany	9	Italy
2	Britain	6	Netherlands	10	Greece
3	Denmark	7	Belgium	11	Spain
4	Luxembourg	8	France	12	Portugal

FIGURE 5.1 The European Union (1994)

and instituted harmonization programmes, such as the Common
Agricultural and fisheries policies, and development aid to
depressed areas within its borders. Britain's poorer regions have
benefited considerably from regional funds. In 1986 the member
states formed an internal or Single European Market, in which
goods, services, people and capital could operate freely across
national frontiers within the EEC.

Some politicians had always hoped that economic integration
would lead in time to political initiatives and result in a federal
Europe. The Maastricht Treaty of 1991 was a step in this process,
as a result of which the European Community became the

European Union (EU). The Treaty provides, among other things, for a common European currency, a European Bank, and common defence, foreign and social policies.

The British Conservative government, however, prefers a slower and more pragmatic process, and has opted out of Maastricht's monetary and Social Chapter provisions (which give social and employment protection to EU workers). It has also withdrawn from the Exchange Rate Mechanism (ERM) of the European Monetary System (EMS), which had been intended to promote currency stability and to draw European currencies closer together. Some politicians in Britain want full economic and political integration on federal lines, while others see the EU as a free-trade area in which national legal rights and interests are firmly retained. Over half of Britain's trade is now with other EU countries.

The EU is currently enlarging its potential membership to include Sweden, Finland, Norway and Austria by 1995, and is attempting to join Eastern European nations to the EU system. The actual and potential growth of the Union has been seen as providing an important political voice in world affairs and a powerful trading area in global economic matters.

The institutions involved in the running of the EU are the European Council, Council of Ministers, European Commission, European Parliament and European Court of Justice.

The European Council consists of government leaders who meet several times a year to discuss and agree on broad areas of policy. The Council of Ministers is the principal policy-implementing body, and is normally composed of Foreign Ministers (or their equivalents) from the member states.

The Commission, under a rotating presidency, is the central force of the EU, proposes programmes and policy to the Council of Ministers, and is responsible for the administration of the EU. It comprises commissioners (of whom there are two from Britain) chosen from member states to hold certain portfolios, such as agriculture or competition policy, for a renewable four-year period. Their interests then become those of the EU and not of their national governments.

The European Parliament (in which Britain has 87 seats – see table 5.1) is directly elected for a five-year term on a party-political basis from the EU-wide electorate. Its functions are to advise the Council of Ministers on Commission proposals, to determine the EU budget and to exert some political control over the Council and the Commission. Its powers of veto over EU policy have now been extended by the Maastricht Treaty, and in the 1994 British EU Parliament elections the Conservatives did very badly compared with the Labour Party, while the Liberal Democrats suffered because of the 'first past the post' system.

TABLE 5.1 European Union Parliament: election results (Britain), 1994

Party	Seats	Vote (%)
Conservative	18	26.9
Labour	62	42.7
Liberal Democrats	2	16.1
Scottish National Party	2	3.1
Northern Irish parties	3	7.1

The Court of Justice comprises judges from the member states. It settles disputes concerning EU law, and is a very influential factor because it also determines the application of EU law in the domestic systems of the member states.

Critics argue that the Council of Ministers and the Commission should be more democratically accountable, and that the Parliament, as the only elected body, should have more power. But the EU is a new structure on the world stage. It will take time before its institutions achieve their final shape, and before the member states agree as to what that shape should be.

Britain's membership of the EU has been a difficult one. It has complained in the past about its contribution to the budget, and has received rebates; objected to the workings of the Common Agricultural and fisheries policies; and opposed movements towards political federalism and monetary harmonization. Critics maintain that Britain's sovereignty and independence are threatened by EU developments. But all the major political parties are officially pro-European, although there are opposition groups within the Labour and Conservative Parties. The country is now so closely tied to Europe in economic and institutional ways that withdrawal would be very difficult in practical terms. But there are divided views about the pace and direction of future developments.

Opinion polls reveal that while there is support for the EU among the British public, that support tends to be lukewarm and indifferent. The turnout for British EU Parliament elections is the lowest in Europe, and there is still a lack of knowledge about the EU and its institutional realities. But Europe is considered to be more important to Britain than the USA and the Commonwealth.

Eire and Northern Ireland

Northern Ireland (also known as 'the six counties', or Ulster after the ancient kingdom in the north of the island) is constitutionally a part of the United Kingdom. But its history is inseparable from that of the Republic of Ireland (Ireland or Eire). Historically, mainland Britain has been unable to accommodate itself successfully to its next-door neighbours. During the twentieth century, as Britain has detached itself from empire and entered the European Union, its relationship with Northern Ireland and Eire has been problematic.

A basic knowledge of the island's long and troubled history is essential in order to understand the present situation in Northern Ireland, for any solution to the problems there cannot be simplistic. Ireland was first attacked by England in the twelfth century. Since then there have been continuous rebellions by the native Irish against English colonial, political and military rule.

The situation worsened in the sixteenth century, when Catholic Ireland refused to accept the Protestant Reformation, despite much religious persecution. The two seeds of future hatred, colonialism and religion, were thus early sown in Irish history. A hundred years later, Oliver Cromwell crushed rebellions in Ireland, and continued the earlier 'plantation policy', by which English and Scottish settlers were given land and rights over the native Irish. These colonists also served as a police force to put down any Irish revolts. The descendants of the Protestant settlers became a powerful political minority in Ireland as a whole, and a permanent majority in the northern counties of Ulster. In 1690, the Protestant William III (William of Orange) crushed Catholic uprisings at the Battle of the Boyne and secured Protestant dominance in Northern Ireland.

Ireland was then, as now, mainly an agricultural country, dependent upon its farming produce. But crop failures were frequent, and famine in the middle of the nineteenth century caused death and emigration, with the result that the Irish population was halved. The people who remained demanded more Irish autonomy over their own affairs. Irish MPs in the Westminster Parliament called persistently for 'home rule' for Ireland (control of internal matters by the Irish through an assembly in Dublin). The home rule question dominated late nineteenth- and early twentieth-century British politics. It led to periodic outbreaks of violence as the Northern Irish Protestant majority feared that an independent and united Ireland would be dominated by the Catholics.

Eventually, in 1921 Ireland was divided (or partitioned) into two parts as a result of political decisions, uprisings and violence. This attempted solution of the historical problem has been at the root of troubles ever since. The 26 counties of southern Ireland became the Irish Free State and a dominion in the Commonwealth. It later developed into the Republic of Ireland (Eire), remained neutral in the Second World War and left the Commonwealth in 1949. The six counties in the north became known as Northern Ireland, and remained constitutionally part of the United Kingdom. They had their own Protestant-dominated Parliament (at Stormont outside Belfast), which was responsible for governing the province.

After the Second World War, Northern Ireland developed agriculturally and industrially. Urban centres expanded and more specifically Catholic districts developed in the towns. But the Protestants, through their ruling party (the Ulster Unionists) at Stormont, maintained an exclusive hold on all areas of life in the province, including employment, the police force, local councils and public services. The minority Catholics suffered systematic discrimination in these areas.

The years 1968–9 marked the beginning of the present troubles in Northern Ireland. Marches and demonstrations were held to call for civil liberties. Although they were initially non-sectarian, the situation deteriorated, fighting broke out between Catholics and Protestants, and violence quickly escalated. The Stormont government asked for the British army to be sent in to restore order. The army, although welcomed at first, was soon attacked by both sides of the conflict. Relations between Catholics and Protestants grew worse, and political attitudes became polarized. Violence has continued since 1968; the political situation is still unresolved; and outrages have come from both sides of the sectarian divide.

On one side of the divide is the Provisional wing of the Irish Republican Army (IRA), which is supported by some republicans and Catholics. The IRA, which is illegal in both Eire and Northern Ireland, is committed to the unification of Ireland, as is its legal political wing, Provisional Sinn Fein. It has fought to remove the British political and military presence from Northern Ireland by a campaign of bombing, shootings and murders.

The Protestant paramilitary groups and their Unionist Parties, such as the Democratic Unionists under the leadership of Ian Paisley, are equally committed to their own views. They are loyal to the British Crown, and insist that they remain part of the United Kingdom. The Protestants have consistently refused to accept any reform that would give Catholics some genuine participation in Northern Ireland's political and public life. Their extremist members, partly in retaliation for IRA activities and partly to emphasize their demands, have also carried out sectarian murders and other terrorist acts. British troops and the Royal Ulster Constabulary (the police force in Northern Ireland) are supposed to control the two hostile populations and to curb terrorism. But they have also become targets for bullets and bombs, and have been accused of perpetrating atrocities themselves.

At present, responsibility for Northern Ireland lies with the British government in London (direct rule), because the Stormont Parliament was dissolved in 1972. Since then, there have been various assemblies and executives in Northern Ireland, which were attempts to give the Catholic minority some political representation in cooperation with the Protestant majority (power-sharing). But all these efforts have failed, largely because of Protestant intransigence, although some of the earlier injustices to Catholic civil liberties have been removed.

The signing of an Anglo-Irish Agreement in November 1985 was another attempt to resolve the troubled situation. It was hoped that the Dublin and London governments, working through a shared conference, would discuss common problems to a greater extent than in the past. The agreement aims to solve practical difficulties (such as border security and extradition arrangements), in order to achieve a devolved power-sharing government for Northern Ireland. The Republic of Ireland had to make some political concessions as the price for the agreement, but now has a significant role to play in the resolution of the Northern Irish situation. However, the Republic's cooperation with Britain was seen by Northern Irish Protestants as the first step to reunification of the island, and they have opposed the agreement and its work. The Republic now sees unification as a long-term aim. The British government states that no change in Northern Ireland will take place unless a majority of the inhabitants agree.

The level of violence in the province had been rising since 1990, although it has now been reduced. The emergency legislation employed in the conflict, the reduction of normal legal rights for suspected terrorists, and the infringement of some basic civil liberties were criticized. Many moderates of all political persuasions, who were squeezed out as political polarization grew, were appalled by the outrages and the historical injustices. Outsiders often feel that a rational solution should be possible in Northern

Ireland. But this is to underestimate the deep emotions on both sides, the historical dimension and the extremist elements.

There have been recent initiatives by the British government to persuade the Northern Irish political parties (except Sinn Fein) and the Irish government to meet in order to discuss the realistic possibilities of power-sharing in Northern Ireland. The Downing Street Declaration of 1993 by the Irish and British governments was a further attempt to halt the violence and bring all parties (including Sinn Fein) to the conference table in order to discuss the future of the whole of the country. These initiatives have produced some changes in attitudes but profound difficulties remain. However, the IRA and Protestant paramilitaries declared a 'cessation of military operations' in 1994, and this may help the peace process.

Public opinion polls in recent years indicate a weariness on the part of the mainland British population with both sides in Northern Ireland, and a desire to be rid of the problem. A majority of people seem to be in favour of the unification of Ireland, rather than Northern Ireland continuing to be part of the United Kingdom; support the withdrawal of British troops; are against Britain's continued presence in the province; and do not accept the British government's strategy of withdrawal only with the consent of the majority in Northern Ireland. The mainly Protestant majority, however, wish to remain part of the United Kingdom and oppose union with the Republic.

■ **Explain and examine the following terms:**

Commonwealth	Falklands	Treaty of Rome
decolonization	Boyne	NATO
direct rule	Stormont	referendum
power-sharing	Trident	'special relationship'
WEU	Maastricht	European Commission
EFTA	IRA	pro-marketeer

■ **Write short essays on the following questions:**

1   Does the Commonwealth still have a role to play today?

2   Discuss possible future developments of the European Union.

3   What solution(s) would you suggest to the present situation in Northern Ireland? Give your reasons.

Chapter 6

The legal
system

■ English legal history   149
■ Sources of contemporary English
    law   150
■ The court system in England and
    Wales   152
■ Civil and criminal procedure in
    England and Wales   161
■ Punishment and law enforcement   168
■ The legal profession in England
    and Wales   173
■ *Attitudes to the legal system*   176
■ *Exercises*   177

U NLIKE MANY COUNTRIES, Britain does not have a common legal system. Instead, there are three separate elements – those of England and Wales (with which this chapter is mainly concerned), Scotland, and Northern Ireland. They differ from each other in their procedures, legal professions and courts. There are also some laws which are peculiar to one of the nations and not to the others, although most Westminster legislation is applicable to all of Britain.

Again unlike most countries, Britain does not have criminal and civil codes written down in separate documents. British court cases are of two kinds: civil and criminal. Civil law involves the claim for compensation (financial or otherwise) by an individual (the plaintiff) who has suffered loss or damage (like a breach of contract or a negligent act) at the hands of another (the defendant). The object of the civil law is to secure social harmony by settling disputes between individuals or organizations. This may be achieved by settlement before trial, or eventually by a judge after trial.

Criminal law is concerned to protect society by punishing those (the accused or defendants) who have committed crimes against the state, such as theft or murder. It is usually the state which prosecutes an individual or group at a trial in order to establish guilt. This process may result in imprisonment or a fine. The trial and punishment are supposed to act as deterrents to potential offenders, as well as stating society's attitudes on a range of matters.

The legal system is one of the oldest and most traditional British institutions. Its authority and influence are due to its independence from the executive and legislative branches of government. It is supposed to serve citizens; control unlawful activities against them and the state; protect civil liberties; and support legitimate government.

But it has historically been accused of harshness; of supporting vested and political interests; favouring property rather than human rights; maintaining the isolation and mystique of the law; encouraging the delay and expense of legal actions; and showing a bias against the poor and working class. It has been criticized for its resistance to reform and the maintenance of professional privileges which may conflict with the public interest.

Some critics feel that the law has still not adapted to changing conditions, nor understood the nature and needs of contemporary society. Recent well-publicized miscarriages of justice have caused embarrassment to the police, government and judiciary, and increased public concern about the quality of criminal justice. Similar misgivings are also felt about the expense and operation of the civil law system.

However, the legal apparatus has changed over the centuries. Today, consumer demands, professional pressures and government reforms are forcing it to develop, sometimes rapidly and sometimes slowly.

Most people in the past were ignorant of the law. It now affects citizens more directly and to a greater practical extent than previously. Increased demands are made upon it from individuals, the state and corporate bodies. Rising crime has emphasized the control role of the criminal law, while increasing divorce and family breakdown, among other factors, have contributed to a heavier workload for the civil law.

English legal history

English legal history has been conditioned by two basic concerns: first, that the law should be administered by the state in national courts, and second, that judges should be independent of royal and political control.

State centralization of the law means that the same laws should be applicable to the whole country. This aim was realized by Norman rulers in the twelfth century. The early courts were centred mainly in London, where they dealt with canon (or church), criminal, civil and commercial law.

But there was increasingly a need for courts in local areas

outside London. By the end of the twelfth century, London judges were travelling the country and deciding cases locally by applying the national law. In 1327, Edward III appointed Justices of the Peace (magistrates) in each county who could hold alleged criminals in gaol until their later trial by a London judge. The legal and administrative powers of the Justices were gradually extended, and they operated a system of local criminal courts with the London judges.

But there was still no adequate provision for local civil courts. Such courts were not established until 1846, and a fully integrated apparatus of local civil and criminal law was only gradually established nationwide after this date.

Through the centuries, a growing population, an expanding volume of legal work, and an increasing social and economic complexity, necessitated more courts and specialization. But the number of local and London courts in this haphazard historical development resulted in an overlapping of functions and diversity of procedures, which hindered the implementation of the law. The two periods of major reform to alleviate this situation were in 1873–5, when the Judicature Acts carried out a complete court revision, and in 1970–1, when further changes produced the present court system in England and Wales.

The second concern was that the judiciary should be independent of the executive and legislative branches of government. The monarch had been largely responsible for the administration of the law in earlier centuries, and later interfered in the legal process, as well as dismissing unsympathetic judges. Judicial independence was only achieved in 1701, when the Act of Settlement made judges irremovable from office, except by an appeal to the monarch from both Houses of Parliament. This principle has now been relaxed for junior judges, who may be dismissed in certain cases, and all judges who commit offences are expected to resign.

Sources of contemporary English law

The three main sources of English (and British) law today are the common law, statute law and European Union law.

The oldest source is the *common law*, which is based on the customs of successive settlers and invaders from Europe. After the Norman Conquest, it became a uniform body of rules and principles which were decided and written down by judges in court cases (case law). These judgements were recognized as the law of the land, and were applied by common law courts. Today, the same rules guide judges in their interpretation of statutes, and in the expansion of the common law itself.

Common law decisions have formed precedents from which later judges can deduce the underlying principles of law that may be applied to new cases. The doctrine of precedent is strong in English law, and the judges of the lower courts are obliged to follow it. Normally, the power of creating new precedents is reserved to the House of Lords, as the supreme court of appeal. Its rulings represent the current state of the law to be applied by all courts. The tradition of following precedent maintains consistency and continuity. But it can also make the law conservative, and fail to take account of changing social conditions.

Statute law was originally created by the monarch, but by the thirteenth century was gradually made through royal orders in response to petitions from Parliament. Parliament itself later became the legislating authority because of its growing power against the monarch. Modern statutes are a nineteenth- and twentieth-century development, and arose because new rules were required to meet the needs of a rapidly changing society.

Statutes are Acts of Parliament, created after a bill has passed through both Houses of Parliament and received the Royal Assent. Parliament makes new laws, which have usually been initiated by the current government. Acts of Parliament are supreme over all other forms of law (except for some European Union law). Much of British law is now in statute form, and represents the influence of the state in citizens' lives. Most criminal actions and some civil matters are covered by statutes, which also provide for a range of penalties and damages, although civil law is still mainly the province of the common law.

European Union law is the latest element in English (British) law because of Britain's entry into the then European Economic

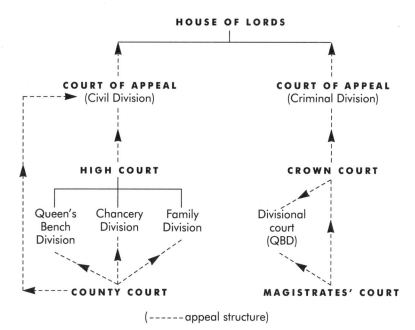

FIGURE 6.1   Civil and criminal courts

Community in 1973. EU law takes precedence over British domestic law in certain areas, and judges must apply EU law when there is a conflict with Acts of Parliament. English (British) law is being increasingly affected by EU developments, so that EU law and British domestic law now coexist, and Britain plays its part in creating EU law.

The court system in England and Wales

The formal court system is divided into criminal and civil courts at various levels (see figure 6.1). But there are other legal processes outside this structure, such as tribunals, inquiries, coroners' courts, and ombudsmen or commissioners, which provide important legal services for citizens.

Criminal courts

There are two levels of criminal courts. The lower and busiest is the magistrates' court, which deals with summary (less serious) cases, and handles 95 per cent of all criminal matters. The more serious (indictable) criminal offences, like murder, are tried by the higher court, the crown court.

Magistrates' courts serve urban and rural local areas in England and Wales. Two types of magistrates sit in these courts: Justices of the Peace and stipendiary magistrates.

Most magistrates' courts are presided over by 30,000 lay Justices of the Peace (JPs or magistrates). They are part-time officials chosen from the general public, who hear cases without a jury, receive no salary for their services (only expenses), and have not had an extensive legal training. Magistrates may be motivated by the desire to perform a public service and sometimes by the

PLATE 6.1 Magistrates' court building, Peterborough
(J. M. Webber/Barnaby)

PLATE 6.2 Inside the magistrates' court *(Priscilla Coleman)*

supposed prestige of the position. They sit daily in the big cities, and less frequently in the rural areas. Magistrates' courts date from 1327, and illustrate a legal system in which the ordinary person is judged by other citizens, rather than by professionals.

Magistrates are appointed by the Crown on the advice of the Lord Chancellor, who receives suitable names from local committees for each county. This procedure has been criticized for its secrecy and exclusivity. Magistrates tended in the past to be white middle- or upper-class males who were prominent in the local community, such as landowners, doctors, retired military officers and businessmen. In recent years, the committees have recruited magistrates from wider and more representative social, ethnic and gender backgrounds.

The magistrates' court has an average of three JPs when it is hearing cases, composed usually of men and women. They decide a case on the facts and also the punishment (if any). Magistrates are advised on points of law by their clerk, who is a legally qualified, full-time official of the court, and a professional element in the system. The clerk is restricted to an advisory role, and must not be involved in the decision-making of the magistrates, nor seek to influence them.

Everyone accused of a criminal offence (defendant) must usually appear first before a magistrates' court. The court can try summary offences, and some indictable/summary offences (known as 'either-way offences') with the defendant's consent. The magistrates may decide that the either-way offence is more suitable for the crown court, and the defendant has no choice in the matter. The magistrates will then, and in the case of other indictable offences, hold committal proceedings to decide whether evidence of the alleged crime is strong enough for committal (sending on) to the crown court for trial.

The magistrates have a limited power of punishment, and may impose fines of up to £2,000 for each offence, or send people to prison for six months on each offence up to a maximum of one year. There is, however, a preference not to imprison if a fine or other punishment is sufficient, and the large majority of penalties are fines.

There is an obvious need for uniform punishments in the magistrates' court. But benches can vary in competence, and sentences can differ considerably in different parts of the country. This factor, in addition to alleged bias and the amateur nature of the JPs' role, has led to frequent criticism of the magistrates' system. There have been proposals to replace it with lawyers or other professional experts, and to centralize the system. But these suggestions have been opposed by those who are against the professionalization of the legal process, and argue that such a step would not necessarily result in greater competence or justice.

An important function of magistrates is to decide criminal cases involving young persons under the age of 17. Youth Courts, from which the public are excluded, comprise experienced magistrates of both sexes. Media reports of the case must not normally identify the accused, and there is a range of punishments for those who are found guilty. The Youth Courts have a central role to play, particularly at a time when so many crimes are committed by young people.

Magistrates' courts also handle limited civil matters involving family problems and divorce; road traffic violations; and licence applications for public amenities such as restaurants, clubs, public houses (pubs) and betting shops.

Stipendiary magistrates are qualified lawyers and full-time officials, who are paid by the state and usually sit alone to hear and decide a case. There are some 63 of them, and they work mainly in the large cities. Since the magistrates' system is divided between JPs and professional stipendiaries, it is sometimes argued that the latter should be used to replace the amateurs on a national basis. But this proposal has been resisted by those critics who wish to retain the civilian element in the magistrates' courts.

The higher *crown courts* are situated in about 90 cities in England and Wales, and are administered by the Lord Chancellor's Department in London. They are divided into levels of importance, with serious criminal cases being heard by the top-level courts, such as the Central Criminal Court in London (popularly known as the Old Bailey).

The crown court has jurisdiction over all indictable criminal offences, and innocence or guilt after a trial is decided by a jury of 12 citizens. After it has reached its decision on the facts of the case, sentence is passed by the judge who is in charge of proceedings throughout the trial.

In Scotland, some minor criminal cases are tried summarily in District Courts but mainly in sheriff courts. The sheriff sits alone to hear summary offences and has the help of a jury (15 members) for indictable cases. More serious cases are handled by the High Court of Justiciary. Northern Irish criminal courts generally follow the system in England and Wales. But the emergency situation there has led to the establishment of special 'Diplock' courts to deal with alleged terrorists. These courts do not

---

PLATE 6.3 The Old Bailey *(Tony Parry/Barnaby)*

PLATE 6.4 Inside the Old Bailey *(Priscilla Coleman)*

have a jury, and a single judge decides the case and pronounces judgement. Such procedures have been criticized for their denial of normal legal rights.

Criminal appeal courts in England and Wales

The appeal structure (see figure 6.1) is supposed to be a safeguard against mistakes and miscarriages of justice. But there have been an increased number of such cases in recent years, which have attracted widespread publicity and concern. They have been caused by police tampering with or withholding evidence; police pressure to induce confessions; and the unreliability of forensic evidence. Appeal courts have been criticized for their inadequate handling of some appeals, and there are proposals to set up an independent appeal authority.

Appeals to a higher court can be expensive and difficult, and permission must usually have been granted by a lower court. Appeals may be made against conviction or sentence, and can be brought on grounds of fact and law. If successful, the higher court may quash the conviction, reduce the sentence or order a new trial. The prosecution can also appeal against what it regards as an insufficient punishment, and a heavier sentence may be substituted.

The crown courts are appeal courts from the magistrates' courts, and both may appeal on matters of law to a divisional court of the Queen's Bench Division. Appeals from the crown court are made to the Criminal Division of the Court of Appeal, and heard by two judges. Appeals may then go to the House of Lords as the highest court in England and Wales. But permission is only granted if a point of law of public importance is involved. Up to five Law Lords hear the case and their decisions represent the current state of the law.

In Scotland, the High Court of Justiciary in Edinburgh tries criminal cases and also hears criminal appeals. There is no appeal from it to the House of Lords. Northern Ireland has its own appeal courts, but the Court of Appeal and the House of Lords in London may also be used.

Civil courts

Civil law proceedings can be brought either in the county court or in the High Court (see figure 6.1). The main difference between the two is that actions up to a value of £50,000 can be dealt with in the county court, whereas more expensive and complicated cases are decided in the High Court.

England and Wales are divided into 300 districts with a *county court* for each district, and a county court or circuit judge has responsibility for a number of courts. The judge will usually sit alone when hearing cases.

The county court handles actions to recover money and property, and some family affairs. It is much busier than the High Court, and is equivalent to the magistrates' court. In Scotland, the

PLATE 6.5 Law Courts *(Barnaby)*

sheriff court deals with most civil actions, because its jurisdiction is not financially limited, although the higher Court of Session may also be used for some cases.

The *High Court of Justice* has its main centre in London, with branches throughout England and Wales. It is divided into three divisions which specialize in specific matters.

The *Queen's Bench Division* deals with contract and negligence cases, and claims for the recovery of land and property. The *Chancery Court Division* is mainly concerned with commercial, financial and succession matters. The *Family Division* deals with domestic issues such as marriage, divorce, family property and the custody of children.

Civil appeal courts in England and Wales

The High Court hears appeals from magistrates' courts and county courts. But the main avenue of appeal is to the Court of Appeal (Civil Division), which deals with appeals from all lower civil courts on questions of law and fact. It can reverse or amend decisions, or sometimes order a new trial.

Appeals from the Court of Appeal may be made to the House of Lords. The appellant must normally have obtained permission either from the Court of Appeal or the House of Lords. Appeals are usually restricted to points of law where an important legal issue is at stake. In Scotland, civil appeals can be made first to a sheriff-principal, then to the Court of Session, and finally to the House of Lords in London.

Civil and criminal procedure in England and Wales

Civil procedure

A civil action in the county court or the High Court is started by the plaintiff serving documents, which contain details of a claim, on the defendant. Should the defendant defend the action, the court is informed; relevant papers are prepared, circulated to all parties, and the case proceeds to trial and judgement. A decision in civil cases is reached on the balance of probabilities. The court also decides the expenses of the action, which may be considerable, and the loser is usually expected to pay both his own and the opponent's costs. This is a very simplified account of a civil action and, in practice, different procedures are used in the county court and High Court.

Civil litigation can be relatively cheap, quick and efficient in the county court. But it can be complicated, expensive and subject to great delay in the High Court. It is therefore advisable for disputes to be settled out of court, or before the case actually comes to trial, in order to avoid the high costs and uncertainty of the result. In practice, many claims are settled during a process of negotiation, and sometimes even outside the court building just before the parties are due to start the trial.

Attempts are being made to reorganize civil law procedures because of concern about the efficiency of the system, with its delays, expense and complexity. Much of the High Court's work has been transferred to the county court, and cheaper, quicker alternative forms of settlement have been implemented, particularly those dealing with business matters.

Criminal procedure

Similar criminal procedures are used throughout Britain. Crimes are offences against the laws of the state, and it is the state which usually brings a person to trial. A private individual may initiate criminal proceedings, but the Director of Public Prosecutions (DPP) normally takes over such cases, and also has the final word in deciding whether to proceed with cases which may not result in conviction.

Prior to 1986, the police were responsible for prosecuting cases. But a Crown Prosecution Service (CPS) is now in operation, which is independent of the police, financed by the state, staffed by state lawyers, and responsible for prosecuting criminal charges made by the police. There is criticism of the performance of the CPS, which has suffered from understaffing and underfunding. In

Scotland, prosecution duties rest with the Crown Office and Procurator-Fiscal Service, and in Northern Ireland with the police and the DPP.

Arrests for most criminal offences are made by the police, although any citizen can make a 'citizen's arrest'. Many arrests of suspects and searches of property can now be made by the police without applying to the magistrates' court for arrest and search warrants, although in some cases they must still follow this procedure.

The police operate under codes of practice, which lay down strict procedures for the protection of suspects. The police have no authority to question people, nor to detain them at a police station, if they have not been arrested or charged. Once a person has been arrested, and then charged with an offence, he or she must be brought before a magistrates' court, normally within 24 hours. But this period can now be extended up to 96 hours without charge in serious cases by applications to a senior policeman or magistrate. After 96 hours, the police must release the suspect if no charges are brought against him or her. The police have been heavily criticized in recent years for their arrest, questioning and charging practices.

When a person appears before a magistrates' court prior to a trial, the magistrates can grant or refuse bail (freedom from custody). If bail is refused, a person will be kept in custody in a remand centre or in prison. If bail is granted, the individual is set free until his or her later court appearance. The court may require certain assurances from the accused about conduct while on bail, such as residence in a specific area and reporting to a police station.

The application for bail is a legal right, since the accused has not yet been found guilty of any crime by a court, and there should be strong reasons for refusing it. There is concern that many people who are refused bail are, at their later trial, either found not guilty or are punished by a fine, rather than imprisonment. The system is thus keeping alleged criminals in custody for a lengthy period waiting for trial, and increasing the overcrowding in British prisons. But there is also public concern about accused persons who commit further serious offences while free on bail.

Many people charged with minor offences, such as road traffic violations, are not arrested. They are summoned to appear in court to hear the charges against them. It is often suggested that the summons procedure could be used more widely in order to avoid bail problems and prison overcrowding.

Criminal trials in the magistrates' and crown courts are, with a few exceptions, open to the public. But the media can only report the court proceedings, and must not comment upon them while the trial is in progress (the *sub judice* rule).

The accused enters the dock, the charge is read out, and he or she is asked to plead 'guilty' or 'not guilty'. On a 'guilty' plea, the person is usually sentenced after a short presentation of the facts by the prosecution. On a 'not guilty' plea, the trial proceeds in order to establish the person's guilt or innocence. In English law, an individual is innocent until proved guilty, and it is the responsibility of the prosecution to prove guilt beyond all reasonable

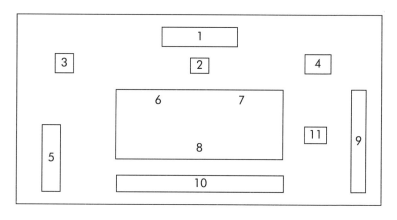

1	Magistrates	5	Press seats	9	Witnesses who
2	Clerk to the	6	Defending lawyer		gave evidence
	Justices	7	Prosecuting	10	The public seats
3	Defendant		lawyer	11	Court ushers
4	Witness	8	Probation officers		

FIGURE 6.2 A typical magistrates' court in action

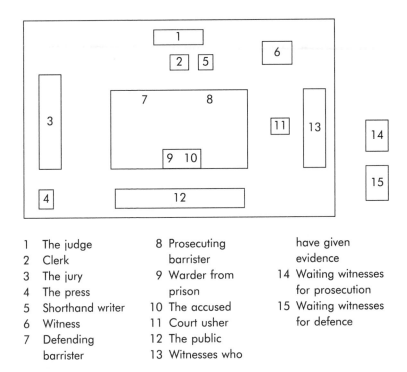

1 The judge
2 Clerk
3 The jury
4 The press
5 Shorthand writer
6 Witness
7 Defending barrister
8 Prosecuting barrister
9 Warder from prison
10 The accused
11 Court usher
12 The public
13 Witnesses who have given evidence
14 Waiting witnesses for prosecution
15 Waiting witnesses for defence

FIGURE 6.3 A typical crown court in action

doubt. If this proof is not achieved, a 'not guilty' verdict must be returned by the magistrates in the magistrates' court or by the jury in the crown court. In Scotland, there is an additional possible verdict of 'not proven'.

The prosecution and defence of the accused are usually performed by solicitors in the magistrates' court and by barristers and solicitor-advocates in the crown court. But it is possible to defend oneself. An English trial is an adversarial contest between defence and prosecution. Both side call witnesses in support of their case, and these may be questioned by the other side. The rules of evidence and procedure in this contest are complicated and must be strictly observed. The accused may remain silent throughout the trial, need not give evidence, and silence does not imply guilt. However, the right to silence has now been abolished for terrorist trials in Northern

Ireland. The Conservative government proposes to limit it in all British courts, or at least to allow the judge to comment on silence and for the jury and magistrates to give it weight in their decision.

Critics argue that the adversarial nature of criminal trials can result either in the conviction of innocent people or the guilty escaping conviction. They maintain that the inquisitorial system of other European countries would be better. This allows the questioning of suspects and establishing of facts to be carried out by professional impartial interrogators rather than the police.

The judge in the crown court and the magistrates in the magistrates' court are controlling influences in the battle between defence and prosecution. They apply the rules of the court and give directions on procedure and evidence. But their powers of intervention are limited, and they should not interfere too actively, nor show bias. After the prosecution and the defence have concluded their cases, the magistrates decide both the verdict and sentence. In the crown court, the jury delivers the verdict after the judge has given a summing-up, and the judge pronounces sentence. Before the final sentence on a 'guilty' decision, details of other admitted crime may be taken into account, and the defence may offer a plea of mitigation in an attempt to reduce the sentence.

The jury

Trial by jury is an ancient and important feature of English justice. Although it has declined in civil cases (except for libel and fraud), it is the main element in criminal trials in the crown court. Jury membership was once linked to the ownership of property, which resulted in male and middle-class dominance. But now most categories of British residents are obliged to undertake jury service when summoned.

Before the start of a criminal trial in the crown court, 12 jurors are chosen from a list of some 30 names randomly selected from local electoral registers. They listen to the evidence at the trial and give their verdict on the facts, after having been isolated in a separate room for their deliberations. If a jury cannot reach a decision, it will be discharged and a new one sworn in. The accused can thus be tried twice for the same offence (as also in appeals which order a new trial). Such results are an exception to the English principle that a person can only be tried once for the same offence. In most cases, the jury is able to reach a decision. Until 1967 the verdict had to be unanimous. But now the judge will accept a majority verdict after the jury has deliberated for more than two hours, provided that there are no more than two dissentients (that is, ten to two). The jury does not decide the punishment or sentence, except in some civil cases where it awards damages.

The jury system is the ordinary citizen's link with the legal process. It is supposed to safeguard individual liberty and justice because a commonsense decision on the facts either to punish or acquit is taken by fellow citizens rather than by professionals. But the system has been criticized because of its high acquittal rates; allegedly unsuitable or subjective jurors; intimidation of jurors;

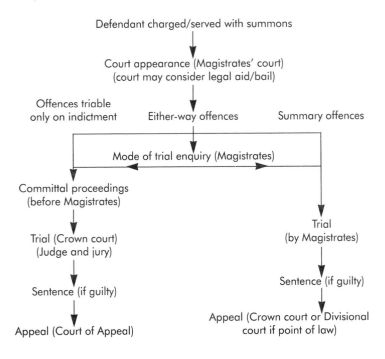

FIGURE 6.4 Criminal procedure

and administrative reason for saving time and costs. Critics would like to replace the jury with panels of experts in relevant fields. But, after widespread opposition to such proposals, it seems as though the jury will continue in its present form.

Legal aid

The legal aid system was established in 1949. It enables those persons who are unable to afford legal representation and advice in criminal and civil matters to have their bills paid by the state. Applicants must prove that they have a suitable case, and that their income falls below certain financial limits. Generally, only those with very low incomes or who are already receiving state welfare benefits qualify.

There have been frequent demands that the income limits be raised to include more people. At present, given the high costs of legal actions, only the poor or the very rich can afford to resort to litigation without hardship. Government reductions in the legal aid fund mean that fewer people in future will be eligible for legal aid. This is seen as a serious development in the provision of justice, especially when the demand for legal aid is constantly rising.

A recent government reform may help to alleviate the pressures on both legal aid and those people who wish to initiate legal actions but who cannot afford the cost. Clients may now enter into conditional agreements with lawyers, in which payment of legal fees on a percentage basis is only made if the client wins. But such cases are restricted to personal injury and other specialized areas, and will only affect people who feel that they have a strong case and are willing to take the gamble of going to court.

Punishment and law enforcement

Crime and punishment

Law and order in Britain is a controversial issue, on which the political parties base their claims for public support. But a problem in this area is the reliability of statistics and the non-reporting of offences such as burglary and rape. Although there has been a recent decrease in overall notifiable crime, official statistics again show an increase in crimes such as violence against the person (assaults), robberies, sexual offences, thefts from vehicles and non-domestic property, and criminal damage. There has also been a greater use of firearms in criminal acts, leading to demands that the police be armed. The number of unsolved crimes remains at a high level, with a clear-up rate of 34 per cent.

A disturbing aspect of the statistics is the amount of drug-related crime and the number of offences committed by young people. Britain has a serious problem with young offenders, the peak age for committing crime is 15, and one in four criminal offences is committed by teenagers under 16.

However, research based on individual experience of crime suggests that offences (including violent crime) in England and Wales are on average below those of many other western nations. The findings indicate that the very real and increasing fear which many British people feel about potential crime does not relate to its actual incidence or reality.

Interviewees in a MORI public opinion poll in 1990 considered that the main causes of crime in Britain today were lack of parental discipline (75 per cent); drugs (71); alcohol (62); too lenient sentencing (62); unemployment (61); lack of school discipline (51); poverty (40); television (27); poor policing (20); and national newspapers (10).

A person found guilty of a first offence may receive no punishment, or be placed on probation for a period under the supervision of a probation officer. Other punishments for adults are usually fines or imprisonment (over 21), which vary according to the severity of the offence and any previous convictions. There have been attempts to avoid giving prison sentences because prisons are overcrowded and Britain has the largest prison population in Western Europe (51,785 prisoners in 1992). But 18 per cent of convicted persons are imprisoned, a higher rate than in comparable European countries, and much depends on the attitudes of magistrates and judges.

An alternative to prison is community service, where the offender serves the community in some capacity for a number of hours. Prison sentences may also be suspended for a period, if no further offences are committed. Young people under 21 may be punished by penalties such as fines (under 17), being taken into local authority care, confinement in a young offenders' institution for those between 17 and 20, or supervision in the community. Re-offending among young people who serve a custodial sentence is high, but supervision outside institutions reveals a decrease in re-offending patterns.

The death penalty by hanging for murder and some other crimes was discontinued for a trial period from 1965, and was abolished in 1969. The House of Commons has since voted on several occasions against its re-imposition. But opinion polls, despite recent miscarriages of justice, consistently show that a majority of the public are in favour of the death penalty, especially for terrorist offences and the murder of policemen. The general public seem to support harsh treatment of criminal offenders, and argue that more sympathy and aid should be given to the victims of crime. The government has tried to support such victims with financial compensation, but its programmes have not satisfied the critics or the victims.

Many British people feel that the penalties for criminal offences are inadequate as deterrents to prevent crime. But most prisons are old and decaying, lack humane facilities, are largely unfitted for a modern penal system, are understaffed and their personnel overworked. Prison conditions have resulted in serious disorder and riots in recent years, and low morale among prisoners and prison staff. Debates about punishment as opposed to the rehabilitation of offenders continue. But proposals to improve the situation for prison officers and prisoners usually encounter the problems of expense, although the government is building more courts and prisons. Some prisons and prison services (such as escorting prisoners to court) have now been privatized.

It is clear that the majority of prisoners are not reformed by their sentences, nor does fear of prison or punishment act as a deterrent. Some critics argue that the main concern of the criminal system should be punishment and not rehabilitation. However, there are frequent proposals to humanize institutions and give prisoners a sense of purpose. Alternatives to custodial sentences, such as supervised housing, probation hostels, community service schemes and supervised work projects, are also advocated.

Law enforcement and the police

There has been no tradition in Britain of military involvement in law enforcement. The armed forces are subordinate to the civilian government, and are used only for defence purposes. An exception to this principle has been the deployment of the army in Northern Ireland since 1969, where they support the police force (the Royal Ulster Constabulary). The armed forces have also sometimes been used to maintain essential supplies and services during strikes.

The maintenance of law and order rests with the civilian police. The oldest police force is the Metropolitan Police, which was founded in 1829 by Sir Robert Peel to combat crime in London, and from which the modern forces have grown. Today there is no national police force, although there have been proposals to establish one. Instead, there are 52 independent forces, which undertake law enforcement in local county or regional areas, with the Metropolitan Police being responsible for policing London. The regional forces are under the political control of police committees composed of local politicians and other appointees, although their direct influence is small. Authority rests with the head of each regional force (Chief Constable), who has organizational independence and responsibility for the actions of the force. But the Home Secretary is responsible for the Metropolitan Police, which is centred on Scotland Yard in London.

There are about 140,000 policemen and women in Britain, or one officer for every 400 people in the population. Only a disproportionately small number are from ethnic communities. Many of their members are hostile to or sceptical of the police, although attempts have been made to recruit more of them to the forces, with varying degrees of success.

Members of the police forces are not allowed to join trade unions or strike. But they do have staff associations to represent their interests. The police are subject to the law, and can be sued or prosecuted for any wrongdoing in the course of their work. But it is usually difficult to bring successful prosecutions against them, although individuals can appeal to the Police Complaints Authority. This body does have a greater civilian component than previous models, and is some improvement upon earlier situations where the police tended to act as judge and jury in the investigation of complaints against them. But critics argue that the procedures are still unsatisfactory and lack impartiality. In their view, democratic control of the police in practice does not properly exist.

The police, with their distinctive helmets and lack of firearms, have been traditionally regarded as a typical British institution. They have embodied a presence in the local community by 'walking the beat', and have supposedly personified fairness, a certain stolidity, friendliness, helpfulness and incorruptibility. These virtues still exist to a degree, and there is a desire in some forces to return more strongly to them. The traditional view is that the police should control the community by consent rather than force, and that they should be visible in local areas.

But, in recent years, the police have been taken off foot patrols; put into cars to increase effectiveness and mobility; and more are now armed and trained in riot-control programmes. They have been accused of racism, corruption, brutality, sexism, excessive use of force, perverting the course of justice and tampering with evidence in criminal trials. Some of these accusations have been proved in a number of cases. They have lowered the image of the police as well as their morale, and have contributed to a loss of public confidence. Government attempts to impose performance-related contracts and other structures upon them have also provoked fierce resistance.

The police tread a thin line in community activities, strikes and demonstrations. They are in the middle of opposing forces, much is expected of them, and uncertain law has sometimes hindered their effectiveness. However, reforms have been made in recent years, and there have been successful attempts to purge some police forces of corrupt officers. The problems of rising crime, relations with ethnic communities and an increasingly complex society have made the police job more difficult than in the past. The police are trying to find ways of adequately and fairly controlling a changing society. They are concerned about their image, but insist that they also have a duty to maintain law and order.

The legal profession in England and Wales

The legal profession in England and Wales is divided into barristers and solicitors. Each branch has its own vested interests and jurisdiction, and fiercely protects its position against external opposition. This system has been criticized because of the duplication of services, delay in the legal process, and expense. But the Conservative government is reforming the legal profession and legal services in order to benefit consumers and promote easier access to the law.

There are some 60,000 *solicitors*, who practise mainly in private firms, but also in local and central government, legal centres and industry. Most are now organized by their self-regulating professional body, the Law Society. The solicitors' branch is a middle-class profession, but it is increasingly attracting members from a relatively wide spectrum of society.

Solicitors deal with general legal work, although many now specialize in one area of the law. Their firms (or partnerships) offer services such as conveyancing (the buying and selling of property); probate (wills and succession after death); family matters; criminal and civil litigation; commercial cases; and tax and financial affairs. Conveyancing, which used to be a monopoly for solicitors, may now be done by licensed conveyancers, banks and building societies. This reform has caused difficulty for some solicitors' firms which rely upon conveyancing fees as their chief source of finance.

Complaints by dissatisfied clients against solicitors, of which there are an increasing number, are investigated by the Solicitors' Complaints Bureau, which is supposed to provide an independent investigation into complaints, and is separate from the Law Society.

The client with a legal problem will first approach a solicitor, who can usually deal with all aspects of the case. But the solicitor in the past was only able to appear (rights of audience) for his or her client in the lower courts (county and magistrates' courts). Because he or she could not appear in the higher courts, the case had to be handed to a barrister if it was to be heard in a superior court. This practice, which was criticized as expensive and inefficient, is being changed to allow qualified solicitor-advocates to appear in the higher courts. Barristers will then lose their exclusive rights of audience in the higher courts.

In order to become a solicitor, it is now necessary to have a university degree, not essentially in law. After passing additional professional examinations organized by the Law Society, the student will serve a practical apprenticeship as a trainee solicitor with an established solicitor for some two years. After this total period of about six years' education and training, the new solicitor can practise law.

There are about 6,000 *barristers*, who have the right to appear before any court in England and Wales, although in future this will be shared with qualified solicitor-advocates. Barristers belong to the Bar, which is an ancient legal institution controlled by the self-regulating Bar Council and four legal societies or Inns of Court in London (Gray's Inn, Lincoln's Inn, Middle Temple and the Inner Temple). Barristers have two main functions: first, to give specialized advice on legal matters and, second, to act as advocates in the courts. The general public cannot approach a barrister directly, but must be introduced by a solicitor.

In order to become a barrister, one must usually have a university degree, pass professional examinations organized by the Council of Legal Education, and become a member of one of the Inns of Court. The student must dine in his or her Inn for a number of terms before being 'called to the Bar', or accepted as a barrister. He or she must then serve for a one-year period (pupillage) under a practising barrister.

Barristers are self-employed individuals who practise the law from chambers (or offices), together with other barristers. The barrister's career starts as a 'junior' handling minor briefs (or cases). He or she may frequently have difficulty in earning a reasonable living or in becoming established in the early years of practice, with the result that many barristers drop out and enter other fields. However, should the barrister persist and build up a successful practice as a junior, he or she may then 'take silk' and become a Queen's Counsel (QC). A QC is a senior barrister who can charge higher fees for his or her work, but who is then excluded from appearing in lesser cases. Appointment as a QC may lead to a future position as a judge, and it is regarded as a necessary career step for the ambitious.

The *judges* constitute the judiciary, or independent third branch of the constitutional system. There are a relatively small number of judges at various levels of seniority, who are located in most large cities and in the higher courts in London. But there is no judicial profession as such, and judges are appointed from the ranks of senior barristers, although solicitors have now become eligible for some of the lower posts. The highest appointments are made by the Crown on the advice of the Prime Minister, and lower positions on the advice of the Lord Chancellor. This appointments procedure has been criticized because it rests with the Lord Chancellor, who holds much power and patronage. But he has now decided that judgeships will be advertised for open competition.

The Lord Chancellor is a political appointee of the sitting government; effective head of the legal system and profession; a member of the Cabinet; presiding officer (or Speaker) of the House of Lords; and a Law Lord. But other judgeships are supposedly made on non-political grounds. Once appointed, senior judges cannot be removed from office until the retiring age of 75, although junior judges can be dismissed by the Lord Chancellor for good reasons before retirement age at 72. There have been proposals that complaints against judges and their possible dismissal should be handled by a complaints board. It is argued that judges should be more easily removable from office. But the existing measures have been designed to ensure the independence of the judiciary and its freedom from political involvement.

Judges are felt, in some quarters, to be socially and educationally élitist and remote from ordinary life. They are usually people who will not cause embarrassment to the establishment, although there are exceptions to this rule. They generally tend to support the accepted wisdom and status quo, and are overwhelmingly male. Although over half of law students are female, there are few women judges, QCs or senior partners in solicitors' firms. While judges often appear to support the policies of the sitting government, they are also capable of ruling against it. But British judges are not supposed to be political animals seeking to change the established order, and their freedom to speak out in public on a range of issues is restricted. However, the judiciary is gradually changing to admit more women, members of ethnic communities and people with lower-class and educationally diverse backgrounds.

The judiciary tends to be old in years because judgeships are normally awarded to senior practising lawyers, and there is no career structure that people may join early in life. A lawyer's income will often be greatly reduced on accepting a judgeship, but the honour and added security are supposed to be some compensation. There are promotional steps within the judiciary from recorder to circuit judge to High Court judge, and thence to the Court of Appeal and the House of Lords.

ATTITUDES

Attitudes to the legal system

Britain is not usually thought of as a litigious society. Most people avoid the difficulty and cost of legal actions if possible, and regard the law and lawyers as a last resort. Public opinion polls reveal that fear of crime and physical assaults is increasing; crime, law and order, vandalism and violence are a main concern for many British people; a large number are dissatisfied with the legal system as a whole; but a considerable majority are satisfied with the police. There is majority support for the government's reforms of the legal system and profession, and a desire to see further government action on the law's delays, risks and costs.

EXERCISES

■ Explain and examine the following terms:

civil law	plaintiff	conveyancing
barrister	legal aid	Crown Prosecution Service
indictable	Inns of Court	common law
solicitor	Lord Chancellor	Metropolitan Police
jury	crown court	county court
JP	statute law	bail

■ Write short essays on the following questions:

1   Describe and comment critically on the structure of the legal profession in England and Wales.

2   How is the courts system in England and Wales organized?

3   Discuss the role of the police in law enforcement.

Chapter 7

Economic
and industrial
institutions

■ The modern economy: policies,
structure and performance   179
■ Economic policy and performance
since 1979   182
■ Social class, the workforce and
employment   190
■ Financial institutions   197
■ Industrial and commercial
institutions   202
■ Consumer protection   208
■ *Attitudes to the economy and*
economic structure   209
■ *Exercises*   211

B RITAIN WAS A PREDOMINANTLY RURAL COUNTRY until the end of the eighteenth century, and its economy was mainly based on agricultural production. But there had also been industrial and manufacturing developments over the centuries, which were located in the larger towns. Financial and commercial institutions, such as banks, insurance houses and trading companies, were gradually founded to finance and service the expanding and increasingly diversified economy.

By the nineteenth century, Britain was established as an economic power, and its wealth was based on international trade and the payments that it received for its exported goods. Governments believed that free trade was essential and that a country increased its wealth as long as exports exceeded imports. This view of international commerce is still central to the balance-of-payments situation in Britain today.

The growth of a colonial empire contributed to the national economy as Britain capitalized on its worldwide trading connections to sell its products abroad. Overseas markets grew quickly because British merchants and traders were privileged and protected at home and abroad. They exploited the colonial markets, and became virtual monopolies by controlling foreign competition. The colonies supplied cheap raw materials, which were then converted into manufactured goods in Britain and exported.

This trading system and its financial institutions benefited the later industrial revolutions, which had begun in the eighteenth century with the invention of new manufacturing methods. In the nineteenth century, Britain was transformed into an urban and industrialized country. The rich supply of domestic materials and energy sources, such as coal, iron and water, stimulated industrial production and the national economy. Manufacturers, who had gained by foreign trade and the demand for British goods abroad, invested their profits in the new industries and in more efficient technology.

Bigger factories were built, industrial towns expanded, and a transport infrastructure of roads, railways and canals developed. Improved and efficient manufacturing methods made British products competitively priced and attractive to buyers on the world market. By the middle of the nineteenth century, Britain had become the world's first industrial nation, and capitalized on its worldwide influence to sell its goods.

But industrialization was opposed by some people. The Luddites, for example, destroyed new machinery in an attempt to halt progress and preserve their traditional jobs. Industrial development had its negative effects, such as long working hours for low wages, and bad conditions in mines and factories. It also resulted in the depopulation of rural areas, and the decline of traditional home and cottage work. The industrial conditions produced social and moral problems in towns and the countryside, and mechanization was often regarded as exploitative and dehumanizing. The situation was worsened by the indifference of many manufacturers, employers and politicians to the human cost of industrialization.

However, the industrial changes did transform Britain into a rich and powerful nation, despite economic slumps and resulting hardship in the nineteenth century. Manufacturing output was the chief generator of wealth; production methods and technology advanced; and domestic competition improved the quality of goods and services.

But this industrial leadership and dominance of world trade did not last long. They decreased by the end of the nineteenth century, as other countries like Germany and the USA industrialized and became more competitive. Financial expertise in the City of London continued to be influential in global commercial dealings. But in most other fields, Britain progressively lost more of its international economic standing during the early decades of the twentieth century, although this downturn was disguised by an apparent prosperity.

The modern economy: policies, structure and performance

Britain's relative economic performance has continued to decline. It has suffered from problems created by two world wars; international recessions; increased global competition; structural changes in the national economy; a lack of competitiveness in industrial and commercial life; and a series of 'boom-and-bust' cycles in which economic growth has fluctuated greatly. Essential elements in understanding this situation are government policies and the structure of those organizations which own and manage the economy.

Economic policies

Governments since the 1940s have tried in varying degrees to balance intervention in the national economy with 'free-market' considerations. They have generally become more involved in economic planning and management, and the performance of the economy has been tied to their policies.

Keynesian economic theory was the dominant school of thought in the mid-twentieth century. It was based on stimulating demand by injecting money into the economy, and was employed by all British governments as either a small or large governmental intervention in economic life. Keynesian economics was the basis for a consensus between the two major parties on how the economy and society should be managed. This included the ideal of full employment and support for the welfare state, but opinions differ about its real extent. It was dependent upon a growing economy, and a lack of sustained expansion since 1945 has caused strains in the consensus.

The Conservative Party has traditionally insisted on a policy of non-interference (*laissez-faire*, or letting things take their own course). But this has only been partially achieved in practice, and government intervention was necessary as international competition grew and the demands of the domestic market became more complex. The Labour Party, on the other hand, has argued that the economy should be centrally organized and planned, and its essential sectors should be owned and managed by the state.

Labour governments since 1945 have nationalized (transferred to state or public ownership) the railways, water, gas and electricity, ship-building, coal-mining, the iron and steel industries, the Post Office and telecommunications, airlines and the health service. This means that essential public services and central industries are run by the state, and are responsible to Parliament. They are subsidized by taxation for the benefit of the country as a whole, rather than for private owners or shareholders. Today the few remaining nationalized industries are managed by government-appointed boards, and political and financial control rests with government ministers. Nationalized industries are expensive, require considerable capital investment, and governments have been expected to rescue any which ran into economic trouble. But this mentality has changed in respect of Conservative governments.

The Conservatives have often denationalized state industries and returned them to private ownership. They have argued that the public industries and services are too expensive and inefficient; have outdated technology and bad industrial relations; suffer from lack of investment in new equipment; are dependent upon tax subsidies; and are run purely as state services with too little attention paid to profit-making, consumer demand or market forces.

Conservative denationalization has since 1979 been called 'privatization' or 'deregulation'. Deregulation means the loosening of controls over industries so that they can operate more freely within a more competitive atmosphere. For example, the stock market and public transport have been deregulated, so that there is greater diversity in the City of London, and bus companies operated by local authorities now compete with private bus firms for customers.

The Conservative government has privatized a number of state industries such as British Telecom, British Airways, British Petroleum, British Gas, and the water and electricity supplies. British Coal, British Rail and other state businesses will also be privatized. Privatization means that ownership of industries is transferred from the state to private owners or companies mainly through the sale of shares. The industry is then run as a profit-making concern, and is regulated in the public interest by independent regulators, although the effectiveness of the regulators is criticized.

The Conservative government believes that privatization improves efficiency, reduces government spending, increases economic freedom and encourages share ownership. The public has been eager to buy shares in the new private companies and share-owning has increased, if largely by financial institutions. But many people consider that privatization has now gone too far. The private industries have become virtual monopolies with little effective competition. There have been frequent complaints about their services, prices and products, although some of them are now more profitable and many of the initial problems have been solved. But opinions differ as to whether Conservative economic policies have meant a total break with the traditional consensus, since the government from 1979 has argued that it still supports public services.

Debates over economic policy and how the economy should be organized continue between the political parties. But it seems that many of the privatized industries will continue should there be a Labour government after the next general election. All the parties in varying degrees have accepted 'market economics', and there may not be such violent reversals of policy in future. The essential question is how to manage the 'market' or 'capitalist' economy effectively, while maintaining public or state services. But there is often a gap between the policy rhetoric of political parties and their actual implementation of programmes when in government.

Economic structure

Government policies have given Britain a mixed economy, divided into public and private sectors. The public sector includes the nationalized industries and public services which are provided by local and central government. These now amount to under one-third of the total goods and services in the economy, and employ about one-third of the national workforce. Two-thirds of the economy is in the private sector, although this will increase as more privatization is implemented.

Unlike public sector concerns which are owned by the state, the private sector belongs to those people who have a financial interest in a company. It consists of small private businesses which are owned by individuals; 'public' companies whose shares are sold to the general public through the Stock Exchange; and larger private companies whose shares are not offered for sale to the public. The majority of companies in Britain are private and most are small or medium-size. They are important to the national economy because they generate 50 per cent of new jobs. Some 10 per cent of the economy is controlled by foreign private corporations, which employ 10 per cent of the workforce. These percentages will grow as more overseas firms buy into the British economy, since Britain is seen as an attractive low-cost country for foreign investment.

The shareholders are the real owners of those companies in which they have invested their money. However, the daily organization of the business is left to a board of directors under a chairman/chairwoman or managing director. In practice, most shareholders in larger companies are more interested in receiving profit dividends on their shares from a successful business than in being concerned with its running. But shareholder power is occasionally mobilized if the concern is doing badly, or if the directors are not performing well.

National and foreign companies are sometimes associated with takeovers and mergers in the private sector. A takeover occurs when a larger company takes over (or buys) a smaller, often loss-making, firm. Mergers are amalgamations between companies of equal standing. Such battles for control can be fiercely fought, and have resulted in sections of the economy, such as cars, hotels, media concerns and food products, being dominated by a relatively small number of major groups.

Takeovers and mergers in the private sector can be a source of concern, particularly since the methods used are not always beneficial to the companies or workforces involved. An independent Monopolies and Mergers Commission is supposed to control this situation by preventing any one group forming a monopoly or creating unfair trading conditions. It examines potential monopolies and restrictive practices, and reports to the Secretary of State for Trade and Industry, who may rule against the proposed takeover or merger. Some ministers have ruled against undesirable developments. But others have allowed situations which amount to near-monopolies, and the role of the Commission continues to be criticized.

Economic performance

Britain's economic problems since the Second World War have resulted in periods of expansion followed by periods of recession; fluctuations in the number of manufactured goods; inflation running at high levels; and unemployment.

These difficulties have been associated with the balance-of-payments situation. The economy suffers when exports do not exceed imports, because a deficit in trade, or negative 'trade gap' between exports and imports, is created. Deficits have been consistently large since 1987, and would often be worse if it were not for the support given by 'invisible exports'. These are financial services, insurance charges, tourism, shipping and aviation revenues, which are not calculated in the balance equation. But the value of such earnings is often insufficient to cover the trade gap totally, although they still contribute substantially to the national economy.

Devaluation of the pound (reduction of its exchange value) has sometimes been used to improve the economic situation. Devaluation encourages exports by making them cheaper on the world market, while raising the cost of imports, and thus dissuading people from buying expensive foreign goods. But this measure has been unsuccessful because it does not address the structural problems of the economy, and there are difficulties in generating sufficient exports of the requisite cheapness and quality. Devaluation has not therefore been used recently as a formal economic weapon.

Instead, since 1972 the pound has been allowed to 'float', and find its own market value in competition with other world currencies. But the British authorities, through the Bank of England, often intervene to prevent the pound falling below certain levels. They do this either by raising interest rates to encourage foreign investment in the pound, or by themselves buying pounds on the currency markets in order to boost the exchange rate. The pound is vulnerable to changing demands in the market, political instability and currency speculation. A drop in its value leads frequently to higher domestic interest rates, increased costs, higher prices and a worsening of the balance of payments.

In an attempt to improve the economy, Britain joined the European Exchange Rate Mechanism (ERM) in 1990 which, by linking European monies, is supposed to stabilize currencies and prevent wide fluctuations. This move was expected to cut interest rates, reduce inflation and boost the national economy. But, following heavy speculation against a weak pound in 1992 which resulted in an effective devaluation, Britain withdrew from the ERM and again allowed the pound to float.

Such features have forced structural changes in the industrial and commercial fields, as the economy has adjusted itself to different circumstances. The introduction of new technology and production methods has resulted in the growth of specialized industries and the service sector (banking, insurance, catering, leisure and financial services), allied to an increased use of information technology. But such changes have also hastened a process of deindustrialization in Britain as traditional industrial bases, such as steel, iron, coal and textiles, have contracted.

The location of British industry, which was dictated by the earlier industrial revolutions, has been a factor in manufacturing and industrial decline. Industries were situated in areas where there was access to natural resources and transport systems, and where there was often one major industry. They could be easily destroyed in a changing economic climate, unless they managed to diversify. But even regions which had diversified successfully in the past were affected by further deindustrialization and recession.

Many manufacturing industries were unable to adapt to new markets and demands. They had not diversified or produced goods efficiently and cheaply enough to compete, and had often priced themselves out of the world market. This situation was not improved by the number of cheap imports flooding the traditional trades. In 1938, Britain still produced 22 per cent of the world's exports of manufactured goods. But this figure slumped to 6.5 per cent by 1989, due to world competition and the rundown of manufacturing industries.

The process of industrial decline has badly affected the north of England, the English Midlands, industrial Scotland and South Wales. Industries such as textiles, steel, iron, ship-building and coalmining have been considerably and permanently reduced. Successive governments, helped by European Union grants, have tried to revitalize the depressed areas with financial aid, relocation of industry, enterprise and development zones, and the creation of new industry. But these policies have taken time to produce a widespread and positive effect, although there have been recent improvements in places such as Liverpool, Glasgow, Birmingham and Newcastle.

However, Britain is still an important industrial and manufacturing country, despite its relative decline, and employs about one-fifth of the national workforce in manufacturing industry. It remains a major exporter of manufactured goods, despite its reduced share of the world market. Manufacturing production had increased impressively in the late 1980s, but then slumped and is only now slowly improving again. Manufactured goods comprise some 80 per cent of Britain's exports, even though they only amount to some 24 per cent of gross domestic product compared to the 69 per cent for construction and the service sector. Engineering equipment, machinery, food, drink and tobacco, together with chemicals and man-made fibres, are the largest groups of manufactured goods. Britain's trading patterns have also changed somewhat, and its chief trading partners are now the European union (over 50 per cent), North America (13 per cent) and other Western European countries (11 per cent).

The discovery of North Sea oil and gas, together with their associated industries, have contributed greatly to the British economy, and made it less dependent upon imported energy supplies. But this development has disguised the true state of the economy, made the pound very vulnerable to oil price fluctuations, and emphasized that gas and oil are finite. Britain is left not only with the problem of finding alternative energy sources when these diminish, but must also fill the financial gap with new revenues. Critics argue that oil income has been unwisely spent on social targets, rather than being used more positively for investment in new industry and in creating a modern industrial infrastructure.

Economic policy and performance since 1979

British economic performance since 1979 should be seen against this background. The situation was poor when the Conservatives achieved power in 1979. They have subsequently dominated policy and attempted to reverse consensus ideas about economic management, first under Margaret Thatcher and then John Major. Opinions differ sharply on their record, which has staggered between 'boom' and 'bust'.

The government saw its main task initially as reducing inflation by limiting and tightly controlling the money supply (or amount of money in circulation in the economic system). This involved cutting government and public spending over a wide area, including social welfare, health and education. Income tax was to be reduced, government involvement in the economy was to be restricted, and industry and commerce were left to fend for themselves under market forces. The government believed that this programme would persuade industry and commerce to restructure themselves; increase their growth rates and productivity; cut down overmanning in the workforce; and become more efficient.

Such deflationary measures, combined with a continuing world recession, resulted in the 1980 British economy falling to very low levels. Inflation was 22 per cent and interest rates were high, so that companies could not borrow money to re-equip or modernize. The exchange rate of the pound fluctuated and British goods were expensive on the world market. Many businesses went bankrupt, while others had to cut back drastically on their workforces and production in order to survive. By 1982, some 3 million people were unemployed (12 per cent of the workforce). But public spending had fallen, and inflation had been reduced to 6 per cent. Government policy and the depressed state of the economy provoked fierce arguments through the mid-1980s. There were calls for reflationary programmes to boost the economy, and in 1986 the government admitted that the economic recovery which it had promised was taking longer than expected.

Yet, by the end of 1986, things had started to improve, and economic indicators and performance throughout 1987 and early 1988 were positive, suggesting that an 'economic miracle' was in progress. Unemployment and interest rates had been reduced; there was increased investment in industry; manufacturing productivity improved; inflation continued to fall; and the economy was growing at a high rate.

But, from mid-1988 and through 1989, there were signs that the economy was overheating. Under the impetus of a consumer boom, the balance of payments assumed record deficits, the pound was under attack, and inflation increased again. The government responded by raising interest rates to reduce inflation. This did not help industry and business, which require low interest rates for expansion. Consequently, in the period 1989–93, and due to domestic and international factors, Britain experienced its worst recession since the 1930s depression. Only in 1993–4 were there signs that the country was slowly and unsurely coming out of recession, with manufacturing, financial and industrial performance improving, and unemployment, inflation and interest rates falling. But government spending, in spite of cuts in public services, continues to be high, and points to the continuing problem of how to manage a 'social economy' and a 'free-market' system.

Social class, the workforce and employment

Social class

Class in Britain has been variously defined by money and material wealth; ownership of the means of production as against the sellers

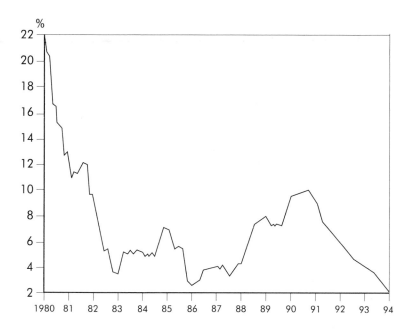

FIGURE 7.1 Inflation rate, 1980–94

of labour; education and professional status; accent and dialect; birth and breeding; and sometimes by lifestyles. But today it still seems to be mainly associated with economic and employment status.

Historically, the British class system has been divided into upper, middle and working classes. In earlier times, hierarchies based on wealth, the ownership of property, aristocratic privilege and political power were rigidly adhered to. But a small middle class of traders, merchants and skilled craftsmen began to make inroads into this system. Industrialization in the nineteenth century further fragmented class divisions. The working class divided into skilled and unskilled workers, and the middle class split into lower, middle and upper sections, depending on job classification or wealth. However, the upper class was still defined by birth, property and inherited money rather than by association with any particular profession.

The spread of education and gradual expansion of wealth to greater numbers of people in the twentieth century allowed greater social mobility (moving upwards out of the class into which one was born). The working class was more upwardly mobile and, owing to a loss of aristocratic privilege, the upper class merged more with the middle class. This process resulted in further distinctions between skilled and unskilled workers, and between the upper- and lower-middle class.

There was consequently a feeling in the 1960s and 1970s that the class system was breaking down. But class structures still exist. They are exploited by politicians, advertisers and manufacturers, and are acknowledged by the British people themselves. *British Social Attitudes: 1984* reported that a majority of people interviewed felt that Britain is still a class-divided society; considered that people are aware of class differences; and thought that social class affects a person's opportunities in life and employment. Few believed that class would be less important in the near future.

It seems that the social and educational provisions of the welfare state have not led to substantially greater equality of opportunity and achievement, nor to the absolute decline of the class system. But there has clearly been some upward mobility in Britain in the twentieth century, with more people advancing socially and economically because of general economic progress and changes in the employment and occupational structures.

Indeed, the British themselves feel that they are becoming increasingly middle class, and that class is now as much a matter of different social habits and attitudes as it is of occupation and money. Social commentators also maintain that more people in Britain have the sort of jobs, income and lifestyle which would classify them as middle class. A MORI opinion poll in 1990 supported these findings, and reported that 30 per cent of those interviewed considered themselves to be middle class and 67 per cent working class.

An adequate definition of class is difficult, and depends upon variable factors. The old absolute gaps between the classes have obviously lessened, and class today is a more finely graded hierarchy. The traditional boundaries have fragmented into smaller units, which are dependent upon a range of characteristics. The gaps between skilled and professional workers, and between manual and non-manual workers, are not as great as they used to be. But inequalities of wealth, the majority ownership of the means of production and services, difficulties of social mobility, poverty, and question of prestige still continue.

Researchers and advertisers build class models based on occupation, standing in the community and economic purchasing power, although lifestyle factors are now often included. Some employ a six-class model based on occupation:

1   Higher-grade professional, managerial and administrative workers (e.g. doctors and lawyers).
2   Intermediate professional, managerial and administrative workers (e.g. schoolteachers and sales managers).
3   Non-manual skilled workers (e.g. clerks and shop assistants).
4   Manual skilled workers (e.g. coalminers).
5   Semi-skilled workers (e.g. postmen)
6   Unskilled workers (e.g. dustmen, cleaners and labourers).

This model indicates three broad social/occupational groupings for contemporary Britain: a professional class made up of classes 1 and 2; an intermediate skilled class consisting of classes 3 and 4; and a skilled–unskilled class composed of groups 5 and 6. In addition a further group has been controversially used in recent years, the underclass. This consists of people who fall outside the usual classes, and includes the unemployed, single-parent families, the very poor and those with alternative lifestyles.

The workforce and employment

The total British workforce in 1992 was 28.2 million. Of these, 21.8 million were classed as employees actually in employment, nearly 3 million (or 10 per cent of the workforce) were self-employed, and the rest comprised the unemployed, the armed forces and people on work-related training programmes.

Despite changes in work patterns and business structures in the twentieth century, the majority of British people at most class levels, and whether part-time or full-time, are employed by an organization. It may be a small private firm, a large company, a public sector industry or service, or a multinational corporation. In this sense, most people are workers who sell their labour in a market dominated by concerns which own and control the means of production and services. The class-defining boundaries of employees and employers have remained relatively constant, and the top 1 per cent of British society still own more than 20 per cent of marketable wealth, and the top 10 per cent have 56 per cent.

However, there has been an increasing complexity in work processes and changes in employment patterns. Manufacturing industry has declined; unemployment has grown; self-employment has risen; the service trades have increased; and the managerial and professional fields have expanded. The number of manual workers has decreased; non-manual occupations have increased; and the old working-class bases have been eroded by the growth of salaried jobs. The British workforce has also become increasingly 'white-collar' and better educated, so that some 70 per cent of workers between 25 and 29 now have some educational qualifications.

Women have entered the workforce in greater, if largely part-time, numbers. They constitute some 45 per cent of the total, and 49 per cent of wives are now employed compared with 22 per cent in 1951. But their average weekly wage is only 79 per cent of the average paid to men. The majority of female workers are badly paid, part-time and often unprotected by the trade unions or the law. Although women form a 52 per cent majority of the population, and are increasing their numbers in higher education (where they form a slight majority of students) the professions and white-collar jobs, they have problems in progressing to the senior ranks.

Since the 1960s, women have been campaigning for greater equality with men in job opportunities and rates of pay. Legislation from the 1970s to the present has attempted to redress the balance. Equal Pay Acts stipulate that men and women who do the same or similar kinds of work should receive the same wages.

The Sex Discrimination Act makes it unlawful for the employer to discriminate between men and women when choosing a candidate for most jobs. The Equal Opportunities Commission is supposed to monitor this legislation, bring cases when there has been a breach of the Acts, and prepare reports and recommendations. Despite Acts of Parliament, however, men remain better paid than women in many occupations, particularly in industry and service trades.

There has been a recent need for more women to enter the workforce at all levels, in order to compensate for a reduced birthrate and the shortage of skilled labour. This situation requires improved financial, social and child-care benefits for women to enable them to work, as well as more flexible employment arrangements. There are signs that some employers, if not the government, are responding positively in these areas. But *British Social Attitudes: 1988–89* reported that the rapid changes in women's activity in the labour market 'have been accompanied by less rapid changes in attitudes to women's work. Even so, Britain seems to be much more egalitarian on women's issues than it was, say, twenty years ago. As on so many matters, circumstances tend to change first and attitudes lag behind. Put another way, such long-standing aspects of culture change only slowly and, it seems, reluctantly' (p. 193).

Unemployment, although continuing to be a major source of public concern, dropped steadily from mid-1986, but started to rise again in 1990, and was still 2.6 million in 1994. It remains proportionally high in Northern Ireland, the industrial English Midlands, Merseyside, north-east England, Scotland and South Wales. But since the late 1980s it has also affected the normally affluent south of England, and includes professional and higher-grade workers.

The creation of jobs is seen by all political parties as an important aim, but their various policies seem unlikely to improve the situation without a significant upturn in the economy and resulting expansion. Most vacant jobs at present are low-paid and part-time. Other positions are in technical areas, for which the educational and industrial systems have not provided. There is consequently a shortage of trained workers in many fields, which coincides with a drop in the birth-rate. Traditional apprenticeships have been greatly reduced, and technical education suffers from a lack of investment and facilities. However, the Conservative government has established some technological colleges in the major cities, which are financed jointly by government and private companies.

In order to provide the unemployed with job experience and training, the government has introduced a number of employment-related programmes under the control of Training and Enterprise Councils, such as Employment Training and Youth Training. These attempt to train the unemployed workforce, in the hope that permanent jobs may be found for them. But many programmes have been criticized for their lack of relevant training provisions and there is no guarantee that trainees will obtain a job afterwards. The government has also stipulated that young people between the ages of 16 and 18, who become unemployed on leaving school,

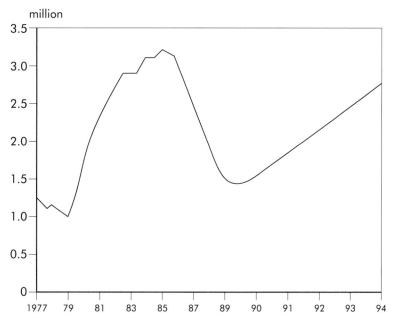

FIGURE 7.2 Unemployment rate, 1977–94

will not receive social security benefits but must undertake a training scheme or further education. Critics argue that Britain is still lagging behind other countries in appropriate training schemes for the young and unemployed. The result is that the potential workforce is inadequately equipped in those technical areas which are essential for a modern industrial state.

Traditional manufacturing industry has been progressively reduced in Britain. But an industrial infrastructure with different methods and products, in addition to some of the heavier manufactures, will continue to be important. It will not be as labour-intensive as in the past, because of technical advances. As the economy improves, high-technology industry and the service trades are set to expand. It is also likely that job opportunities for professional and skilled workers generally, particularly in managerial, supervisory, personal and financial services, will increase. However, unemployment and an inadequately trained workforce will still be problems in this post-industrial society, and will entail revisions of the work ethic and concepts of leisure, as well as more flexible employment arrangements.

Financial institutions

Financial institutions are central actors in the economy. In the 1980s, they responded to new developments in British economic life, which allowed them more freedom of operation. Banks, building societies, insurance firms, money markets and the London Stock Exchange expanded and diversified. They entered new fields and reorganized their traditional areas of expertise, as competition between the institutions increased. But they also had problems when the economic situation fluctuated in the late 1980s and early 1990s: unemployment in financial concerns was high; and the future of London as a European financial centre looked insecure.

Many of the major financial institutions have their headquarters in London, but also have branches throughout Britain. The square mile of the *City of London*, with its banks, insurance businesses, legal firms and financial dealers' offices, has always

PLATE 7.1 The Bank of England *(COI London)*

been a centre of British and world finance. In the past, its monetary resources have financed royal wars, military and colonial exploration and trading companies. Today it provides financial and investment services for commercial and industrial interests in Britain and overseas. Many of the City's institutions were founded in the seventeenth and eighteenth centuries, as Britain's prosperity and overseas trade grew, such as the insurance firm of Lloyd's (1680s), the London Stock Exchange (1773) and the Bank of England (1694).

The *Bank of England* is popularly known as 'the old lady of Threadneedle Street', and is the country's central bank. Although it is nationalized and closely tied to the government, which it advises on financial matters, it operates with some independence.

It is organized by a governor and directors who are appointed by the government, and is the government's banker and the agent for British commercial and foreign central banks. It prints and issues money notes for use in England and Wales, manages the national debt and supervises the country's gold reserves. It supports the pound by buying pounds on foreign currency exchanges, and indicates to the financial markets and commercial banks when interest rates should be lowered or raised. The Bank is the contact between the government and the other financial institutions, and supervises the implementation of government policies.

The other main banks which provide banking services throughout Britain are the *central clearing banks*, of which the most important are the Midland, National Westminster, Barclays, Lloyds and the Royal Bank of Scotland. They provide their customers with current and deposit (savings) accounts, loans and financial advice. But they have been criticized for their banking charges to clients and their unwillingness to provide funds for small businesses. They are involved in international finance, and have foreign interests, investments and branches. In recent years they have expanded their traditional activities, and moved into home loans, property sales, tax consultation and commercial advice.

In addition to these high street banks, there are the long-established *merchant banks*, which are mainly located in London. They give advice and finance to commercial and industrial businesses, both in Britain and overseas. They advise companies on takeovers and mergers; provide financial assistance for foreign transactions; and organize a range of financial services for individuals and corporations.

The City of London has a considerable range of financial markets. The *International Stock Exchange* is a market for the buying and selling of quoted (or listed) stocks and shares in British public companies, and a few overseas. Dealings on the Stock Exchange reflect the current market trends and prices for a range of securities, which may go up as well as down.

The Stock Exchange was revolutionized in 1986 by new developments, known popularly as the 'Big Bang'. The changes deregulated the old financial boundaries and restrictions, resulting in greater freedom of operation. Rules on membership were changed, negotiated fees for services were introduced, and financial dealers were given greater powers of dealing for themselves and their clients. Competition increased and large-scale computerization took place. Financial transactions are organized from computer screens by dealers in their corporate offices, rather than as previously on the floor of the Stock Exchange. However, some companies were too ambitious, over-expanded, and consequently suffered from the effects of the world stock market crash of 1987. The London market has only now returned to the profitability levels of 1987, after many redundancies among dealers and closure of some companies.

The *Foreign Exchange Market* is also based in London. Brokers in corporate or bank offices deal in the buying and selling of foreign currencies by telephone or computer. The London market in 1989 was the largest in the world in terms of average daily turnover of completed transactions.

Lloyd's of London is a famous name in the insurance market, and has long been active in its traditional fields of shipping and maritime insurance. But it has now diversified into many other areas, and insures against a multitude of events. Lloyd's operates as a market, where individual underwriters (or insurers), who are all members of Lloyd's, carry on their business. Underwriters normally form groups to give themselves greater security, because they have to bear any loss which occurs. Membership of Lloyd's is restricted to those who possess financial capacity, and who also satisfy standards of business integrity. But many underwriters have suffered in recent years as a result of heavy insurance losses.

In addition to the Lloyd's market, there are many individual insurance companies with headquarters in London and branches throughout the country. They have international connections and huge assets. They play an important role in British financial life because they are the largest investors of capital. Their main activity has traditionally been in life insurance. But many have now diversified into other associated fields, such as pensions and property loans.

Other London money markets arrange deals on the Euromarkets in foreign currencies; trade on financial futures (speculation on future prices of commodities); arrange gold dealings on the London Gold Market; and conduct international transactions in the commodity, shipping and freight markets.

British financial institutions have traditionally been respected for their honesty and integrity. But, as money markets have expanded and become freer, there have been a number of fraud cases, collapse of financial organizations and financial scandals. Such features, which give the City a bad image, have forced governments and the City ruling bodies to institute legislative and self-regulatory provisions, such as a Securities and Investments Board (SIB), a Financial Services Act and a Serious Fraud Office, in order to tighten the controls on financial dealings.

But critics argue that such provisions do not go far enough, and that there must be stronger independent controls of the City's dealings. The Labour Party has traditionally fought for the nationalization of financial institutions. It has argued that they should be more nationally and socially conscious, and forced to invest in British industry rather than overseas. The institutions maintain that they should be allowed to invest how and where they like in order to make a profit. However, it does seem that most City organizations are conscious of the negative criticisms, and are prepared to put their houses in order.

The composition of those who create and control wealth in Britain has changed since the Second World War. Bankers, aristocrats, landowners and industrialists were the richest people in the nineteenth and early twentieth centuries. Today the most affluent are retailers and those who service the consumer society, although holders of inherited wealth are still numerous. The number of millionaires has trebled since 1979 to an estimated 30,000. A large percentage of them are self-made, with lower-middle- and working-class backgrounds. The Labour Party feels that anyone earning more than £27,000 a year should be classified as rich (and taxed accordingly), while opinion polls suggest that the general public considers earnings above £30,000 a year to be real wealth. Talking about what one earns and about money generally has been traditionally regarded as unseemly in Britain, and too much involved with the cruder elements of existence and survival. But this mentality has slowly changed, particularly since the arrival in the 1980s of 'yuppies' (young upwardly mobile professional people) in business and the money markets. However, the yuppies have also been affected by the 1987 Stock Market crash and the economic downturn from mid-1988.

Industrial and commercial institutions

The workforce, whether as employees, managers or self-employed persons, and their representative organizations are important actors in the national economy.

The trade unions

Trade unions have achieved their present status only after a long and bitter historical struggle. They obtained legal recognition in 1871. But the fight for the right of workers to organize themselves originated in the trade guilds of the fourteenth century, and later in social clubs which were formed to give their members protection against sickness and unemployment.

The modern trade unions are closely associated with the Labour Party, and campaign for better working, health and pay conditions for their members. The trade union movement is highly organized, and has a membership of some 9 million people. But this marks a fall from over 12 million in 1978. The reduction has been due to rises in unemployment; changing attitudes to trade unions among workers; industrial decline; and regulatory legislation from the Conservative government.

Today there are some 350 trade unions and professional associations of workers, which vary considerably in size and influence. They represent not only skilled and unskilled workers in industry, but also white-collar workers in a range of businesses, companies, and local and central government. Other professional associations like the Law Society, the Police Federation and the British Medical Association carry out similar representational roles for their members.

Members of trade unions pay annual dues (money) to their unions and frequently to the Labour Party, unless they elect not to pay this latter amount. The subscriptions provide the finance for union activities and services, such as legal, monetary and professional help, as well as support for the Labour Party. The richer unions are able to give strike pay to members who are taking part in 'official strikes', which are those legally sanctioned by members and are distinguished from 'unofficial strikes'. Trade unions vary in their wealth and in their political orientation, ranging from the far left to the right wing of the political spectrum.

Some unions admit as members only those people who work in a specific trade or profession, such as miners or teachers. Other unions comprise workers who are employed in different or more general areas of industry or commerce, such as the Transport and General Workers' Union. Smaller unions have frequently joined with others in similar fields to form new unions, such as Unison, which comprises public service workers and which is now the largest in Britain.

Some industries chose in the past to operate a 'closed shop' policy, whereby a factory or business employed only workers who were members of recognized trade unions. Although the unions argued for the solidarity of the scheme, the closed shop was widely attacked, both from inside and outside the labour movement. Conservative legislation now allows individual workers to choose, without victimization, whether they should belong to a particular union or none at all.

Many trade unions are affiliated to the Trades Union Congress (TUC), which was founded in 1868 and serves as an umbrella organization to coordinate trade union interests. It holds an annual conference and, although it has no power over individual unions, can be successful in promoting cooperation among workers. In the past, it exerted some political pressure on government, usually when Labour governments have been in power. It is currently seeking to extend its contacts in industry and commerce, and with employers as well as workers.

But the influence of the TUC and the trade unions has

declined. This is due to the effects of unemployment; the restructuring of industry attempting to recover after recession; and to Conservative legislation. Laws have been passed to enforce secret voting by union members before strikes can be legally called and for the election of union officials. The number and rights of pickets (union strikers) outside business premises have been curtailed, and secondary (or sympathy) action by other unionists outside the immediate conflict are effectively banned. Unions may now be fined by the courts if they transgress legislation.

Such laws (most of which the Labour Party now accept) and the economic climate forced trade unions to be more realistic in their wage demands in the 1980s. But pay claims are now escalating again, and raise fears of increased inflation.

The legislation has controlled some of the more extreme and dubious union practices, as well as introducing more democratic procedures into union activities. The grassroots membership has become more independent of the union bosses and activists; has become more determined to represent its own wishes; and is concerned to cure abuses in the labour movement. The initiative in industry has shifted gradually to the employers and moderate unions, who have been moving away from the traditional 'class-war' image of unionism and are accepting new technology and working patterns in an attempt to improve competitiveness and productivity.

A MORI public opinion poll in 1990 found that while 80 per cent of those interviewed believed that unions are essential to protect workers' interests, 38 per cent felt that unions still have too much power in Britain today, and 50 per cent believed that the unions are dominated by extremists; 43 per cent of trade unionists themselves agreed with this latter point of view, and 44 per cent disagreed.

Any strike action by the unions can be very damaging to the British economy, and has been used as an economic and political weapon in the past. In some cases, strikes are seen as legitimate and will find public support. But others which are clearly political or unpopular will be rejected. Britain seems superficially to be prone to industrial disputes. But domestic and international statistics consistently show that fewer working days are lost in Britain each year than in several other leading industrial nations. On average, the large majority of manufacturing plants and businesses are free of strikes, and media coverage is sometimes responsible for giving a distorted picture of industrial relations.

Industrial problems should be placed in the context of financial rewards. Britain has a low-wage economy, compared with other major European countries, with an average gross wage in 1993 of £317 per week. Many workers (especially women) receive less than this amount, and all are taxed at the lower rate of 20 per cent and the basic rate of 25 per cent. The British tend to believe that they are over-taxed. But their basic rates of taxation, and a

PLATE 7.2   Coal miners' demonstration, 1992 *(Jacky Chapman/Format)*

top rate of 40 per cent, are in fact lower than in many other western countries, although the Conservatives have recently increased indirect taxation.

Employers' organizations

There are some 140 employers' and managers' associations in Britain, which are associated with companies and organizations in the private sector. They promote good industrial relations between businesses and their workforces; try to settle disputes; and offer legal and professional advice.

Most are members of the Confederation of British Industry (CBI). This is an umbrella body which represents its members nationally; negotiates on their behalf with the government and the TUC; supports industrial growth and planning; campaigns for greater investment and innovation in industry and new technology; and is more sympathetic to Conservative governments than Labour ones. However, it can be very critical of Conservative policies. It also acts as a public relations organization; relays the employers' points of view to the public; and has considerable economic influence and authority. The number of interest groups controlling the CBI today is less than in the past because of takeovers and mergers, and the decline of manufacturing industry. But their influence is consequently much greater.

Industrial relations

Complaints are often raised about the quality of industrial relations in Britain. This has tended to be confrontational rather than cooperative, and based on notions of 'class-warfare' and 'us-and-them', which have not benefited either commerce or industry. Trade union leaders can be extremist and stubborn in pursuing their members' interests. But the performance of management also continues to be criticized. Insensitive and incompetent managers can frequently be responsible for strikes arising in the first place, and then continuing. Relations between management and workers still leave much to be desired and industrial unrest, which was largely dormant in the 1980s, has broken out again in recent years. A MORI public opinion poll in 1990 found that 58 per cent of those people interviewed believed that bad management is more to blame than the unions for poor industrial relations and Britain's economic problems.

The Advisory, Conciliation and Arbitration Service (ACAS)

ACAS is an independent, government-financed organization, which was created in 1974 in an attempt to improve industrial relations. It may provide, if requested, advice, conciliation and arbitration services for the parties involved in a dispute in both the public and the private sectors. But ACAS does not have any binding power, and the parties may disregard its advice and solutions. Nor is there any legal requirement to bring ACAS into the dispute, for industrial relations in Britain have been traditionally seen as consisting of free collective bargaining between employers and workers. It has been argued that this situation should be reformed, that arbitration should be made compulsory, and that findings should be binding on the parties concerned. On the other hand, strike action is not illegal for most workers if legally called, and the government has no power to intervene. Nevertheless, ACAS has performed much valuable work even within the present framework, and has been responsible for settling a wide range of disputes.

ACAS also oversees the operation of employment law and can examine abuses of workers' rights under various legislation. These may involve complaints of unfair and unlawful dismissal; claims under the Equal Pay Acts of 1970 and 1984; grievances under the Sex Discrimination Acts of 1975 and 1986; and unlawful discrimination under the Race Relations Act of 1976. There is now a large body of employment and regulatory law in Britain, which makes conditions of work more secure and less arbitrary than they have been in the past, particularly in the cases of women, ethnic minorities, the low-paid and part-time workers. But there is still concern about the real effectiveness of such legislation.

Consumer protection

In a competitive market, consumers should be given a choice of goods and services, together with information to make that choice, and enough protective legislation to safeguard their purchases. Statutory protection for consumers in the industrial and commercial markets has grown steadily in Britain, and is now harmonized with strong European Union law. The public can complain to tribunals and the courts about unfair trading practices, dangerous goods, misrepresentation, bad service, unsafe products and misleading advertising. The Consumer Protection Act of 1987 imposes strict liability for personal injury and deaths resulting from defective products, and generally improves consumer protection.

The Office of Fair Trading is a government department which, under a Director-General, oversees the behaviour of trade and industry in the consumer field. It promotes fair trading and the protection of consumers. The Office is an active body, and has helped to improve consumer protection. It has drawn up codes of practice with industrial and commercial organizations. It keeps a close watch for any breaches of the codes and publishes its findings, often to the embarrassment of the manufacturers concerned. It can suggest legislation to the government in areas where improvement is needed, and provides information on consumer rights for the public, in order to create a wider consumer awareness.

Organizations which provide help on consumer affairs at the local level are Citizens' Advice Bureaux, specialist Consumer Advice Centres and the consumer protection departments of local councils. Private consumer protection groups, which investigate complaints and grievances, may also exist in some localities.

At national independent level, the National Consumer Council conveys consumers' attitudes to relevant authorities, although there is doubt about its effectiveness. A more positive body is the Consumers' Association, funded by the subscriptions of its 1 million members. Its magazine *Which?* is a champion of the consumer in Britain, and examines a variety of consumer products by applying rigorous tests to anything from television sets to insurance and estate agents. *Which?* is the 'buyers' bible', and its reports have raised the standards of commercial products and services in Britain.

But critics argue that much remains to be done in the consumer field to achieve minimum standards and adequate protection. In 1991 the Conservative government introduced a Citizens' Charter programme which, by promoting greater openness and providing more information, is intended to improve standards of service for the consumer. It gives rights to members of the public to complain about state businesses, such as education, health, the Post Office, transport and employment. The scheme is being expanded to other fields, but its effectiveness has yet to be proved. However, the British are being encouraged to complain more about the quality of goods and services they receive, in an effort to raise standards.

ATTITUDES

Attitudes to the economy and economic structure

Public opinion polls have reflected the changing economic climate since 1979, with its considerable ups and downs. People generally are satisfied with the Conservative government when the economy has performed well, but dissatisfied when things are bad. There has been a recent lack of faith in the Conservative ability to manage the economy, but little optimism that Labour could do any better. This was shown in the 1992 general election when the Labour Party failed to win crucial support partly because of its high taxation policies.

The economic situation is a source of great concern for a majority of British people, particularly unemployment, factory closures, the decline of industry, inflation, prices and taxation. It is generally felt that the government could do more about unemployment and invest more in industry. Job security has become the first priority of job seekers, and is ranked ahead of work satisfaction, promotion opportunities and working conditions. But, in terms of job satisfaction, a 1990 MORI opinion poll found that, of those people interviewed, 82 per cent were very or fairly satisfied with their jobs, and only 10 per cent were either fairly or very dissatisfied.

However, a majority of respondents to opinion polls also believe that business and economic arrangements in Britain are unfair, and that the values of managers and workers are opposed. They feel that the country's wealth is unfairly distributed, and that this situation favours the owners and the rich at the expense of employees and the poor. A growing number of people now support the idea that workers should be given more control over and say in the organization of their places of work.

Critics argue that Britain's economic ills are largely due to cultural factors; that there has been a traditional reluctance for educated and qualified people to enter trade and industry; that the workforce has a lower productivity rate than other comparable competitors; that there has been insufficient investment in industry; that management is weak and unprofessional; and that there has been too little investment in and encouragement of the technical, scientific and research fields.

■ **Explain and examine the following terms:**

diversify	privatization	monopoly	invisible exports
merger	Lloyd's	shares	balance of payments
private sector	deficit	TUC	service industries
laissez-faire	Barclays	ACAS	deindustrialization
the City	inflation	Which?	mixed economy
devaluation	consumer boom	CBI	Stock Exchange

■ **Write short essays on the following questions:**

1   Examine British economic policy and performance from 1979 to the present.

2   Consider the financial institutions in Britain. Should they be more closely regulated by government? If so, why?

3   Discuss the role of the trade unions in British life.

Chapter 8

Social security, health and housing

- Welfare history   215
- Changing family and demographic
  structures   217
- Social security   221
- The National Health Service (NHS)   223
- The personal social services   228
- Housing   231
- *Attitudes to social security, health
  and housing*   235
- *Exercises*   237

S TATE PROVISIONS FOR SOCIAL SECURITY, health, social services and housing are very much taken for granted by British people today. But it was not until the early twentieth century that the state gradually accepted more responsibility for providing basic assistance to its citizens. In earlier centuries there had been few public facilities, and it was felt that the state was not obliged to supply welfare services.

British social amenities have developed considerably since the mid-twentieth century, as society and government policies have changed. They are now divided between the state and private sectors. State provisions include services and benefits for sick, old, needy, unemployed and poor people. They are provided by local agencies under the central direction of the Departments of Health and Social Security. The cost of this welfare state is financed mainly by public taxation and partly by a national insurance scheme to which employers and employees contribute.

In the private sector, there are many voluntary organizations which continue the tradition of charitable help in various areas of need, and which depend for their funding upon public donations. Other private welfare and health services are financed by personal insurance schemes and by those people able to pay for their facilities.

The Conservative government is introducing reforms in the state sector in an attempt to reduce expenditure, improve efficiency and target benefits to those most in need. Critics argue that such a market orientation is a return to the old mentality on welfare. Government policies have been widely attacked, some reforms are unpopular with the public, and state provision is an area of debate and controversy. This situation emphasizes the difficulties of trying to reconcile social services with a 'free-market' national economy.

Welfare history

In earlier centuries, welfare provisions were virtually non-existent for the majority of the British population. The churches, charitable institutions, the rural feudal system and town guilds (organizations of skilled craftsmen) did give some protection against poverty, unemployment and illness. But this help was limited in its application and effect. Most people were therefore thrown upon their own resources, which were often minimal, in order to survive.

During Elizabeth I's reign (1558–1603), a Poor Law was established in England. The state took over the organization of charity provisions from the church. Each parish became responsible for its own poor, sick and unemployed, and was supposed to provide them with material aid, housing and work opportunities. The Poor Law marked the start of state welfare legislation in Britain. But it was grudging, limited in its application, and actively discouraged people from relying on the parish relief system. Poverty and need were assumed to be the result of an unwillingness to work and provide for oneself. The state was not considered to have extensive responsibility in welfare areas.

These attitudes persisted in later centuries. But urban and rural poverty continued. Conditions became worse in the eighteenth and nineteenth centuries under the impetus of the industrial revolutions, and as the population increased rapidly. The urban workforce was often obliged to work long hours in bad conditions in low-quality factories for low wages. Families frequently inhabited slums of overcrowded, back-to-back dwellings which lacked adequate sewage, heating or ventilation. The situation of many rural agricultural workers was just as bad.

Public health became an inevitable problem, and the poor conditions resulted in infectious epidemics in the nineteenth century, such as diphtheria, typhoid, tuberculosis and smallpox. Disease remained endemic in the British population into the twentieth century because of bad housing and the lack of adequate health facilities.

The Elizabethan Poor Law was eventually replaced by the Poor Law Amendment Act of 1834. This was designed to prevent the alleged abuse of the existing social relief provided by the parishes. It created a system of workhouses in which the destitute and needy could live. But the workhouses were unpleasant places, and people were discouraged from relying upon them. They were dreaded by the poor, and accepted as a last alternative only when all else failed. Since nineteenth-century Britain was subject to economic slumps and unemployment, the workhouse system often resulted in misery and the separation of families.

Successive governments until the end of the nineteenth century also refused to allow workers to organize themselves into trade unions, through which they might agitate against their working and living conditions. This forced workers into establishing their own social and self-help clubs and Friendly Societies, in order to provide basic protection for themselves. Some employers were more benevolent than others, and provided good housing and health facilities for their workforces. But these examples were few, and life continued to be harsh for the majority of the people.

The social misery of the nineteenth century persuaded some towns to establish local boards to control public health and initiate health schemes. But an effective apparatus was not created until the Public Health Act of 1848, and a national system of public health was not effective until a second Public Health Act in 1875. Other legislation was passed to clear slum areas, but large-scale slum clearance was not achieved until the middle of the twentieth century. Further reforms relating to housing, health, factory and mine conditions, sanitation and sewage, town-planning and trade unionism were accomplished during the course of the nineteenth century. But they were limited in their effects, and have been described as paternalistic in their intention.

The social welfare problems of the nineteenth century were substantial. The failure of the state to provide for a reasonable security against illness, unemployment and poverty made the situation worse. The prevailing mentality was that suffering was the fault of the destitute themselves and that, like businessmen and manufacturers, the remedy for their ills was in self-help.

Humanitarian social reformers, who were largely responsible for legislation which gave some relief from the effects of nineteenth-century industrialization, had to struggle against the apathy and hostility of the vested interests in Parliament and the country.

However, some small victories had been won, and it was gradually admitted in the early twentieth century that the state did have social responsibility for society as a whole. But this admission was not universally accepted. It was left to the Liberal government between 1906 and 1914 to introduce reform programmes on old-age pensions, national insurance, employment, trade unionism and medicine. These formed the basic structures of the future welfare state. But such measures only affected a minority of people, and the state was unwilling or unable to introduce further provisions in the early twentieth century. The financial and physical exhaustion resulting from the 1914–18 World War and the economic crises of the 1920s and 1930s halted welfare expansion.

But the underlying need for more state help continued. The model for the welfare state appeared in the Beveridge Report of 1942. It recommended that a comprehensive system of social security and free health care for all should be established to overcome the obvious suffering and need experienced by many people. It was intended that the system would be largely financed by a national insurance scheme, to which workers would contribute, and out of which they and their families would receive benefits when required. Although Conservative governments passed some of the necessary legislation to implement these proposals, it was the Labour government from 1945 to 1951 that radically altered the social and health systems, and created the present welfare state.

Changing family and demographic structures

Contemporary social provisions, in both public and private sectors, should be seen partly within the context of changes in family structures. These, and other demographic factors, influence governmental responses to welfare needs and the availability and cost of social services.

It is often argued that the British family structure is falling apart; failing to provide for its elderly and disabled; suffering from social and moral problems; and looking automatically to the state for support. The pattern of family life in recent years has changed considerably as nuclear families (two parents and children) have decreased, and new family structures have emerged. However, certain traditional features continue.

Marriage is still popular in Britain, despite a decline in recent years. In 1991 there were 340,500 marriages, and 37 per cent of the ceremonies were remarriages of one or both parties. Of the English and Welsh population aged 16 and over, 58 per cent are married, 27 per cent are single, 9 per cent are widowed and 7 per cent are divorced.

But more people are delaying marriage until their mid- to late twenties, with an average age of 27 for men and 25 for women. This suggests that the British are postponing marriage for a number of reasons, such as career considerations, rather than rejecting it as a social institution. Denominational weddings still remain popular, with some 70 per cent of those marrying for the first time having a religious ceremony.

But four out of every ten marriages end in divorce; Britain has one of the highest divorce rates in the European Union; remarriages are at greater risk than first marriages; and people who marry under 21 are statistically the most susceptible to divorce. The average duration of marriages which end in divorce is ten years, and the average divorce age is 36 for women and 38 for men.

Divorce is based on the irretrievable breakdown of a marriage and, unless one party can prove fault such as adultery, desertion or unreasonable behaviour, the couple must wait two years before a divorce can be finalized. Divorce is painful for most people, and affects a considerable number of children under 16. The difficulties are increased by the confrontational nature of the divorce system, with conflicts over property, financial support and custody of children. But the government is reforming divorce procedures by providing better conciliation, counselling and mediation services.

Despite the popularity of marriage, there has been a considerable increase in cohabitation (couples living together outside marriage). This new structure occurs mostly in the cases of separated or divorced women, although an increasing number of single women now cohabit. Many of these relationships are stable and long-term, and half of the resulting births are registered by both parents, rather than one as previously.

Non-marital (or illegitimate) births arising from cohabitation and single mothers are now 31 per cent of all live births. The situation has created controversy and concern, since illegitimacy retains some of its traditional stigma. However, government legislation has improved the legal standing of such children by removing restrictions in areas such as inheritance.

There were 781,000 live births in Britain in 1992, and this birth-rate outnumbered deaths at 634,200. The average family size had been declining in previous years and is still below 2.1 children per family, or the level necessary to replace the population in the long term. The proportion of young people under 16 fell from 25 per cent in 1971 to 20 per cent in 1991. But it is estimated that the number of school-age children and young people in the population will increase again from the mid-1990s.

The relatively low birth-rate is due to several factors. Childbearing is being delayed, with an average age of 27 at which women have their first child in marriage. Some career women are delaying even longer, and there has been an increase in the number of single women and married couples who choose to remain childless, or to limit their families. Contraception has become more widespread, voluntary sterilization of both sexes is more common, and legal abortions have increased.

Increased divorce, separation and choice of individual lifestyles have led to a growth in the number of one-parent families, which add another element to the family structure. It is estimated that some 2 million children are being raised in 1.3 million one-parent units, where 90 per cent of the parents are women. Of the women bringing up one-parent families 16 per cent are single, 34 per cent are divorced, 22 per cent are separated and 17 per cent are widowed. Many of these families, the highest proportion of which is in inner London, are struggling with poverty and reduced living standards, and are dependent upon social security benefits.

The proportion of married women in employment is now some 49 per cent, and more women are returning to work more quickly after the birth of a child. But although Britain has a high percentage of working mothers and wives, provisions for maternity leave and child care are the lowest in Europe.

The various nuclear, one-parent and extended families have to cope with increased demands upon them, which may entail considerable personal sacrifice. Families (usually the women) still carry out the greater share of the caring roles in British society, rather than state professionals. Only 5 per cent of people over 65 live in state or private institutions, and only 7 per cent of disabled adults live in communal establishments. The majority of handicapped children and adults are cared for by their families, and the majority of the elderly are also cared for by families or live alone. This is a considerable saving to the state without which the cost of state health and welfare care would rise steeply.

But the burden upon families and state resources will grow as the population becomes more elderly, the ranks of the disabled (currently some 6 million) and the disadvantaged swell, and unemployment remains high. Some 18 per cent of the population are over the current state retirement ages of 60 for women and 65 for men. Life expectancy of men is 73 years and women 78 years, so that there are more women among the elderly. It is estimated that Britain will have 4.5 million people over 75 and 0.5 million over 90 by the year 2001. Critics argue that more government aid should be given to families and local authorities to lighten their burden.

The picture that emerges from these overall statistics is one of smaller families; more people living alone; an increase in one-parent families and non-marital births; rising divorce rates; more people living longer and contributing to an ageing population; more working mothers and wives; more couples cohabiting before and outside marriage; but with the institution of marriage itself remaining popular.

However, the traditional nuclear family is surviving despite changes in family structure. Most adults marry and have children inside marriage, most children are raised by their natural parents, and most marriages continue until ended by the death of one of the partners. These features form a background to the contemporary state and private provisions for social security, health, social services and housing.

Social security

The social security system is operated by the Department of Social Security (DSS) and provides benefits for workers who contribute financially to the scheme while employed (contributory) and also for those people who are unable to make contributions (non-contributory).

The finance in the contributory sector comes from compulsory national insurance payments which are deducted from the wages of workers over 16 and under 65 (under 60 for women); contributions from employers; fixed amounts from self-employed workers; and the state.

The system gives benefits and pensions, such as sickness benefit for people who are absent from work because of sickness; unemployment benefit following the loss of a job, up to a limit of 12 months; state retirement pensions for women at 60 and men at 65; a widow's pension and benefits to support the wife and children of a deceased worker; maternity pay for pregnant working women; and invalidity benefit for a worker who is unable to work because of incapacity. The Conservative government intends to cut unemployment benefit to six months, to restrict invalidity benefits, and to equalize state retirement pensions for both sexes at 65.

The two most important non-contributory benefits, which are financed from government expenditure, are Income Support and Family Credit. Income Support is provided for some 5.3 million people in great financial need, which usually includes the unemployed (after 12 months' unemployment), one-parent families and the elderly. This benefit is supposed to cover the basic living requirements, although the sums involved are relatively low, and the government has further reduced them. It also includes free prescription drugs, dental treatment, opticians' services and children's school meals. Family Credit is a benefit whereby families with children and at least one parent in work receive an additional sum to their low wages, which includes the same extra free benefits as Income Support.

A further non-contributory benefit, Housing Benefit, is paid to people on Income Support and other low-income claimants. It covers the cost of rented accommodation, but the amounts have been reduced by the Conservative government. Child Benefit is another non-contributory benefit (currently £10 per week for the eldest child and £8 for each other child), which is paid to the mother for each of her children up to the age of 18, irrespective of family income, and which is tax-free. This benefit may eventually be abolished or distributed only to families below a certain income.

In the past, people in great need and who suffered hardship were also able to claim a wide range of non-contributory single payments, such as the cost of clothes, cookers and children's shoes, in the form of grants or loans. But these have now been sharply cut by the government, and replaced by a very limited Social Fund, to which people have to apply. The Fund is being applied restrictively, and has been widely attacked as an example of the government's alleged reduction of social security aid.

The social security system does provide a degree of security in both the contributory and non-contributory sectors. It is supposed to be a safety-net against the most urgent needs, but even this does not prevent hardship. It is estimated that some 10 million people in Britain exist on the poverty line, which is sometimes measured on European Union scales as half the average national income. But accurate figures of poverty are difficult to obtain, because of the variable presentation of official statistics, and because there are different definitions of what constitutes poverty.

Social security costs almost one-third of total government spending (£61,500 million). It is very expensive to run, and will become more so as the old-age population grows, and as the numbers of the long-term sick, disadvantaged, poor and unemployed persist. It has in the past also been very complicated with its large array of benefits. Since 1988 the government has reshaped and supposedly simplified the whole system, as well as reducing benefits. It has argued that these reforms will save public money, preserve the safety-net commitment and target those people with the greatest needs. Critics argue that the changes have meant a reduction in the provision of social security, particularly under the Social Fund, Housing Benefit and Income Support. The young unemployed between 16 and 18 have also been affected since they are now ineligible for unemployment benefit until they are 18. But the government maintains that it is increasing its expenditure in real terms.

It is also concerned that people should look after themselves more, without automatic recourse to the state for help, and that they should seek employment more actively. Employees are encouraged to take out personal pension insurance to add to their state pensions, and to insure privately against other welfare contingencies. But the record of the insurance companies in these areas has been criticized.

Government reforms of the social security system, which are influenced by cost considerations and a market ideology, are controversial and bitterly criticized. But it is difficult to create a satisfactorily simple and fair system which will protect the genuinely needy and still encourage people to become more self-reliant and economically independent.

The National Health Service (NHS)

The National Health Service Act of 1946–7 was based on the Beveridge Report recommendations. It established the NHS to replace the previous private system of payment for health care. The NHS now provides a comprehensive range of free medical and some free dental services for the whole country. It includes hospitals, doctors, dentists, nurses and other health facilities, and is financed out of public taxation and some contributions from the national insurance scheme.

There was considerable opposition to the NHS from the

medical profession, which wished to retain private medicine. But such objections were countered by the Labour government. In its first years of operation, the NHS covered 95 per cent of the population and cost some £400 million a year to run. This cost currently stands at £36,000 million, or some 14 per cent of total government expenditure, and the NHS is also the biggest single employer of labour in Western Europe. Yet total health expenditure in Britain as a percentage of the gross domestic product (GDP) is some 6 per cent and lower than other major western industrialized countries.

The NHS in England is divided into central government, regional and district health authorities. The Secretary of State for Health has overall responsibility for policy, and for supervising the regional and district authorities. Secretaries of State do a similar job in Scotland, Wales and Northern Ireland. The district authorities in England and Wales, health boards in Scotland, and health and social service boards in Northern Ireland, organize health in their local areas. In England, because of its size, the additional 14 regional authorities (which the government wants to abolish) are centred on university medical schools, and are a link between the Department of Health and the districts.

It was originally intended that the NHS would be completely free of charge in its provision of consultations, treatment and medicines. But prescriptions, which are written notes from a doctor enabling patients to obtain drugs from a chemist, now have to be paid for, as do some dental work, dental checks and eye tests. Such payments are, however, dependent upon employment status, age and income, so that children under 16, recipients of social security benefits and most old-age pensioners usually receive free health services. In practice, some 80 per cent of medical prescription items are supplied free. Similarly, hospital care and treatment under the NHS is free for British and European Union citizens.

Most people who require health care will first consult their local NHS or state-employed doctor, who is a GP or non-specialist general practitioner, and of whom there are about 35,000 in Britain. Such doctors have an average of about 1,900 registered patients on their panel (or list of names), although they will see only a small percentage of these on a regular basis. The majority of GPs are now members of group practices, where they share larger premises, services and equipment. However, a patient will usually be on the panel of one particular doctor, who will often be a personal choice.

If the patient requires further treatment or examination, the GP will refer him or her to specialists and consultants, normally at the local NHS hospital. These hospitals have some 370,000 beds and provide medical, dental, nursing and midwifery staff. Britain has some of the world's most modern hospitals, expertise and facilities, and more hospitals are being constructed. But it also has many buildings which were erected in the nineteenth century, and which are in urgent need of modernization and repair. There is a shortage of beds in some hospitals, wards and hospitals are being closed, and waiting times for admission to hospital can be long, although these have been reduced in recent years. The blame for this situation has been placed on government spending cuts, and an alleged unwillingness to spend more public money on health.

The NHS occupies an ambivalent position in the public imagination. On the one hand, it is praised for its work and status as a free service, and for its achievements. It is perceived to be a success in terms of consumer demand, especially when contrasted to earlier provisions for medical care. Today people are in general receiving help when they need it, and many who would previously have died or suffered are surviving and being cared for. The standards of living and medicine have risen, better diets have been devised and there is a greater health awareness in the population at large.

On the other hand, the NHS is criticized for its alleged inefficiency, inadequate standards and bureaucracy. Its objectives are sometimes considered too ambitious for the money spent on it. The media are constantly drawing attention to shortcomings and forecasting breakdown. Workers within the NHS, such as doctors, nurses and non-medical staff, have frequently complained about low pay, long hours, bureaucracy and the levels of staffing. They and other critics seem to feel that many of the problems could be solved simply by injecting more finance into the NHS. It is also argued that the government is cutting services and resources.

The government main-
tains that it has in fact increased
spending in real terms, and that
the NHS is safe in its hands. But
this position has to acknowl-
edge the facts of inflation, rising
costs and increased demand,
which arguably contribute to
an alleged underfunding. The
NHS is in many ways a victim
of its own success, and of the
demands that the British place
upon it as of right. It is inevitable that a free, consumer-led
service will either require
increasing levels of expenditure, or better management of
existing resources, particularly
at a time when increasing
demands, due in part to an ageing population and medical
advances, are made upon it.
Yet despite these problems,
the NHS has worked well and
gives great value for the money
spent on it. Foreign observers
often feel that the British do not
always appreciate what a good health system they have compared
with many other countries.

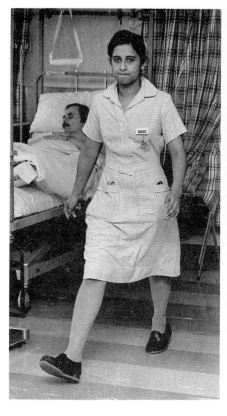

PLATE 8.1 Hospital nurse *(Judy Harrison/Format)*

Conservative government state health reforms

The British public has since 1991 been concerned about
Conservative health reforms in the state sector. The government
had already put out to local tender (or privatized) such items of the
NHS as hospital laundry, cleaning and catering services, in order
to save money and introduce competition. The latest reforms have

altered the way in which the NHS is managed and funded. They are intended to create a competitive and demand-led 'internal market' for health in which money is supposed to follow patients, in order to provide better health facilities and greater choice.

Local health authorities are now purchasers of health care for their local residents rather than providers of hospitals and services; are funded according to the size of their population; and arrange and prioritize services on the basis of needs within existing resources. They can buy health care for their local population from hospitals and other units in both the public and private sectors.

The funding of hospitals is now based on contracts with local health authorities, and is tied to the number of patients they treat. Some hospitals have been allowed to opt out of local health authority control after a ballot of staff and authorization by the Secretary of State for Health. These hospitals then become 'self-governing trusts', and are responsible for managing their own affairs with their own budgets. But they are still state hospitals within the NHS.

Doctors (GPs) belonging to large practices may apply to become 'fundholders'. This means that they receive an annual budget directly from the local health authority; are free to determine the need for patient services; and are able to buy these from hospitals inside and outside their area. There are now two types of GPs (fundholders and non-fundholders), who effectively compete against each other. Critics maintain that patients receive better services from fundholders.

These reforms have aroused fierce controversy, but also some acceptance as ways of simplifying the bureaucratic procedures of the NHS. The government hopes that they will result in competitive, patient-led services, where finance is diverted to real needs and skills. However, critics argue that patient-care will be reduced as opted-out hospitals and fundholding doctors concentrate on finance generation and balancing the economic books, and more money will be spent on management activities than health.

Many people are confused and concerned about what the NHS reforms will actually mean for them. The essential debate is one of how to manage limited resources more efficiently, and

whether this should be done through traditional local planning or the new competitive units. Much will depend on how the reforms work out in practice in the 1990s before final judgements can be made. Independent research (OECD, 1994) indicates that the changes may be creating a more efficient system.

The private medical sector

The Conservative government has also encouraged private health institutions and private medical insurance. Concern about waiting lists and standards of health care in the NHS has persuaded many individuals, trade unions, companies and industrial groups to take out health insurance from specialists such as the British United Provident Association (BUPA). Some 5.5 million people, or 10 per cent of the population, are now covered by private medical insurance.

The insurance policy pays for treatment in the case of illness, either in private hospitals and clinics, or in NHS hospitals which provide 'pay-beds'. These are beds for the use of paying patients, which still exist in NHS hospitals, despite opposition and the political threat (mainly from the Labour Party) to stop the practice. Pay-beds were a concession in 1946 to those doctors who agreed to join the NHS but who still wished to keep a number of private patients.

The private health sector is seen as an alternative to the NHS. The Conservative government maintains that private medicine is complementary to the NHS and releases pressure on public funds, as well as giving greater choice to the public. Critics argue that health care should not be a matter of who can pay for it, but a responsibility of the state.

The personal social services

The social services provide a wide range of facilities for assisting people, like the elderly, the disabled, the mentally ill, families, single parents and children. Trained staff, such as district visitors,

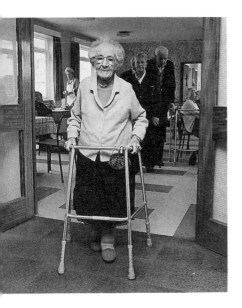

PLATE 8.2 Woman with walking frame in local authority home for the elderly *(Raissa Page/Format)*

home nurses and social workers, cater for many of these personal needs in the community. The services are organized and run by local health and government authorities with central government funding, which currently amounts to some £6,103 million a year.

An increasing pressure is being put upon the social services and families as the elderly population grows and the number of the disadvantaged rises. Critics argue that greater financial resources should be devoted both to family carers and the social services.

However, the government has now introduced a 'Care in the Community' programme. This allows financial and material support to be given to families caring for elderly or disabled relatives in the latters' own homes, or for handicapped children and adults in the family home. It also allows hospital patients who do not need long-term care to be transferred to the community under the supervision of the social services, and for some elderly and disabled people to be cared for in their own homes by the social services. The aim is to prevent the institutionalization of people and to give them a measure of independence.

The scheme is financed by central government and operated by local government authorities. But it has caused controversy and difficulties, such as mentally ill and handicapped patients becoming homeless or housed in inadequate temporary accommodation. Critics argue that there needs to be more support for local authorities and a greater awareness of implementation problems if the policy is to be more successful than at present.

The private social services sector

While there have been substantial improvements in welfare provisions in the twentieth century, there is still a shortage of finance to support the needy in a comprehensive fashion. It is therefore important that voluntary charities and agencies have continued. They are a complementary welfare service to the state facilities, and provide an essential element in the total aid pattern. The state system would be unable to cover all needs without them, particularly in the present financially restricted circumstances.

Most of the voluntary agencies have charitable status, which means that they receive tax concessions on their income, but receive no (or very little) financial support from the state. However, some groups, such as those dealing with drug and alcohol addiction, do receive financial grants from central and local government. There are many thousands of voluntary organizations in Britain, operating at national and local levels, and varying considerably in size. Some are small and collect small amounts of money from the public. Others are very large and have professional staffs, who collect millions of pounds from many different sources. Some groups, such as Oxfam (for the relief of famine) and the Save the Children Fund, have now become international organizations.

The following are examples of the voluntary agencies. Barnardo's provides care and help for needy children, organizes homes for orphans and facilitates the adoption of children; The Church of England Children's Society also cares for children in need and is Britain's largest adoption agency; the Cancer Research Fund gathers finance and carries out research into potential cures for cancer; the People's Dispensary for Sick Animals (PDSA) provides medical and veterinary aid for people's pets; the Samaritans give telephone help to the suicidal; and women's groups have founded refuges for abused women. The functions of such organizations as Help the Aged and the Child Poverty Action Group are self-evident.

Housing

Housing in Britain is divided into the public and private sectors. Of the 22 million domestic dwellings, the great majority are in the private sector, with 67 per cent being owner-occupied and 7 per cent rented out by private landlords. The remaining 26 per cent are in the public or subsidized sector and are rented by low-income tenants from local government authorities which provide council flats and houses, or from housing associations. These are non-profit-making organizations which are becoming the main providers of new or refurbished housing in the subsidized rented sector, although the government is now cutting their public funding.

In both public and private sectors, it is estimated that over 80 per cent of the British population live in houses or bungalows (one-storey houses), and the remainder in flats and maisonettes. Houses have traditionally been divided into detached, semi-detached and terraced housing, with the greater prices and prestige being given to detached property.

Public sector or social housing in England is controlled centrally by the Department of the Environment, and by Secretaries of State in Wales and Scotland. A declining amount of the actual organization and provision of public housing is done by local government authorities. However, should public sector tenants be dissatisfied with the services provided by their local authorities, they can by ballot substitute the local authority for another landlord, which may be a cooperative, a trust, a private company approved by the Housing Corporation, or their own Tenant Management Organization.

Since 1979 the Conservative government has encouraged the growth of home ownership in the housing market, as part of its programme to create a property- and share-owning democracy in Britain. In the public sector, it introduced (1980) a right-to-buy policy by which local government sells off council housing to sitting tenants at below-market prices. This policy has increased the number of homeowners by over 1 million, and relieved local authorities of the expense of decoration, upkeep and repair. But they are not allowed to use the proceeds, which go to central government. The Labour Party, after initially opposing the policy, has now accepted it, mainly because it has proved attractive to tenants.

The Conservative government has been critical of local government housing programmes. It intends that local authorities should divest themselves of council housing management by 1996. Instead, they would work with housing associations and the private sector to increase the supply of low-cost housing for rent without necessarily providing it themselves. They would then concentrate their resources on improving the management of their existing housing stock.

But the construction of new publicly funded houses has been radically reduced, and the private sector is not building enough low-cost properties. Critics argue that government housing policies have contributed to a serious shortage of cheap rented accommodation in towns and rural areas for low-income groups, single people and the unemployed, at a time when demand is increasing.

Home ownership in the private sector has increased by 10 per cent since 1979. The normal procedure when buying a house or flat is to take out a loan on the security of the property (a mortgage) from a building society, bank or other financial institution. The amount of money advanced on a loan depends mainly on the borrower's salary, and it is usual to borrow twice one's gross annual salary. This long-term loan is usually paid off over a 25-year period, and includes interest. Currently tax relief is given on the interest on loans of up to £30,000 for each property, so that a government subsidy helps the purchasers of private property. But mortgage relief is being reduced and may be totally abolished in the future.

House prices can vary considerably throughout the country, with London and south-east England normally having the highest prices, and the north of England, Scotland and Wales having the lowest. Prices increased dramatically at the beginning of the 1970s, and much property speculation occurred. Price increases then stabilized for some years, usually between 7 and 10 per cent each year.

But there was a price boom from 1986 to 1988, followed by high interest rates, and an increase in mortgage foreclosures. This means that, when people cannot afford to continue their repayments on the loan, the lending institution takes over the property, and the occupier becomes homeless. The number of foreclosures has now been reduced. There was also a fall in house prices, and a property slump which has been only slowly reversed from 1994 as interest rates were reduced.

British homes still have variable construction standards. Many of them are old, cold and suffer from condensation; are frequently badly built; and lack central heating and adequate insulation. But there has been some improvement in housing standards in recent years, and most new houses have a high percentage of the basic amenities. Greater attention has been paid to insulation, energy saving and quality. However, as building costs rise and available land becomes scarcer, the trend in new property construction has been towards flats and smaller rooms in houses.

Nevertheless, there are still districts, particularly in the centres of the big cities, where living conditions are bad and the equivalent of contemporary slums. Nearly half of the property in the inner-city areas was built before 1919 and, in spite of large-scale slum clearance in the 1950s and 1960s, much existing housing here is in barely habitable shape. Some recently completed high-rise blocks of council flats and estates in the public sector have had to be demolished because of defective and dangerous structures. According to the National Housing Forum, one in thirteen British homes (or 1.8 million) are unfit for human habitation.

Twentieth-century town renovation and slum clearance policies from the 1930s were largely devoted to the removal of the populations of large city centres to new towns, usually located in the countryside, or to new council estates in the suburbs. The new towns, such as Crawley and Stevenage, have been seen as successes, although they initially had their share of social and planning problems. The same cannot be said of many council estates, which have tended to degenerate very quickly. The bad design of some housing estates, their social deprivation and lack of upkeep are often blamed for the crime and vandalism which affect some of them. However, some local councils are now modernizing decaying housing stock, rather than spending on new development, in an attempt to preserve local communities. Similar work is also being done by housing associations (with government grants) and by private builders.

The provision of sufficient adequate and varied housing in Britain, such as one-bedroom properties for young and single persons, has been a problem for many years. Young people on low wages, whether married or single, are often unable to afford the cost of a mortgage, even for suitable private property. It is frequently difficult for them to obtain council housing because of long waiting lists, which contain people with priority over them. Additionally, the government's right-to-buy policy has reduced the number of available council houses and flats for low-income groups and the unemployed. An alternative for many was either to board with parents, or to rent property in the private sector.

But Rent Acts and other legislation have strictly controlled rents and security of tenure. These measures have resulted in the private rented sector being greatly reduced, because landlords could no longer charge true market prices and were unwilling to put up with the restrictions. The Conservative government has now lessened the effects of the Rent Acts by introducing new lease structures, and has encouraged landlords and other agencies to provide more privately rented accommodation. But the relaxations have led to accusations of exploitation of tenants by landlords.

The inadequate overall housing market has partly contributed to the considerable number of homeless people, particularly in London and other large cities, which in turn has led to increased social problems. It is admitted officially that there are some 142,000 homeless people, who must be housed in temporary accommodation, which is usually inadequate. But unofficial figures put the real homeless total for all age groups at about 300,000, some of whom are clearly visible on the streets of Britain's large cities, especially London. The causes of homelessness are complex and affect all age groups and types of people, but critics suggest

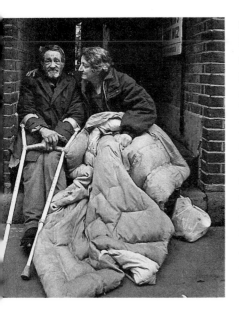

PLATE 8.3 Homeless men
(Brenda Prince/Format)

that the problem could be better handled than at present. Independent research suggests that there are some 870,000 homes in Britain in both the private and the public sectors which remain empty and unoccupied for a variety of reasons. They could eradicate the problem of homelessness and the housing shortage if they were refurbished and if private renting was made more attractive to landlords.

Charities such as Shelter and religious organizations like the Salvation Army provide accommodation for the homeless for limited periods and campaign for the cause of the homeless. Local organizations, such as Housing Advice Centres and Housing Aid Centres, also provide help. But the problem of housing in Britain is still a major one, and a focus of public concern. The high prices of many private houses, the mortgage interest rates and persisting unemployment suggest that the problem will remain. Additionally, the number of new starts for construction in both the public and private sectors has decreased, although the slump in building did improve slightly from 1994.

Attitudes to social security, health and housing

Opinion polls consistently show that a large majority of the British people demonstrate a concern for and dissatisfaction with the condition of the National Health Service and hospitals. Respondents place a high priority for increased public spending on health and medical provisions.

There has also been opposition to government reforms in the NHS, with fear expressed that the government intends to privatize health services. Respondents do not consider that the NHS is as well run as other national institutions, and there has been growing support for a comprehensive, better-funded state health-care service. However, doctors and nurses always head the lists of those professionals with whom the public are most satisfied.

Concern is also felt about the provision of public housing, social security benefits, the personal social services and the community care programme. Most people, at least in response to poll questions, indicated that they would be willing to pay higher taxes in order to ensure better social and health welfare.

■ **Explain and examine the following terms:**

welfare state	chemist	'fundholder'	social services
Social Fund	benefits	GP	charities
'pay-beds'	rent	Shelter	council housing
workhouses	landlord	Oxfam	Beveridge Report
Poor Law	bungalow	mortgage	Income Support

■ **Write short essays on the following questions:**

1   Does the social security system provide a comprehensive service for the needy in Britain?

2   Describe the structure and condition of the National Health Service.

3   Discuss the different types of housing in Britain and the mechanics of buying property.

Chapter 9

Education

■ English school history   240

■ The present state school system   246

■ The independent (or private
fee-paying) school sector   249

■ School organization and
examinations   251

■ Higher education   255

■ Further and adult education   260

■ *Attitudes to education*   261

■ *Exercises*   263

239

T HE BRITISH SCHOOL SYSTEM is complicated because, like the law, there is no one common organization. England and Wales (with which this chapter is mainly concerned), Northern Ireland, and Scotland have different school systems. But the general debates on education are similar in all the nations, and higher education is more or less the same.

A knowledge of school history is essential in order to understand current controversies and concerns. State involvement in the school system, except for Scotland, was relatively late, and the first nationwide attempt to establish state elementary schools came only in 1870. It was not until 1944 that the state supplied a comprehensive system of free and compulsory primary and secondary school education.

However, independent (private) schools have existed for many centuries, and they influenced the later state system. The mixture of state and independent institutions contributes to the complicated diversity of contemporary British schooling, particularly in England. It also illustrates the continuing debates about alleged educational elitism and attempts to create a more representative school system.

English school history

The church's central position in earlier centuries enabled it to create the first English schools in the sixth century, after the country had been converted to Christianity. It maintained its educational role in succeeding centuries, and its schools were chiefly intended to prepare boys for the priesthood.

But other types of school were also periodically established, either by rich individuals or monarchs. Such schools were variously known as grammar, high and public schools, and were later to be associated with both the modern independent and state educational sectors. But these schools were largely confined to the sons of the rich, aristocratic and influential. The vast majority of the population consequently received no formal schooling, and most people remained illiterate and innumerate.

In later centuries, the church created more elementary schools, and a few local areas developed secular schools for young children. Elementary school opportunities were also provided by wealthy industrialists and philanthropists, who established different types of school for working-class boys and girls in towns and the countryside. But the minority of children in the population attending these various schools received only a basic instruction in reading, writing and arithmetic. Educational opportunities for the majority of children were still non-existent. By the early nineteenth century, England had a haphazard and fragmented school structure. At a time when the industrial revolutions were proceeding rapidly and the population was increasing dramatically, the state did not provide a system which could educate the workforce.

But changes had occurred within the existing school framework. The Church of England lost its domination of education, and had to compete with the Roman Catholic Church, the Nonconformist churches and other denominations. Although they had their own separate schools, and protected their independence from state and secular interference, they did provide much of the available schooling and a religious framework which affected later developments in education.

Meanwhile the ancient high, grammar and public schools continued to train the sons of the middle and upper classes for leadership and professional roles in society. But many members of the working class still received no formal or adequate education. Until the late nineteenth century the state played no central role in the school system.

However, local and central government had gradually begun to show some regard for education in the early nineteenth century, although new developments were limited. Grants were made to local authorities for use in their local areas, and in 1833 Parliament supplied finance for the construction of school buildings. But it was only in 1870 that the state became more actively involved at the national level. An Education Act (the Forster Act) created school boards for all local areas in the country, which had authority to provide schools in their neighbourhoods. By 1880 a national system of education provided free elementary schooling for all children between the ages of 5 and 10.

The 1870 Act established a dual system of schools. The new state elementary schools supplied non-denominational training, while the religious voluntary schools, which now received increased financial support from the state, served denominational needs. By 1900 the various schools were able to provide education for children up to the age of 13/14.

Despite developments in the late nineteenth century, advanced secondary education remained largely the province of the independent sector, and consequently of those people who could pay for its provisions. After a period when the old public schools had declined in quality, they revived in the nineteenth century. Their weaknesses, such as the narrow curriculum and lack of discipline, had been reformed by progressive headmasters like Thomas Arnold of Rugby, and their reputations increased. The grammar and high schools, which imitated the classics-based education of the public schools, also expanded. But these schools drew their pupils from the sons of the middle and upper classes, and were the training grounds for the established elite and the professions.

However, a number of Acts in the early twentieth century marginally extended secondary education to those children whose parents could not afford school fees. The Balfour Act of 1902 provided scholarships (financial grants) so that clever elementary schoolchildren could enter fee-paying secondary schools. An education Act of 1918 (the Fisher Act) established a few state secondary schools. But this increased state help did not appreciably expand the provisions for secondary education, and only a small number of children were able to enter the secondary school system on a non-fee-paying basis.

The English school system in the early twentieth century was consequently still inadequate for the demands of society, and governments avoided any further large-scale involvement. It was only in 1944 that a new Education Act (the Butler Act) radically reorganized and developed the state primary and secondary school system in England and Wales.

The Act was an imaginative piece of legislation, and profoundly influenced future generations of schoolchildren. It created a Ministry of Education, headed by a Minister of Education, who established a national educational service in all areas of the country. A decentralized educational system resulted, in which the Ministry drew up policy guidelines, and local education authorities (LEAs) decided which specific forms of schooling would be used in their areas.

State education was divided into three stages: primary schools (5–12 years old); secondary schools (12–15); and further post-school training. State schooling was free and compulsory up to the legal school-leaving age of 15.

Two main types of state schools resulted from the Act: county and voluntary. Primary and secondary county schools were provided by the local authorities of each county. Voluntary schools were mainly those elementary schools which had been founded by religious and other groups, and which were now partially financed and maintained by local authorities, although they still retained their religious affiliation. Today some non-Christian groups, such as Muslims and Hindus, are trying to establish voluntary schools for their children on the same lines. The 1944 changes consequently resulted in non-denominational state schools coexisting with maintained voluntary schools. Today the ratio is two to one.

The 1944 Act allowed LEAs to organize the new system, and different schools developed. But most state county schools at the secondary level were divided into grammar schools and secondary modern schools, with some areas having a third type, the secondary technical school or college. Some of the grammar schools were new, while others were old foundations, which now received direct state financial aid. But other ancient grammar schools decided to become independent, and stayed outside the state system. The independent sector of education was largely untouched by these state developments and the Act.

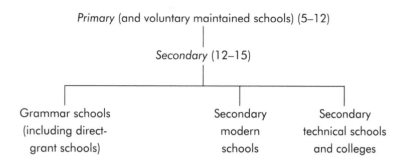

FIGURE 9.1 The 1944 organization of state schools

The secondary division involved a choice between the different types of school, which was dependent upon an examination result. The 11-plus examination, which was adopted by most LEAs, consisted of intelligence tests which covered linguistic, mathematical and general knowledge, and was taken in the last year of primary schooling. The object was to select between academic and non-academic children. Those who passed the examination went to grammar school, while those who failed went to the less academic secondary modern school and technical college. Although these schools were supposed to be equal in terms of their educational targets, the examination led parents, teachers and pupils to equate the grammar schools with a better education and a socially more respectable role.

The grammar schools prepared children for national examinations like the Matriculation Certificate, which later became the General Certificate of Education (GCE) at ordinary and advanced levels. These examinations qualified children for the better jobs and entry into higher education and the professions. Education in secondary modern schools was based on practical schooling without examinations, although GCE and other examinations were later introduced.

The intention of the 1944 Act was to provide universal and free state primary and secondary education. In addition, day-release training at local colleges was introduced for employed people who wanted further education after 15, and local authority grants were given to students who wished to enter higher education. It was hoped that such equality of opportunity would expand the educational market, lead to a better-educated society, and achieve greater social mobility.

However, it was widely felt in the 1950s that these aims were not being achieved under the selective system of secondary education. The concerns turned education into a party-political battlefield, on which ideological battles are still fought. The Labour Party, among other critics, argued that the 11-plus examination was wrong in principle, socially divisive, and had educational and testing weaknesses. It was maintained that the 11-plus regime allowed middle-class children to predominate in the grammar schools and in higher education, so that the class system was perpetuated.

The Labour government in 1964 was committed to abolishing the 11-plus and secondary school divisions. These would be replaced by non-selective 'comprehensive schools'. They would provide schooling for children of all ability levels and from all social backgrounds, ideally under one roof.

The party-political battle for the different systems was waged between 1964 and 1979, accompanied by fierce debate. Labour governments tried to introduce comprehensive schools, while Conservative governments fought to retain grammar schools and the selective system. The debate also involved LEAs in the choice between selective and non-selective secondary schooling in their areas.

The Labour government in 1965 invited the LEAs to submit plans for introducing the comprehensive system. Many had done so by 1970, but others fought the change, and the government threatened to impose comprehensive education by law. But a Conservative government was elected in 1970, and decided against legislative compulsion. Instead, the LEAs were allowed to choose the type of secondary education which was best suited to their local needs. Some authorities decided for comprehensives, while others retained selection. The next Labour government introduced an Education Act in 1976, which was intended to establish a national system of comprehensive schools and to phase out the direct-grant grammar schools, many of which, when faced with the threat, chose to become fully independent of the state apparatus.

However, before a totally comprehensive system could be implemented, a Conservative government came to power in 1979. The comprehensive/selection debate continues, and education is still subject to party-political and ideological conflict. The state secondary school sector remains divided, although with greatly reduced effect, between the selective and non-selective options, since some LEAs do not have comprehensives.

A MORI public opinion poll in 1987 found that only one parent in three supported comprehensive education; 62 per cent of parents with children in state secondary schools wanted a return to a selective system of grammar schools and secondary moderns. However, only 17 per cent favoured the 11-plus, and 45 per cent wanted entry to grammar schools to be determined by continuous assessment rather than by examination. It is often argued that the unceasing arguments about the relative merits of different types of schooling have not benefited schoolchildren or the educational system as a whole.

The present state school system

State schooling before the age of 5 is not compulsory in Britain, and there is no statutory requirement on the LEAs to provide such education. But more parents are seeking school provisions for young children: there is considerable concern about the lack of opportunities; and the government proposes to improve the situation. At present only some 25 per cent of 3- and 4-year-olds benefit from a state nursery education.

Otherwise, state education is free (except for some specialist individual instruction) and compulsory for children between the ages of 5 and 16. Over 90 per cent of all children in England and Wales are educated in the state sector. The Department for Education (DFE), under a Secretary of State, originates broad educational policies, and the LEAs retain for the time being a degree of decentralized power and choice in educational matters. They are controlled by the education committees of local councils, and organize much school planning and the hiring of teachers in their areas. Although most of the finance for local education is provided by central government, governments in the past have interfered very little in the activities of the LEAs and the schools. The LEAs have also traditionally left the academic organization of schools to headteachers. These have allowed freedom to the staffs of their schools to organize their own programmes, books and methods of teaching. Many state schools also have boards of unpaid governors, who are usually local citizens prepared to give help and guidance, and who may also be involved in the hiring of headteachers and teachers.

This overall situation has been considerably changed by the Conservative government's Education Acts of 1986 and 1988. Headteachers have been given financial control over their school budgets and have taken on management roles; greater powers of decision-making have been transferred to school governors; and parents now have a greater voice in the actual running of schools, as well as a right to choose a particular school for their children. Schools are now allowed to opt out of (transfer from) local authority control if a majority of parents vote for such a move, and the Secretary of State authorizes the proposal. Such schools are still state schools, but are self-governing; receive their funding directly from the DFE; and the headteachers and governors have responsibility for their own school budgets and management.

As a result of these reforms, and although only a few schools have completed the opting-out process, LEAs have lost their educational monopoly in the state sector. But greater responsibilities are now held by headteachers, governors, teachers and parents. This has meant a shift from purely educational to management roles, and involves increased burdens of time and administration.

State pupils move automatically from primary to secondary schools normally at the age of 11. Some 90 per cent of secondary schoolchildren go to state comprehensives from the ages of 11 to 16/18, and there are only a small number of grammar and

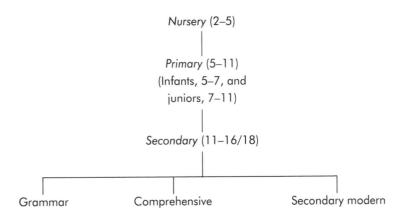

FIGURE 9.2 The current state school system

secondary modern schools left in the state system. The continued existence of these latter schools depends partly upon local government decisions, partly upon parent power, and partly upon whether they are candidates for the opting-out process.

Comprehensive school pupils are of mixed abilities, and come from a variety of social backgrounds in the local area. There is still much argument about the quality and performance of the system. Some critics argue that bright academic children suffer, although streaming into different ability classes occurs, and examination results can be excellent. There are some very good comprehensive schools, which are not necessarily confined to privileged areas. But there are also some very weak ones, which suffer from a variety of social, economic and educational problems.

Scotland has an ancient separate educational system, with colleges and universities which are among the oldest in Europe. Its school system, under a Scottish Education Board which decides policy, has long been comprehensive, and it has different school examinations from those in the rest of Britain. The Scottish 'public schools' are state and not private institutions, and children transfer from primary to secondary education at 12.

In Northern Ireland the state schools are mostly divided on religious grounds into Catholic and Protestant, and are often single-sex. However, there are some tentative movements towards integrated coeducational schools. The comprehensive principle has not been widely adopted, and a selective system with an examination at 11 gives entrance to grammar schools. Performances at these schools have been generally superior to their counterparts in England and Wales, although examination results in the other secondary schools are comparatively poor.

The independent (or private fee-paying) school sector

The independent school sector is separate from the state educational system, and caters for some 7.6 per cent of all schoolchildren, from the ages of 4 to 18 at various levels of education in some 2,500 schools.

Its financing is dependent partly upon investments and partly upon the fees paid by the pupils' parents for their education, which vary somewhat between schools and can amount to several thousand pounds a year. There is a small minority of scholarship holders, whose expenses are covered by their schools, and the government also provides funds (the assisted places scheme) so that gifted children from poorer families can benefit from independent education. The independent sector is dependent upon its charitable and tax-exempt status to survive. This means that the schools are not taxed on their income if it is used only for educational purposes.

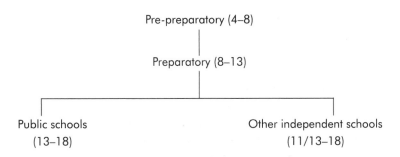

FIGURE 9.3 The independent school sector

PLATE 9.1 Pupils of Harrow public school preparing for cricket
(Raissa Page/Format)

The roughly 250 public schools, such as Eton, Harrow and Winchester, are the most famous of the independent schools, and are usually defined by their membership of the Headmasters' Conference. They were originally created to provide education for the sons of the rich and aristocratic. Such schools are mainly boarding establishments, where the pupils live and are educated during term time, although many of them now take day-pupils who do not board in. But boarding generally in the independent sector as a whole has now declined.

Public schools play a significant role in British education, and many leading figures have been educated at them. Entry today is competitive, normally by an entrance examination, and is not confined to social class, connections or wealth, although the ability to pay the fees is obviously important. Independent preparatory schools (primary level) prepare their pupils for public school entrance, and parents who decide to send their children to a public school will often give them a 'prep school' education first. There are many other independent schools in addition to the public schools, which can vary considerably in quality and reputation. The independent sector has grown, and has an attraction despite its size and increasing fees. Insurance schemes for the payment of school fees mean that there are opportunities for independent education for the less affluent, and parents frequently make great financial sacrifices so that their children can be independently educated. In a 1987 MORI poll, 48 per cent of parents said that they would send their children to an independent school if they could afford it.

The independent sector is criticized for being elitist, socially divisive and based on the ability to pay for education. In this view it perpetuates the class system. The Labour Party argues for the abolition of independent schools; has tried to remove their tax and charitable status; and is committed to phasing out the assisted places scheme. But independent schools are now firmly established, and for many provide an element of choice in what would otherwise be a state monopoly on education.

School organization and examinations

The school day in most state and independent schools, except for infant and junior schools, usually runs from 9.00 a.m. until 4 p.m., and the school year is divided into three terms (autumn, spring and summer). There have been proposals to introduce four-term years and school hours with an earlier start and finish, but these have not been implemented. Classes in British schools used to be called 'forms', and in secondary schools were numbered from one to six. But now many schools have adopted year numbers from 7 to 11 in secondary schools, with a two-year sixth form for advanced work. Corporal punishment was abolished in state schools in 1986, but is still allowed in the independent sector.

PLATE 9.2 A science class in a state comprehensive school
(Michael Ann Mullett/Format)

A reduction in the birth-rate in recent years has led to a decrease in the number of schoolchildren at all levels. This decline will continue into the late 1990s, when it will start to increase again. The reduced pupil numbers have led to the closure of schools in rural and urban areas, and the average pupil–teacher ratio for all state schools is now about 17 to 1.

Most teachers are still trained at the universities and other colleges, although the government would like to broaden their training by greater access to the actual school system. There is a shortage of teachers in some areas of the country and in specialized subjects like mathematics, technology and physics. Potential teachers increasingly see the profession as unattractive, and many practising teachers leave for better-paid jobs or retire early. Teachers at present are suffering from low morale after battles with the government over pay, conditions and educational reforms, and from what they perceive as the low status afforded them by government and the general public. The teaching profession has become very stressful and subject to greater pressures than in the past.

The standards of teaching, particularly in state schools, have attracted a good deal of criticism from all quarters in recent years. School inspectors have reported that some 30 per cent of lessons are not being taught at an adequate standard, and the teaching of English, as well as writing and reading skills, have come under particular attack. However, the effect of public spending cuts in education has been considerable, and has attracted much criticism.

PLATE 9.3 Children in an inner city comprehensive school
(Maggie Murray/Format)

They have prevented the building and modernization of schools, especially in inner-city areas. The cuts have also resulted in a shortage of books and equipment for pupils, teachers and libraries, in addition to other reduced services. But the government has increased funds for the training of in-service teachers, is establishing (jointly with local industry) technological colleges in some cities, and is trying to attract more specialist teachers.

As part of government reforms, attainment tests have been controversially set to establish what children should be reasonably expected to know at the ages of 7, 11, 14 and 16. The progress of each schoolchild can then be measured against national standards, assessed and reported. But many teachers are opposed to the extra work involved, doubt the validity of the tests and have boycotted them in recent years.

Another radical reform is the establishment of a National Curriculum. The aim was to create an educational curriculum which was standardized, centrally devised, and appropriate to the needs and demands of the contemporary world. It was to cover all age groups, and include the 'core subjects' of English, mathematics and science, as well as the 'foundation subjects' of history, geography, technology, music, art, physical education and (at the secondary level) a modern foreign language. But this reform has generated much controversy, opposition, difficulties of implementation, and problems concerning the content and scope of course material. It has now been reduced to a more manageable level, but its future is still uncertain.

The National Curriculum (which is not applicable to independent schools) is tied to a system of national examinations at the secondary level. They may be taken in all types of schools in England, Wales and Northern Ireland. The two main examinations are the General Certificate of Secondary Education (GCSE), which is taken usually by 16-year-olds, and the General Certificate of Education at Advanced Level (GCE A level), which is normally taken at the end of the second year in the sixth form by 18-year-olds.

The GCSE can be taken in a range of subjects, the questions and marking of which are undertaken by independent examination boards. In addition to written examinations, project work and continuous assessment of pupils are also taken into account in arriving at a final grade. The GCSE was intended as a better evaluation of pupils' abilities than pure examinations, and would give prospective employers some idea of the candidate's ability. It can be taken in any subject(s) according to individual choice. But most candidates will usually attempt six or seven subjects, and the basic subjects required for jobs and further education are English, mathematics (or a science) and a foreign language.

The second national examination (GCE A level) is normally associated with more academic pupils, who are aiming for entry to higher education or the professions. Good passes are now essential because the competition for places in the universities and other colleges has become much stiffer. The number of subjects taken at A level varies between one and four, although three are usually required for entry into higher education. Pupils may mix arts and science subjects, but this is now unusual because high marks are crucial. The concentration upon a few subjects reflects the high degree of early specialization in the British system. Supplementary examinations to the A levels (AS levels) may also be taken at the end of the first year in the sixth form, and serve as a lower-level alternative. There is continuing discussion about the format and content of A levels, but it seems that the emphasis upon specialized academic knowledge will continue.

Higher education

Should a pupil obtain the required examination results at A level, he or she may go on to an institution of higher education, such as a university or other college. The student, after a prescribed period of study and after passing examinations, will receive a degree and become a graduate of that institution. In the past only a small proportion of the age group in Britain proceeded to higher education, in contrast to the higher rates in many major industrial nations. But the numbers have now increased to one in five, and the government wishes to increase this to 25 per cent.

The universities

There were 23 British universities in 1960. After a period of expansion in the 1960s and government reforms in 1992 when existing institutions such as polytechnics were given university status, there are now some 83, with 822,800 students in 1991–2. The Open University and the independent University of Buckingham are additional university-level institutions.

The universities can be broadly classified into four types. The ancient universities of Oxford and Cambridge (composed of their many colleges) date from the twelfth century. But until the nineteenth century they were virtually the only English universities and offered no places to women. However, other older universities had been founded in Scotland, such as St Andrews (1411), Glasgow (1450), Aberdeen (1494) and Edinburgh (1583). A second group comprises the 'redbrick' or civic universities such as Leeds, Liverpool and Manchester, which were created between 1850 and 1930. The third group consists of universities founded after the Second World War and in the 1960s. Many of the latter, like Sussex, York and East Anglia, are in rural areas. The fourth group are the 'new universities' created in 1992 when polytechnics and some other colleges attained university status.

The competition to enter universities is now very strong, and some students who do not do well at A level may be unable to find a place. A very small percentage of students leave university without finishing their courses. The majority aim for a good degree in order to obtain a good job, or to continue in higher education by doing research (masters' degrees and doctorates). The bachelor's degree (Bachelor of Arts or Bachelor of Science, BA or BSc) is usually taken in final examinations at the end of the third year of study, although some degree courses do vary in length in different parts of Britain. This degree is divided into first-, second- and third-class honours. Some degrees are dependent entirely upon the examination results, while others include continuing assessment over the period of study.

Universities are supposed to have uniform standards, although there are centres of excellence in particular subjects, and students can usually choose from an impressive array of subject areas. Teaching is mainly by the lecture system, supported by tutorials (small groups) and seminars. The student–lecturer ratio at British universities is good at about 1 to 13. Most students tend to live on campus in university accommodation, while others may choose to live in rented property outside the university. Until recently few British students chose universities near their parents' homes, and many seemed to prefer those in the south of England. But financial costs are now changing these preferences.

While universities are independent institutions created by royal charter, they are in practice dependent upon government money. This is mainly supplied by the finance allocated by government to the Universities Funding Council for distribution to the universities, largely through university Vice-Chancellors who are the chief executive officers of the universities.

The Conservative government has been concerned to make the universities more accountable in the national interest; has tightly controlled their budgets, and encouraged them to seek alternative private sources of finance. The universities have lost staff and research money; have been forced to adopt more effective management and accounting procedures; must market their resources more efficiently in order to attract students; pay greater attention to performance; and must justify their positions financially and educationally. The government is consequently intervening more closely in the running of the universities than in the past. Such policies have provoked considerable opposition from the universities. But they are being forced to adapt rather than to continue to lose staff, finance and educational programmes.

Other higher education colleges

The 1970s saw the creation of colleges (or institutes) of higher education, often by merging existing colleges with redundant teachers' training colleges or by establishing new institutions. They now offer a wide range of degree, certificate and diploma courses in both science and the arts, and in some cases have specifically taken over the role of training teachers for the schools. They used to be under the control of their local authorities, but the Conservative government has now granted them independence, and some have achieved university status.

There are a variety of other British institutions which offer higher education. Some, such as the Royal College of Art, the Cranfield Institute of Technology and various Business Schools, have university status, while others, such as agricultural, drama and art colleges like the Royal Academy of Dramatic Arts (RADA) and the Royal College of Music, provide comparable courses. All these institutions usually have a strong vocational aspect to their programmes which fills a specialized role in higher education.

Student grants

Most British students who gain a place at a recognized institution of higher education are awarded a financial grant from their local authorities. This is supposed to cover the tuition fees of a first degree course (paid directly to the institution), and maintenance expenses of that course during term time. But the maintenance part of the grant depends upon parental income (means testing). This results in some students with rich parents receiving no maintenance grant, while others with less wealthy parents are given a partial maintenance grant. The parents are expected to make up the short-fall in the full grant by making a direct contribution to their children. However, a relatively large percentage do not do so. Students complain that they should be treated as adults, with no reference to parental income, and that grants have seriously declined in real value.

The government changed the grant system in 1990. The value of the maintenance grant was frozen at its current level and students became eligible to take out an additional 'top-up loan' from a government-sponsored scheme, the Student Loan

Company. In future, and since the value of the grant is frozen, students will have to take out progressively larger loans to finance their studies. The loans are to be paid back once students attain a certain level of employment. The government reform has been controversial and fiercely opposed on two main grounds: first, that it will inhibit poorer students from going on to higher education; and second, that it substitutes a loan structure for the grant tradition which has given generations of students a free higher education. But the National Union of Students has now accepted the loan scheme. The government is also considering imposing tuition charges upon students which, together with the new loan scheme, may mean that future students will largely have to finance their own higher education. Many students are currently in financial difficulties.

The Open University

The Labour Party first broached the idea of the Open University in the 1960s. It would be an educational service, or 'university of the air', which used television, radio and correspondence courses to teach its students. It was intended to give educational opportunities (or a 'second chance') to people who had not been able to proceed to conventional higher education. It was particularly hoped that the courses might appeal to working-class students who had left school at the official school-leaving age, and who now wished to broaden their horizons.

The Open University opened in 1969; its first courses started in 1971; and by 1993 there were 86,000 registered first degree students and an increasing number of postgraduate and research students. About 7,000 students of all ages and from very different walks of life receive degrees from the Open University each year. First degrees (bachelors) are awarded on a system of credits for each course completed.

Dedication, stamina and perseverance are necessary to complete the long, part-time courses of the Open University. Students, who are often employed, do not attend any one institution, but receive their lessons and lectures at home, partly by correspondence courses and partly by special television (BBC 2) and radio broadcasts. Part-time tutors in local areas mark the students' written work, and meet them regularly to discuss their progress. There are also special weekend and refresher courses throughout the year, which are held at universities and colleges, to enable students to take part in intensive study. The various television broadcasts and books associated with the Open University programmes are widely exported throughout the world. The Open University is generally considered to be a cost-effective success, and has provided valuable alternative educational opportunities for many people.

Further and adult education

An important aspect of British education is the provision of further and adult education, whether by voluntary bodies, trade unions or other institutions. The present organizations originated to some degree in the thirst for knowledge which was felt by working-class people in the nineteenth and early twentieth centuries, particularly after the arrival of elementary state education and mass literacy. Today a wide range of educational opportunities is provided by self-governing colleges of further education, technical colleges and other institutions. These offer a considerable selection of subjects at basic levels for part- and full-time students.

Adult education is provided by these colleges, the universities, the Workers' Educational Association (WEA), evening institutes, local societies and clubs. Adult courses may be vocational (relating to employment) or recreational (for pleasure), and cover a wide variety of activities and programmes.

Some 4 million students of very varying ages are taking further and adult education courses in one form or another. In the past a relatively low percentage of the 16–24 age group in Britain were in further and higher education, compared to the much larger percentages in Japan, the USA and former West Germany.

Although the figures have now improved considerably, it is still a matter of concern that too few people are being educated or trained further after the age of 16. This is particularly true at a time when there will be an increasing shortage of well-qualified people in the future workforce, especially in the scientific and technological fields.

Nevertheless, there has been a recent expansion of continuing-education projects and a range of programmes specifically designed for employment purposes and to provide people with access qualifications for further training. For example, the Conservative government initiated an Open College in 1987, which allows students to follow job-related training courses by correspondence, radio programmes and television's Channel 4. Although the service has had some problems in becoming established, it is hoped that students might acquire skills and qualifications which will benefit them on the job market.

Attitudes to education

There have been continuous and vigorous debates about the quality and goals of British education at all levels since the 1970s. Traditionalist critics feel that state comprehensive schools and 'creative/progressive' methods of child-centred teaching are not producing the kind of people needed for contemporary society. It is argued that pupils, 10 per cent of whom leave school with no qualifications, lack the basic skills of numeracy and literacy, and are unprepared for the realities of the world outside school. Employers frequently criticize both the schools and higher education for the quality of their products.

The Conservative government's reforms since 1986 are based on centralizing and consumer-choice policies. They may be seen as an attempt to rectify the general educational situation, and are aimed at producing accountability, improved standards and skills in both the school and higher education sector by more formal learning programmes. The government has attempted to reform the teaching profession, improve pupils' performances, emphasize science and modern language studies, and increase parental choice.

Critics, however, argue that an educational system should not be solely devoted to elitist standards, market considerations and the 'enterprise culture', but should try to combine the academic/liberal tradition, the technical and the vocational. The future of British education will depend in large part on how government reforms work and how they are perceived by teachers, parents and students.

Concerns about quality and educational policy at all levels, particularly in the schools, are consistently voiced by a majority of respondents to public opinion polls. They think that state schools are not run well, and that more public money should be spent on education. Education is likely to continue as a major factor in British life as the political parties develop conflicting policies.

■ **Explain and examine the following terms:**

public schools	grammar schools	WEA
comprehensives	11-plus	tutorial
GCE A level	Open University	scholarships
LEAs	corporal punishment	student grant
Eton	GCSE	'prep school'
the Butler Act	degree	vocational

■ **Write short essays on the following questions:**

1   In what ways have government reforms since 1986 changed educational provisions?

2   Describe the structure of British higher education and its roles.

3   Comment upon the desirability, or otherwise, of British education's division into state and independent sectors.

Chapter 10

The media

- The print media   266
- The broadcasting media   278
- Media ownership and freedom
  of expression   286
- *Attitudes to the media*   291
- *Exercises*   292

T HE TERM 'MEDIA' may include any form of communication through which people are informed, educated and entertained. In Britain today it refers mainly to the press (newspapers), periodicals, magazines, radio, terrestrial (or earth-based) television, cable and satellite television, and video. These communications systems overlap in certain areas, have become profitable businesses, and are tied closely to commerce, industry, advertising and sponsorship.

Media forms have evolved from simple methods of production, distribution and communication to the present sophisticated and technological complexities. They now cover homes and places of business, and their influence is very powerful and an inevitable part of daily life. It is estimated, for example, that some 61 per cent of British people obtain their news and views of current affairs from television, 20 per cent from newspapers and 15 per cent from radio. The growth and variety of media services in the twentieth century have clearly improved information dispersal, news availability and entertainment opportunities.

But they have also resulted in debates about what is socially and morally permissible in terms of content, together with accompanying demands for censorship and restriction of media expression. They have raised questions about the controversial position of advertising; concentrated ownership of media sources; legal and other restraints upon free expression; the quality of the various services; and the responsibility and influence of the media.

The print media

The first of the media to develop historically were the print industries (newspapers and magazines). However, a wide circulation was hindered initially by transportation and distribution problems, illiteracy, and government restrictions in the form of licensing which amounted to censorship. But, over the last 200 years, an expanded educational system, relaxation of government control, new print inventions and Britain's small geographical size have eliminated these difficulties and created allegedly free print media. The growth of mass literacy after 1870 provided the owners of the print media with a greatly increased market. This resulted in the popularization of newspapers and magazines, which had previously been limited to the middle and upper classes. The print media were progressively used not only for news, information and communication, but also for entertainment and, inevitably, the increased earning of profits by the owners. Ownership and new varieties of the print media expanded rapidly in the competitive atmosphere of the late nineteenth and early twentieth centuries, and were helped by financially rewarding advertising. The owners also realized that political and social influence could be achieved through control of the means of communication.

National newspapers

National newspapers in Britain today are those which are available in all parts of the country on the same day, including Sundays. Many of them are delivered direct to the home from local newsagents by newsboys and girls. The good internal communications systems of a relatively small country have enabled a genuine national press to develop, in contrast to the situation in some other larger nations where size and geography are often great obstacles.

The first British newspapers to have some claim to national circulation appeared in the early eighteenth century, and were followed by others, such as *The Times* (1785), the *Observer* (1791) and the *Sunday Times* (1822). But most of them were quality papers, which catered for a relatively small, educated and largely London-based market.

In the nineteenth century, the growth and composition of the population conditioned the types of newspaper which were produced. The first popular national papers were initially and deliberately printed on Sundays, such as the *News of the World* (1843) and the *People* (1881). They were inexpensive and were aimed at the expanding and increasingly literate working class. In 1896, Alfred Harmsworth produced the *Daily Mail*, which was targeted at the lower-middle class and served as a more accessible alternative to the quality dailies. Harmsworth then published the *Daily Mirror* in 1903, which was aimed at the working-class, popular market. Both the *Mail* and the *Mirror* were soon selling more than a million copies a day.

The early twentieth century was the era of the mass-circulation newspapers and the newspaper-owning dynasties, such as those controlled by Harmsworth and Arthur Pearson. There was fierce competition between them as they fought for bigger shares of the market. Pearson's *Morning Herald*, which later became the *Daily Express*, was created in 1900 to compete with the *Daily Mail* for the lower-middle-class readership. The *Daily Express* later changed directions in the 1950s, and was then also aimed at the working class in order to attract larger sales.

The *Daily Mirror* became the largest-selling national daily in the early twentieth century. It actively supported the Labour Party, and was specifically designed for quick and easy reading by the industrial and increasingly politicized working class. The *Daily Herald* (1911) also supported the Labour Party, until it was later sold in 1964, renamed the *Sun*, and developed very different political and news emphases. The competition between the *Express*, *Sun* and *Mirror* continues today, with each aiming for a bigger share of the mass daily market. There are also the same fierce battles between owners or proprietors, since newspaper ownership tends to be concentrated in a few large publishing groups, such as Rupert Murdoch's News International (see table 10.1).

The difference between today and the early twentieth century lies perhaps in the quality of the mass papers. The success of the early popular press was due partly to growing rates of literacy; partly to a genuine desire for knowledge and information by the working class; and partly to an increased political awareness among workers generated by the rise of the Labour Party. The newspaper owners obviously profited by this huge market, but they also supplied a need. The price and content of the mass papers reflected the lower-middle- and working-class readership. This

TABLE 10.1   The main national newspapers (average daily sales), 1994

Name	Founded	Circulation (July 1994)	Owned/controlled by
Popular dailies			
Daily Mail	1896	1,757,982	Associated Newspapers
Daily Express	1900	1,333,908	United Newspapers
Daily Mirror	1903	2,501,421	Mirror Group
Sun	1964	4,173,699	News International
Star	1978	723,202	United Newspapers
Today	1986	626,896	News International
Quality dailies			
The Times	1785	599,358	News International
Guardian	1821	394,862	Guardian Newspapers
Daily Telegraph	1855	1,070,908	Daily Telegraph
Financial Times	1888	282,859	Pearson
The Independent	1986	257,812	Newspaper Publishing
Popular Sundays			
News of the World	1843	4,741,228	News International
People	1881	1,973,858	Mirror Group
Sunday Express	1918	1,495,908	United Newspapers
Sunday Mirror	1963	2,523,684	Mirror Group
Mail on Sunday	1982	1,932,883	Associated Newspapers
Sunday Sport	1989	274,486	Sport Newspapers Limited
Quality Sundays			
Observer	1791	467,933	Guardian Newspapers
Sunday Times	1822	1,165,673	News International
Sunday Telegraph	1961	666,622	Daily Telegraph
The Independent on Sunday	1990	312,830	Newspaper Publishing

Source: Audit Bureau of Circulation, July 1994

287

PLATE 10.1 *Daily Mirror* newspaper building, Central London
(Bill Coward/Barnaby)

emphasis attracted large consumer advertising, and the owners were able to produce cheaply by using modern printing methods and a nationwide distribution network.

The circulation of national newspapers rose rapidly in the early twentieth century, and it is estimated that there were some 5.5 million daily sales by 1920. By 1973 the figure had increased to 17 million. But newspapers and other print products have had to cope first with the competition of radio and films, and later with television. Although they have survived in considerable numbers, there has, since the 1970s, been a large reduction in daily sales and in the number of national and other newspapers. The circulation of some papers has remained steady, while that of others has either increased or decreased in the face of stiff competition, resulting in a succession of papers going out of business.

However, more papers are sold per person in Britain than in many other countries. It is estimated that some two out of three people over the age of 15 read a national daily paper, and about three out of four read a Sunday newspaper. National newspapers now have total sales of nearly 14 million on weekdays and

17 million on Sundays, although the total readership (e.g. family members) is obviously greater than these figures suggest.

The national press in Britain, consisting of 11 daily morning papers and ten Sunday papers, is in effect the London press, because most of the national newspapers have their headquarters and printing facilities in the capital. The majority of them used to be based in Fleet Street in central London, which was the centre of the national newspaper industry. But all have now left the street, and moved to other parts of London, like the dockland area of east London, or even outside London. The reasons for these moves have been high property rents, fierce competition and opposition from the print trade unions to the introduction of new printing technology.

In the 1970s and 1980s all types of newspapers and magazines have had to accommodate themselves first to rising production and labour costs, and second to technological developments in printing and office management. The expense involved has had to be absorbed while competing in a highly competitive market.

The heavy labour costs of the print industries had often been attributed to the overmanning in the businesses and the restrictive practices of the trade unions, particularly in London. This situation forced the owners to consider new and different ways of increasing productivity while cutting costs. The use of new printing technology to hasten this process resulted in job reductions and trade union

PLATE 10.2 *Guardian* newspaper building, Docklands, London
(*Jennifer Fry/Barnaby*)

opposition, which in turn led to industrial action and damaging production losses. The new methods allow journalists' 'copy' to be printed directly through computerization, without having to use the intermediate and traditional 'hot metal' typesetting by printers. This profound change has meant that owners now have greater flexibility in their printing and distribution methods, and cheaper production costs. It has also allowed them to escape from the old trade union dominance and the concentration of the industry in London.

Regional owners outside London pioneered the movement of newspapers and magazines into the new printing technology. They eventually forced the London national newspaper industry to follow. *The Times* had tried to introduce new equipment, but was prevented by union opposition. The paper was closed down for 11 months (1979–80) in an attempt to put pressure on the unions, but this also failed. The paper was then sold to Rupert Murdoch's News International group, which has large newspaper and media holdings in Britain, Australia and the USA. After further problems with the unions, Murdoch sacked his printers, and moved *The Times* and his other papers from Fleet Street to high-technology facilities at Wapping in east London. He then employed only those workers who were prepared to operate the new machinery. These actions provoked bitter opposition and the Wapping plant was heavily picketed by trade unionists. But other Fleet Street and regional newspapers have had to follow *The Times*' lead in order to survive.

The new printing technology, improved distribution technique, and the cutting of labour and production costs have increased the profitability of the press and the print industry as a whole. Despite the competition with other media sources, there still seems to be a considerable future for the print industries. Britain's ethnic minority communities, for example, produce their own newspapers and magazines, which are increasing in numbers and improving in quality. There is a wide range of Jewish, Asian, West Indian (Afro-Caribbean), Chinese and Arabic publications, among others.

The emphasis upon information technology, news gathering

and data dispersal also provided an impetus to the public sale of Reuters to private shareholders in 1984. Reuters is a London-based news agency (founded in 1851), which has traditionally been used by newspapers and journalists worldwide as a source of news.

The newspaper business is very competitive, and papers can suffer from a variety of problems. But the considerable risks involved have not stopped the introduction of new newspapers. For example, the mid-market national daily *Today* was launched in April 1986 and, after serious problems with circulation and technology, is continuing. The quality national daily, *The Independent*, appeared in October 1986, and is surviving despite circulation losses. Sunday nationals, like *The Independent on Sunday*

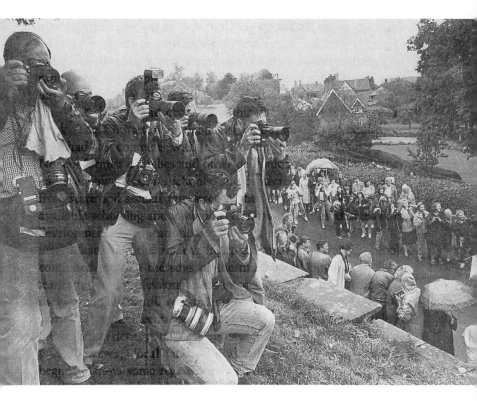

PLATE 10.3 Press photography and coverage: Althorp wedding, 1989 *(Melanie Friend/Format)*

(1990), together with the national the *European* (1990) appearing on Fridays, have also been published in recent years. But a number of other papers have opened up and then quickly disappeared.

The national newspapers are usually termed 'quality' or 'popular' depending on their differences in content and format (broadsheet or tabloid). The quality papers are broadsheets (large-sheet), report national and international news in depth, and analyse current events and the arts in editorials and articles. The popular nationals are mostly tabloid (small-sheet), deal with relatively few 'hard news' stories, and tend to be superficial in their treatment of events. The vocabulary range of some of these papers is limited; the emphasis is upon quick reading; and much of their material is sensationalized and trivialized. It cannot be said that the British populars at the lower end of the market are deeply instructive, or concerned with raising the critical consciousness of their readers. But the owners and editors often argue that their readership demands particular styles, interests and attitudes.

The sales and circulation figures of the populars far exceed those of the quality nationals, both on Sundays and during the week. The qualities are more expensive than the populars, and carry more up-market and costly advertising that generates essential finance for the newspapers. The populars carry less advertising, and cater in the main for more down-market, mass forms of consumer material. The national press in 1992 took 14.8 per cent of total advertising revenue.

The British national press, which is financially independent of the political parties, is often accused of being conformist and reflecting similar views. But it does in fact cater for a wide range of interests and perspectives.

The *Morning Star*, which is an independent Marxist newspaper associated with the Communist Party of Great Britain, follows a particular political philosophy, but has a very small circulation. Most of the other papers also have a political bias, and may support a political party, particularly at election times. It is often argued that the majority of British newspapers are politically right-of-centre, and tend to sympathize in general terms with the

PLATE 10.4   Newspaper rack *(Janine Wiedel)*

Conservative Party. A few, like those of the *Mirror* group, support the Labour Party, some like *The Times* and *The Independent* consider themselves to be independent, while others, like the *Guardian*, favour a left-of-centre position.

But these political slants can vary considerably over time and under the influence of events. It appears in practice that the British public receive a reasonable variety of political views from their newspapers. There is no state control or formal censorship of the press, although it is subject to stringent laws of publication and expression. There are also certain unofficial forms of self-censorship, by which the media attempt to regulate themselves and their conduct.

Since the press does not receive any financial subsidies from the state, it is dependent for its survival upon its circulation figures; upon the advertising that it can attract; and upon financial help from its owners. A paper may face difficulties and fail if advertisers remove their business. But a high circulation does not necessarily guarantee the required advertising and consequent survival, because advertisers today tend to place their mass-appeal consumer products on television, where they will benefit from a larger audience. Most popular papers, which now receive relatively little advertising revenue, are in constant competition with their rivals to increase their sales. They attempt to do this by gimmicks such as bingo games and competitions, price-cutting, or by calculated editorial policies which are intended to catch the mass readership. Owners may refuse to rescue those papers which make continuous losses. A number of newspapers in the twentieth century have ceased publication because of reduced circulation, loss of advertising revenue, refusals of further financial aid, or a combination of all three factors.

Regional newspapers

Regional, or provincial, newspapers are those which are published outside London. Excluding its national newspaper industry, London itself has one major central paper (the *Evening Standard*) with a daily circulation of some 476,000, in addition to about 100 local weeklies, dailies and evening papers which appear in the Greater London districts.

Outside London, a large number of regional papers are widely published in the cities and smaller towns in the mornings and evenings. They tend to contain a mixture of local and national news, and are supported financially by local advertising. The regional press is the second largest advertising medium after television. In 1992 it took 21 per cent of total advertising revenues.

Some of the more famous daily regional papers, such as *The Scotsman* (Edinburgh) and the *Glasgow Herald* in Scotland, the *Western Mail* in Cardiff, Wales, and the *Yorkshire Post* (Leeds) in England, have considerable reputations and a wide circulation both in and outside their particular regions.

A recent development of some note in the regions has been the rapid growth of 'free newspapers', which are delivered direct to homes and for which the consumer does not pay. They are usually published weekly on a local basis and are financed by local advertising, to such an extent that news is often outweighed by the advertisements. It is estimated that they have a weekly circulation of some 35 million.

Periodicals and magazines

There are over 7,000 different periodicals and magazines in Britain, which are published on a weekly, monthly or quarterly basis. They cover the vast majority of trades, professions, sports, hobbies and interests, and are aimed at different markets and levels of sophistication. It is very difficult to break into this established market with a new product. Some attempts, which manage to find a gap in the market, are successful, but most usually fail. For example, there are no illustrated news magazines in Britain, because they have been unable to compete with television and with the existing magazine coverage.

Among the main serious weekly journals are the *New Statesman and Society* (a left-wing political magazine which also comments on social affairs); the *Economist* (dealing with economic and political matters); the *Spectator* (a conservative journal); and

277

New Scientist. The Times publishes several influential weekly magazines, such as the *Educational Supplement*, the *Higher Education Supplement* and the *Literary Supplement*. The lighter side of the market is catered for by periodicals such as *Private Eye*, which satirizes and attacks what it considers to be the short-comings of British society.

The teenage and youth magazine market is fiercely competitive and some new attempts to enter this specialist field succeed while others quickly fail. Women's periodicals, such as *Woman* and *Woman's Own*, have very large and wide circulations. But the best-selling publications are the weekly *Radio Times* and the *TV Times*, which contain feature stories and the scheduled pro-grammes for BBC and independent television. Other magazines cover a varied range of interests, such as computers, rural pas-times, gardening, railways, cooking, architecture, do-it-yourself skills, and a wide selection of sports.

The broadcasting media

Radio was the first broadcasting medium to appear in Britain. Experimental transmissions were made at the end of the nineteenth century, and the systems were further developed in the early twen-tieth century. After a period of limited public availability, national radio broadcasting was established in 1922 when the British Broadcasting Company was formed under the direction of John Reith.

In 1927 Reith became the first Director-General of the British Broadcasting Corporation (the present BBC), and was to set the tone and style for the BBC's future development. The BBC had a monopoly in broadcasting and tended to have a paternalistic image, which still exists today to some extent. Reith was concerned that the BBC should be independent of government and commer-cial interests; that it should strive for quality (as he defined it); and that it should be a public broadcasting service, with a duty to inform, educate and entertain. The BBC has since built up a repu-tation for impartial news reporting and quality programmes, both in its domestic services and through its worldwide radio and television broadcasting on the external services.

The BBC continued its monopoly on broadcasting into the 1950s, in both radio and television (which had started in 1936 for a limited audience). But there was increasing pressure from commercial and political interests to widen the scope of broadcasting. The result was that independent (or commercial) television broadcasting financed by advertising and under the supervision of the Independent Broadcasting Authority (IBA) was created in 1954, and the first programmes shown in 1955. In 1972 the Sound Broadcasting Act ended the BBC's monopoly on radio broadcasting, and allowed the establishment of independent radio stations throughout the country, dependent on advertising for their financing. Historically, therefore, the BBC has been profoundly affected by the establishment of independent television and radio.

Two organizations then covered British broadcasting: the BBC and the IBA. This structure resulted in a duopoly in which broadcasting was shared between the public service of the BBC and the independent (commercial) service of the IBA. This division has now been expanded as cable, satellite and other broadcasting services have developed in recent years. British broadcasting is thus conditioned by the competition between the BBC and the independent organizations.

In 1988 the Conservative government announced that it would make wide-ranging changes to British broadcasting, most of which became operative in the early 1990s (see following sections). The number of television and radio channels was to be increased, and the IBA was to be replaced by an Independent Television Commission (ITC). The plans were intended to provide greater deregulation and competition among broadcasters and to give greater choice to the consumer.

This new broadcasting regime is controversial and has been widely criticized for its alleged emphasis on competition and commercialism, rather than quality. A larger number of channels may not lead to greater choice, but rather to inferior programmes as the BBC and ITC chase bigger audiences. There is a finite number of people to watch television; advertisers' budgets cannot be stretched to cover all the available independent television offerings; and advertisers naturally gravitate towards those programmes which attract large audiences. Nevertheless, television in 1992 accounted for 31.7 per cent of total advertising revenues in Britain.

The BBC

The BBC is based at Broadcasting House in London, but has studios and local facilities throughout the country, which provide regional and national networks for radio and television. It was created by Royal Charter and has a board of governors who, under a chairman or woman, are responsible for supervising its programme structures and suitability. The governors are appointed by the Crown on the advice of government ministers, and are supposed to constitute an independent element in the organization of the BBC. The daily operation of the corporation is controlled by the Director-General, who is chosen by the board of governors in consultation with the Prime Minister.

The BBC is financed by a grant from Parliament, which comes largely from the revenue received from the sale of television licences. These are payable by anyone who owns a television set, and are relatively low by international standards (in 1994 £83 annually for a colour set). Under the government's reforms in the Broadcasting Act of 1990, the BBC, while keeping the licence-fee system, has been encouraged to develop alternative forms of funding, such as subscription and pay services, and must include independent productions in 25 per cent of its television schedules. The BBC also generates considerable income from selling its programmes abroad, and from the sale of a programme guide (*Radio Times*), books, magazines and videos.

The BBC's external services, which consist of radio broadcasts in English (the World Service) and some 39 other languages abroad, were founded in 1932 and receive direct financing from the government, mainly through the Foreign Office. These services have a high reputation for objective news reporting and programmes. But, because of a declining radio audience, the World Service began television services in 1991 to Europe on cable subscription channels, and by satellite links in Africa and Asia. The BBC intends to develop the television service into a world leader.

The BBC is not a state organization, in the sense that it is controlled by the government. But it is not as independent of political pressures as many in Britain and overseas assume. Its Charter has to be renewed by Parliament, and by its terms the Home Secretary can, and does, intervene in the showing of programmes which are alleged to be controversial or against the public interest. The BBC governors, although supposedly independent, are in fact government appointees. Governments can also exert pressure upon the BBC when the licence fee comes up for renewal by Parliament. The BBC in recent years has struggled to maintain its position as a traditional public service broadcaster, funded by the licence fee. It does try to be neutral in political matters, to such an extent that all political parties have periodically complained that the BBC is prejudiced against them. The major parties have equal rights to broadcast on the BBC and independent television.

In 1994, the government recognized that the BBC's recent internal reforms and reorganization had led to a slimmer and more efficient organization. The BBC was given a ten-year extension of the Charter, based on the licence fee, to continue its role as a public service broadcaster. Government pressures upon the BBC have thus now been reduced.

Historically, the BBC has been profoundly influenced by the invention of television, which changed the entertainment habits of the people and created a dominant source of news. The BBC has two television channels (BBC 1 and BBC 2). BBC 1 programmes consist of news, plays and drama series, comedy, quiz shows, variety performances, sport and documentaries. BBC 2 tends to show more serious items such as news analysis and discussion, documentaries, adaptations of novels into plays and series, operas, concerts and some sport. It tends to be a minority channel, watched by 10 per cent of viewers, although it is now increasing its audience. But it is a crucial element in the provision of Open University courses.

BBC Radio audiences have declined somewhat recently, but it still provides an important service. The BBC has five national radio channels; 39 local radio stations serving many districts in

England; and regional and community radio services in Scotland, Wales and Northern Ireland. All of these compete for listeners with independent stations. The national channels specialize in different tastes. Radio 1 caters for pop music; Radio 2 has light music, news and comedy; Radio 3 provides classical and modern serious music, talks, discussions and plays; Radio 4 tends to concentrate on news reports and analysis, talks and plays; and the new Radio 5 (1990) provides sport and educational programmes.

The ITC (formerly IBA)

Independent television and radio were considerably affected by government reforms under the Broadcasting Act of 1990. The ITC (Independent Television Commission) replaced the IBA; controls the activities of the independent television companies (including cable and satellite services); and consists of a government-appointed chairman or woman and other members.

The ITC does not produce or make programmes itself. In addition to supervising cable and satellite television, it issues licences (or franchises) to, and regulates, the transmitting companies who are responsible for making the actual programmes shown on two advertising-financed television channels (the majority ITV/Channel 3 and minority Channel 4), and a proposed new Channel 5.

There are 15 ITV production companies at present, such as Granada (north-west England), Central (the Midland counties of England) and Anglia (East Anglia). London has two companies holding one licence, with one providing programmes during the week (Carlton), the other at weekends (London Weekend). These companies make programmes for the 14 regions into which Britain is divided for ITV television purposes.

The licences granted to the present ITV companies are renewable every six years, and the companies have to compete with any other interested applicants. Although open to competitive tendering, it is by no means certain that a further licence will be granted to an existing company, or a new one to a new company which offers the highest bid. Much will depend on past performance, financial standing and commitment to provide quality and regional programmes. The programme companies receive nothing from the national television licence fee, which is applicable only to the BBC. The companies are consequently dependent upon the finance they receive from advertising and the sales of programmes, videos, books, records and other publications.

ITV is the oldest independent channel, and once seemed only to provide popular programmes of a light-entertainment and sometimes trivial type. But its quality has improved, largely because of competition from the BBC, and it now has a high standard of news reports, drama productions and documentaries. Under the government's new legislation, ITV must provide programmes made in and about the region represented by the production company.

Channel 4 was established in 1982 in order to create an independent alternative to BBC 2. It is now a public corporation, licensed and regulated by the ITC, selling its own advertising time and retaining the proceeds. It was intended to offer something different and challenging in an appeal to minority tastes, and provides programmes in Welsh in Wales. Channel 4 initially had serious problems with advertising and the quality of its programmes, but has now developed a considerable reputation and is a success. The proposed Channel 5 is not yet operative, but franchises to supply its programmes will be awarded by competitive tender.

It had often been argued that the old IBA did not always keep a close watch on independent broadcasting developments; that it lacked sufficient regulatory powers and consistent policies; and sometimes acted arbitrarily in the granting of licences. There was also considerable concern in some quarters at the rapid expansion and dubious quality of independent broadcasting as a whole. It remains to be seen whether the new ITC improves this situation. Already, there has been controversy over the system of awarding ITV franchises, which have often gone to the highest bidder with little apparent regard to quality and production efficiency.

The Radio Authority

A new Radio Authority now controls some 150 local and regional independent radio stations (ILRs) throughout the country, which are supported by advertising and provide mainly pop music, news flashes and programmes of local interest. They operate on a commercial basis, and revenue figures in 1993 suggest that radio is the fastest-growing medium in Britain. Three new commercial national radio stations are being created under government policy to expand radio broadcasting. The licence for the first station was awarded to Classic FM in 1991, which broadcasts popular classical music and news bulletins. The second licence was awarded to Virgin 1215 in 1992, which specializes in rock music. Expansion will also occur at the city, local and community levels because radio broadcasting has been deregulated by the government in its attempt to increase the variety of radio and include more tastes and interests.

Cable and satellite broadcasting

Television and other associated technological developments have become very attractive in Britain, and a rich source of entertainment profits. At one stage, it was considered that cable television by subscription charge would considerably expand these possibilities. But cable in Britain, although growing slowly and potentially capable of further expansion and varied services, has been challenged first by video equipment sales, and second by satellite programmes.

Direct television broadcasting by satellite has been available in Britain since 1989. The biggest satellite programmer is BSkyB (British Sky Broadcasting) which provides 15 channels, consisting of news, light entertainment, sport and feature films, from the privately financed Astra satellite through domestic receiving dishes. The choice of satellite channels is expanding steadily in Britain. But companies do have problems in attracting subscribers; the quality of programmes is often poor; and it is too early to assess whether these satellite ventures will be commercial successes.

However, in those homes which had access to cable and satellite services in 1994, the share of television viewing was 31.6 per cent for cable and satellite; 23.6 per cent for BBC 1; 7.4 per cent for BBC 2; 30.5 per cent for ITV; and 6.8 per cent for Channel 4.

The role and influence of television

Television is an influential and dominant force in modern Britain. It is also a very popular entertainment activity. Over 98 per cent of the population have television sets in their homes. Some 95 per cent of these are colour sets, and over 50 per cent of homes have two sets or more. Some people prefer to rent their sets instead of owning them because rented sets are repaired and maintained free of charge.

A large number of the programmes shown on television are made in Britain, although there are also many imported American series. A few programmes come from other English-speaking countries, such as Australia, New Zealand and Canada. But there are relatively few foreign-language productions on British television, and these are either dubbed or subtitled.

The range of programmes shown is very considerable, but they also vary widely in quality. Although British television has a high reputation abroad, it does attract substantial criticism in Britain, either because of the standard of the programmes, or because they are frequently repeated. News reports, documentaries and current-affairs analyses are generally of a high standard, as are dramatic, educational, sporting, natural history and cultural productions. But there is also a wide selection of series, films, quizzes and variety shows which are sometimes of doubtful quality.

The competition between the BBC and independent television is strong, and the battle of the ratings (the number of people watching individual programmes) indicates the popularity (or otherwise) of individual programmes. But this competition can mean that similar programmes are shown at the same time on the major channels, in order to appeal to specific markets and attract the biggest share of the audience. It is also argued that competition has reduced the quality of programmes overall, and resulted in an appeal to the lowest common denominator in taste.

Voices have been raised about the alleged levels of violence on British television, particularly before the 'watershed' of 9 p.m. in the evenings when young children may be watching. Some private individuals have attempted by their protests to reform and influence the kind of programmes that are shown. Recent research suggests that the public can be morally harmed by watching television for an average viewing time of 26 hours each week. The Conservative government considers that violence, sex and obscenity on television do affect viewers, some more than others. It is concerned to 'clean up' television, and has set up a Broadcasting Standards Council and a Broadcasting Complaints Commission (which in future will operate as one body) to monitor programmes, examine complaints and establish codes of conduct for the broadcasting organizations. The government has banned the sale and rent of so-called 'video nasties', that is, videos which portray extreme forms of violence and brutality, and has tightened rules for the sale of videos. Some 69 per cent of homes now own at least one video-cassette recorder.

There is fierce competition among the increased number of broadcasters to attract viewers and advertising revenue. But the broadcasting debate in Britain is now concerned with whether this entertainments expansion means more genuine choice or declining quality. It is therefore important that the BBC has retained its licence-fee funding and is maintaining its commitment to public service broadcasting.

Media ownership and freedom of expression

The financial and ownership structures of the British media industry are complex, and involve a range of media outlets which include the press, radio and television. Sometimes an individual company will own a number of print products, such as newspapers and magazines, and will specialize in this area.

But this kind of ownership is declining. Today it is more common for newspapers to be owned and controlled by corporations which are concerned with wide media interests, such as films, radio, television, magazines, and satellite and cable companies. Other newspaper- and media-owning groups have diversified their interests even further, and may be involved in a variety of non-media activities. In Britain, only a few newspapers such as the

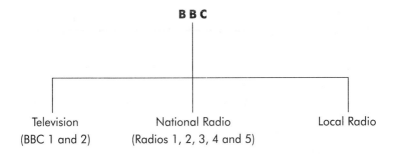

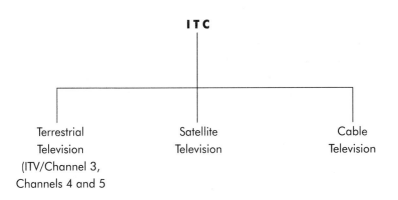

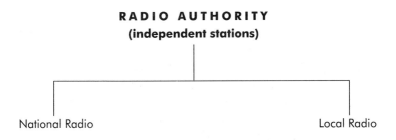

FIGURE 10.1 The structure of British broadcasting

Guardian, the *Morning Star* and *The Independent* have avoided being controlled by multinational commercial concerns.

This involvement of large enterprises in the media business, and the resulting concentration of ownership in a few hands, has caused concern in Britain. For example, more than 60 per cent of total newspaper circulation in 1993 was accounted for by News International and Mirror Group Newspapers. Although these concentrations do not amount to a monopoly situation, there have been frequent enquiries into the questions of ownership and control. Some critics have argued that the state should provide public funds or subsidies to the media industries in order to prevent them being taken over by big-business groups. But this suggestion has not been adopted, and it is felt that there are potential dangers in allowing the state to gain any direct or indirect financial influence over the media.

Today the law is supposed to guard against the risks inherent in greatly concentrated ownership of the means of communication. The purchase of further newspapers by an existing owner is controlled by law, and newspaper owners' shareholdings in independent radio and television stations are restricted. Further restrictions, such as independent directors of newspapers, guarantees of editorial independence from owners' interference, trustee arrangements to allow newspapers to maintain their character and traditions, and special management structures, are usually imposed. These arrangements are intended to prevent the formation of monopolies and undue influence by owners. But such safeguards do not always work satisfactorily in practice, and the Conservative government now allows takeovers of ITV television companies by rival companies and multi-media corporations.

The question of free expression in the media continues to be a central concern in Britain. There are frequent protests that the media do not have sufficient freedom to comment on matters of public interest. But the freedom of the media, as of individuals, to express themselves, is not absolute. Regulations are placed upon the general freedom in order to safeguard the legitimate interests of other individuals, organizations and the state, so that a balance between competing interests may be achieved.

There are several legal restraints upon media freedom of expression. The *sub judice* rule means that the media may not publish comments on court proceedings while these are continuing, and must restrict themselves to the court facts. The rule is intended to protect the individuals concerned, and if a media organization breaks the rule it may be found guilty of contempt of court and fined. Contempt of court proceedings may also be used by judges to obtain journalists' sources of information, or to prevent the media from publishing certain court details and documents.

The obtaining and publishing of certain state and official information is tightly controlled by the Official Secrets Act and by D-notices (directives to the media concerning sensitive items which should not be divulged). The media are also liable to court proceedings for libel and obscenity offences. Libel is the making of accusations which are proved to be false or harmful to a person's reputation. Obscenity covers any action that offends against public morality. In such cases, the media organization and all the individuals involved may be held responsible.

These and other restrictions prevent complete media freedom of expression in Britain. In some cases, it is argued that there is a need for reform if responsible investigative journalism is to do its job adequately. Britain is a secretive society, and campaigns continue for a Freedom of Information Act which might break down some of the secrecy and executive regulation.

On the other hand, the British media can often act irresponsibly by invading individual privacy, behaving in unethical ways, and sensationalizing the news for their own purposes. While the media have won some libel cases brought against them, and have achieved important victories for open information, they have also lost other cases because of their methods. Some media practices do cause concern, and the government may impose statutory restrictions on invasions of privacy unless the media reform themselves in this area. But it is generally felt that freedom of expression could be less restricted than it is at present.

Another restraining media institution, the Press Complaints Commission (PCC), was created in 1990 to replace its somewhat weak predecessor. It is financed by newspaper owners, and is supposed to guard the freedom and independence of the press; maintain the standards of journalism; and pass judgement upon complaints by the public against newspapers. Some critics argue that the Commission is not fighting as hard as it might for more press freedom. Others maintain that it is not strict enough with newspapers when complaints against them were proved. A fear that the government might institute strict legislation against media abuses has led to a tightening of the Commission's procedures. The newspaper owners have also instituted an ombudsman system for each newspaper, through which public complaints can be made and investigated. It remains to be seen whether the Commission and the ombudsman system will be truly effective.

It is sometimes argued that the concentrated ownership patterns of the media might limit freedom of expression by allowing owners undue influence over what is included in their products. Ex-journalists have claimed that there is proprietorial interference in some of the media, which is not being curbed either by editorial guarantees or by legal and government restrictions. On the other hand, editors and journalists can be very independently minded people, who will usually strongly object to any attempts at interference. Owners, in practice, seem to be careful not to tread on too many toes, because there are always competing media sources which are only too willing to publish the facts.

A further concern about limitations on media freedom has been the extent to which advertisers might dictate policy when they place their products. The question of advertisers' influence is complex, and might today be more applicable to the mass-consumer market of radio and television than the press. Advertisers dealing with the press are usually concerned with the type or status of readers rather than with their numbers. Arguably, the media have not succumbed in a substantial degree to the worst manipulations of the advertising agencies, in spite of the media's dependence upon advertising revenue.

Further stresses have also been placed upon the freedom of the media by the influence that the trade unions sometimes bring to bear. They have frequently refused to print or broadcast material to which they object, or have forced owners and editors to insert their particular points of view. These pressures have sometimes been backed by the threat of industrial action.

It is difficult to evaluate absolutely whether the media play a dominant part in influencing public opinion on a range of political and other matters. The left-wing view assumes that they do, and consequently disapproves of the alleged right-wing bias in the British media. But, while some people may have their attitudes directly shaped in these ways, it might be argued that a majority of readers and viewers have already made up their own minds, and react against blatant attempts at indoctrination. On certain occasions and for specific events (such as general elections), the media may have an important effect on public opinion.

But many people learn to read between the lines of newspapers and broadcasts, and are conditioned early in life 'not to believe everything you read in the papers', or hear 'on the telly'. Since television in particular is often accused of being either right-wing or left-wing, depending on which government is in power, it would seem that the British people are receiving enough information from all sides of the political spectrum. In practice, most people object to having politics and other concerns 'thrust down their throats', and many take a sceptical attitude to such matters.

ATTITUDES

Attitudes to the media

According to public opinion polls, the media are not a source of great concern to British people, although they do manifest their dissatisfaction or satisfaction with the various outlets. According to 1990 MORI polls, 39 per cent of people were satisfied with national newspapers and 40 per cent were dissatisfied; 63 per cent were satisfied with the BBC and 20 per cent were dissatisfied; 62 per cent were satisfied with independent television and 17 per cent were dissatisfied.

  British Social Attitudes: 1988–89 found that respondents, on being questioned whether media bodies were well run, rated independent radio and television at 83 per cent, the BBC at 67 per cent, and the press at 39 per cent. But, in terms of who can be trusted for most of the time to serve the public interest, journalists on national newspapers scored only 15 per cent.

EXERCISES

■ Explain and examine the following terms:

media	circulation	'free newspapers'	Reuters
press	tabloid	*Private Eye*	'hot metal'
advertising	broadsheet	ownership	libel
The Times	*Sun*	PCC	*sub judice*
Fleet Street	press dynasties	World Service	BBC
licence	ITC (IBA)	Channel 4	dubbing
Anglia	cable	ratings	John Reith

■ Write short essays on the following questions:

1 Describe and comment critically on the structure of British broadcasting.

2 Examine the problems of media freedom of expression.

3 Discuss the division of British national newspapers into 'populars' and 'qualities'.

Chapter 11

Religion

- Religious history   294
- The Christian tradition   299
- The non-Christian tradition   308
- Cooperation among the churches   311
- Religion in schools   312
- Religious membership and observance   313
- *Attitudes to religion and morality*   314
- *Exercises*   316

B RITISH RELIGIOUS HISTORY has been predominantly
Christian. It has been characterized by conflict between
Catholics and Protestants, and by division into separate Protestant
churches and sects. But it has also included the Jewish community
and other non-Christian denominations, as well as groups with
humanist and special beliefs. Religious life in Britain today still
possesses a diversity of religious denominations. These have been
added to in the twentieth century by the religions of newcomers to
the country.

But despite these features, the country superficially appears to
be largely secular when judged by the relatively low figures (under
20 per cent) for all types (Christian and non-Christian) of regular
religious observance. However, religion is still an important factor
in national life, whether for believers or as a background to the
national culture. It is reflected in active or nominal adherence to
particular denominations; in general ethical and moral behaviour;
and in the stabilizing functions of social institutions. Religiosity
tends to be greater in Wales, Scotland and (particularly) Northern
Ireland than in England.

Religious history

There is little evidence of religious organization in early British history, beyond archaeological discoveries which suggest various
forms of pagan beliefs. Although some Christian influences had
reached England during the Roman occupation, they were not
widespread or long-lasting.

However, Ireland was converted to Christianity around AD
432 by St Patrick, who had brought the faith from Rome. His
followers spread Christianity to Wales, Scotland and northern
England, and established religious centres, such as that of St

Columba on the Scottish island of Iona. In AD 596–7 the Saxons of southern England were converted to Christianity by St Augustine and other monks, who had been sent from Rome by Pope Gregory, and who also founded the ecclesiastical capital of Canterbury in AD 597. English conversion was encouraged by the Saxon kings, who considered that the hierarchical example of the Christian church would support their royal authority. The church also provided educated advisers and administrators, through whom the kings could control their kingdoms more efficiently. The connection between church and state was consequently established at an early stage in English history.

Southern English Christianity was based on the beliefs and practices of the Church of Rome. Although the religion of Ireland, Wales, Scotland and northern England was also founded on Roman doctrines, it had a more Celtic identification. Conflict and divisions inevitably arose between the two branches of Christianity. But these were eventually resolved at the Synod (meeting) of Whitby in AD 663, where all the churches agreed to accept the Roman Catholic form of worship.

Christianity quickly became a central and influential force in national life. The church was an essential part not only of religious culture but also of administration, law and government. But, as its role expanded, it was increasingly accused of worldliness and materialism. It was thought to be corrupt and too concerned with politics at the expense of religion. However, the church remained a part of the Roman Catholic faith, and was based on the traditional hierarchy of monks, priests, bishops and archbishops. The English kings maintained their allegiance to Rome and the Pope in spiritual matters, some with more strength of conviction than others.

But the relationship between England and Rome was becoming more difficult, and by the sixteenth century was at breaking point. English monarchs were jealous of the wealth and power of the English church, and resented the dominant influence of Rome in national affairs. Henry VIII argued in 1529 that as King of England he, not the Pope, was the supreme legal authority in the country, and that the English church and its courts owed their allegiance only to him.

In 1534 Henry finally broke away from the supremacy of Rome and declared himself head of the church in England. The immediate and pragmatic reason for this breach was the Pope's refusal to accept Henry's divorce from his queen, Katharine of Aragon, who had not produced a male heir to the throne. But Henry also wanted to curb the church's legal authority and power. In 1536 he dissolved many monasteries, and confiscated a large part of the church's property and wealth.

However, although Henry had established a national church, that church was still Roman Catholic in its faith and practices. Henry did not regard himself as a Protestant, nor did he consider the English church to be part of the Protestant Reformation, which was then profoundly affecting religious life in continental Europe. Indeed, Henry had defended the papacy against Martin Luther in 1521. The Pope rewarded him with the title of Fidei Defensor (Defender of the Faith), which British monarchs still bear today, and which can be seen on some British coins.

Nevertheless, the influence of the European Reformation caused the English, Scottish and Welsh churches to move gradually away from Rome's doctrines. This movement in England increased under Edward VI (1547–53), when practices and beliefs became more Protestant. John Knox in Scotland also accelerated the process by founding the separate Protestant Church of Scotland in 1560. Meanwhile, Ireland remained firmly Roman Catholic.

Henry VIII's daughter, the Roman Catholic Mary Tudor, had tried to bring back the full Roman Catholic faith during her short reign (1553–8), but did not succeed. Her sister, the Protestant Elizabeth I (1558–1603), established the Protestant status of the Church of England by the terms of her Church Settlement. The Church's doctrine was stated in the Thirty-Nine Articles of Faith (1562), and its rituals and forms of church service were contained in the Book of Common Prayer, which has been revised in later centuries. English replaced Latin in church documents and services, and priests of the Church of England were later allowed to marry. The English church now occupied an intermediate position between Roman Catholicism and the Protestant churches of Europe.

However, this final confirmation of the Protestant Church of England did not stop the religious arguments which were to affect Britain in later years. Many Protestants in the sixteenth and seventeenth centuries argued that the church had not distanced itself sufficiently from Rome. Some left to form their own religious organizations. Initially, they were called Dissenters because they disagreed with the majority view; later they were known as Nonconformists; and today are the members of the Free Churches. Fierce religious conflicts between Protestants and Catholics, often resulting in martyrdom, also continued during the seventeenth century. They culminated in the Civil War (1642–8) between the mainly Protestant Parliamentarians and the largely Catholic Royalists, which led to the Protectorate of Oliver Cromwell.

The collapse of Cromwell's narrowly puritan regime after his death, and the restoration of the Stuart monarchy, did bring some religious moderation. But minority religions continued to suffer. The Roman Catholic Church underwent considerable persecution and exclusion for 300 years after the English Reformation, and Jews and Nonconformists also experienced discrimination. These religious groups were excluded from the universities, the House of Commons and many other public positions. It was not until the mid-nineteenth century that most of the restrictions placed on them were removed. Meanwhile, the Church of England solidified its dominant position in 1688, when the Protestant William III succeeded James II, the last Catholic English king.

But further schisms and quarrels affected religious life in the eighteenth century, as groups reacted to rationalist developments in the Church of England. For example, the Methodists (founded 1739) stressed the emotional aspects of salvation and religion. They initially attempted to work within the Church of England, but opposition to their views eventually forced them to separate. Nevertheless, an Evangelical wing within the church was strongly influenced by Methodism. The Evangelicals based their faith and practice on a literal interpretation of the Bible, and believed in a humanitarian idealism. They accomplished many industrial and social reforms in nineteenth-century Britain. Today, the 'Low

Church' wing of the Church of England is the successor to Evangelical and other Nonconformist influences.

Various other groups reacted to the Church of England in the eighteenth and nineteenth centuries, and founded a variety of Nonconformist sects, such as the Baptists. On the other hand, the Oxford or Tracterian Movement, which developed in the 1830s, emphasized the Church of England's connections with Roman Catholicism, and wanted a closer identification with the Roman Catholic Church. It followed Catholic doctrines, and introduced elaborate ritual into its church services. It influenced succeeding generations, and today is represented by the Anglo-Catholic and 'High Church' wings of the Church of England.

There is complete religious freedom in contemporary Britain; a person can belong to any religion or none; and religious discrimination is unlawful. There is no religious bar to the holding of public office, except that the monarch must always be a member of the Church of England. None of the churches is tied specifically to a political party, and there are no religious parties as such in Parliament.

In recent years, immigrants to Britain have added further religious diversity. Muslim mosques, Sikh and Hindu temples, and West Indian Christian churches, such as the Pentecostalists, are common in areas with large ethnic communities. The growth of fundamentalist Evangelical groups, 'enthusiastic' Christian churches, and a

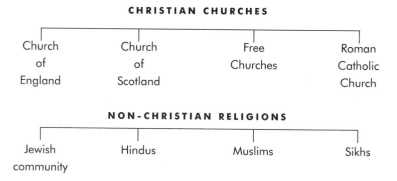

CHRISTIAN CHURCHES

| Church of England | Church of Scotland | Free Churches | Roman Catholic Church |

NON-CHRISTIAN RELIGIONS

| Jewish community | Hindus | Muslims | Sikhs |

FIGURE 11.1 Contemporary religious groups

range of some 500 cults or religious movements have also increased the numbers of people active in religious life.

In Britain today the growth of religious observance and vitality is mainly to be found outside the big traditional Christian churches. The Evangelical movement is the fastest-growing branch of Christianity. It is characterized by a close relationship among members, and between them and God, Christ and the Holy Spirit. It breaks down the barriers of the more traditional worship, places little reliance on church furniture, and has many different meeting places. It has basic Christian beliefs, but expresses them in different ways.

The Christian tradition

Christian religious communities in Britain consist mainly of the Church of England, the Church of Scotland, the Roman Catholic Church and the Free Churches. The two largest churches are the Church of England and the Roman Catholic Church. But the Church of England attracts only a fifth of religiously active Britons, and the Roman Catholic Church does only marginally better. Together they account for only 41 per cent of regular worshippers. Critics argue that these two competing churches built too many buildings for too few people in the nineteenth century. They have since used their resources to subsidize churches that should have been closed, and poorly attended services contribute to decline.

The Church of England

The Church of England is the established or national church in England. This means that its official position in the state has been legally confirmed by the Elizabethan Church Settlement and Parliament. The monarch is the head of the church; its archbishops, bishops and deans are appointed by the monarch on the advice of the Prime Minister; and Parliament has a voice in its organization and rituals. But it is not a state church, such as churches in some other European countries, since it receives no

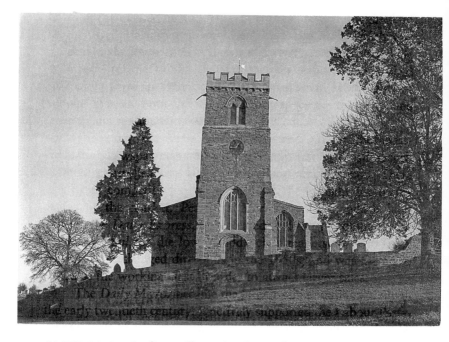

PLATE 11.1 Anglican village church, Northamptonshire *(Maggie Murray/Format)*

financial aid from the state, apart from salaries for public positions and help with church schools.

The church therefore has a special relationship with the state, although there are frequent calls for its disestablishment (cutting the connections between church and state) so that the church might have total autonomy over its own affairs. In spite of low active observance, it plays a central role in national life. Much of its membership is middle and upper class, and it is closely identified with the ruling establishment and authority. But there is considerable conflict within the church at present between traditionalists, who wish to maintain old forms and beliefs, and modernists, who want a more engaged and adventurous church which would attract a contemporary congregation.

The structure of the church is based on an episcopal hierarchy, or rule by bishops. The two Archbishops of Canterbury and

York, together with 24 other senior bishops, sit in the House of Lords and take part in its proceedings. Collectively, they form the senior branch of the church in its connection with Parliament.

Organizationally, the church is divided into the two provinces of Canterbury and York, each under the control of an archbishop. The Archbishop of Canterbury (also called the Primate of All England) is the senior of the two, and is the professional head of the church. The two provinces are subdivided into 43 dioceses, each under the control of a bishop. Many of the bishops' seats are very old, and are situated in ancient cathedral towns, such as Chichester, Lincoln, Durham and Salisbury.

The dioceses are divided into some 13,000 parishes, and each is centred on a parish church. Most parishes, except for those in isolated rural areas, have a priest (called either a vicar or a rector) in charge, and a large parish may have additional assistant priests (curates). A priest must serve first as a deacon for a year before being ordained a priest by the local bishop. The priest usually occupies rent-free accommodation in a vicarage, but does not have a large salary, which in most cases today is paid out of central church funds.

The Church of England is considered to be a 'broad church' in which a variety of beliefs and practices coexist. Priests consequently have a considerable freedom as to how they conduct their church services. The form of these can vary a great deal from the elaborate ritual of High Church worship to the simple, functional presentation of Low Church services. These types represent the two wings of the Church. The High Church or Anglo-Catholic wing, which amounts to some 20 per cent of church membership, lays stress on church tradition and the historical influence of Roman Catholic practices and teaching. The Low Church or Evangelical wing, which amounts to some 80 per cent of church membership, bases faith and practice on a somewhat literal interpretation of the Bible, and is suspicious of Roman Catholic influences.

The two wings of the church do not always cooperate happily, and between them there is a considerable variety of fashions. Some Evangelical priests have introduced contemporary music and dramatic performances into their services, in order to appeal to younger congregations and more modern concerns.

Today priests have to deal with a wide variety of problems and pressures in their work, particularly in deprived and inner-city areas, and cannot easily be restricted to a purely religious role.

The main financial resources of the church come from its substantial property and investment holdings, and it is the third largest landowner in Britain, after the Crown and the Forestry Commission. The total assets of the church, which have been estimated at over £400 million, are administered by the Church Commissioners. This wealth has to finance many very expensive demands, such as salaries for the clergy and administrators, the maintenance of churches and cathedrals, and the provision of a wide range of activities in Britain and abroad. In recent years the financial assets of the church have been seriously depleted because of investment failures which have affected its activities. Appeals have been made to congregations for help in financing church upkeep and the stipends of clergy.

The total membership of the Church of England is difficult to determine, because the church does not have a strict register of members. Membership is usually assumed when a person (usually a baby) is baptized into the church. It seems that perhaps some 40 per cent of the English population have been baptized. This membership may be confirmed at 'confirmation' around the age of 14 or 15. But it is estimated that only a fifth of those baptized have been confirmed and that some 1.8 million people are active members of the church. However, many others who have not been baptized identify themselves with the Church of England, even though they are not active practitioners of any religion.

Lay members of the parish are associated with church organization at the local level through parochial church councils. These councils send representatives to the local diocesan councils (or synods), where matters of common concern are discussed. The matters may then be sent to the General Synod, which since 1970 has been the national governing body of the church. It has spiritual, legislative and administrative functions, and makes the final decisions on subjects like the ordination of women priests.

Women in the past served as deacons and in women's religious orders, but could not be ordained as priests in the church. Much debate and conflict still surround this question, although the General Synod has approved the ordination of women, and the first women were ordained in 1994. The debate has split the church into factions, and driven some members and clergy into the Roman Catholic Church.

The Church of England is sometimes referred to as the 'Anglican Church', in the sense that it is part of a worldwide communion of churches whose practices and beliefs are very similar, and many of which descend from the Church of England. This larger Anglican Communion comprises an estimated membership of 90 million people in the British Isles (with Anglican churches in Wales, Scotland and Ireland) and abroad, such as the Protestant Episcopal Church in the USA. These churches (except for that in Wales) have women priests and bishops. The Lambeth Conference, which is a meeting of Anglican bishops from all over the world, is held every ten years in London, and is presided over by the Archbishop of Canterbury. It has great prestige, and its deliberations on doctrine, relations with other churches, and attitudes to political and social questions are widely considered.

In recent years, the Church of England has been more willing to enter into controversial arguments about social and political problems in contemporary Britain, like the condition of people living in the inner cities, and has been critical of government policies. This has led it into conflict with the Conservative government and its popularity among politicians at present is not high. It has tended to avoid such issues in the past and has been described as 'the Conservative Party at prayer' because of its safe, establishment image. It is still widely felt that the church, like the monarchy, should not involve itself in such questions, and historically it has favoured compromise. However, some critics argue that the church must change its attitudes, organization and values (including adapting theological advances to modern conditions) if it is to continue as a vital force in British life.

The Church of Scotland

The Church of Scotland (or Kirk as it is commonly known) is the second established church in Britain. Its position as the official national church in Scotland has been confirmed by successive legislation from 1707, which has asserted its freedom in spiritual matters and independence from all parliamentary supervision. The church is completely separate from the Church of England, has its own organizational structures, and decides its own doctrines and practices.

It was created in 1560 by John Knox. He was opposed to episcopal rule and considered that the English church had not moved sufficiently far from Roman Catholicism. The Scottish church followed the teachings of Calvin, a leading exponent of the European Reformation, and developed a rather severe form of Presbyterian Protestantism. Presbyterianism means government by ordained ministers and elected elders (who are lay, or non-ordained, members of the church).

The church has a democratic structure. The individual churches are governed locally by a Kirk Session, which consists of the minister and elected elders. Ministers (who include women) have equality with each other. The General Assembly is the supreme organizational body of the church, and comprises elected ministers and elders. It meets every year under the presidency of an elected Moderator, who serves for one year, and is the leader of the church during the period of office. There are some 790,000 adult members of the church.

The Roman Catholic Church

The Roman Catholic Church in Britain experienced much persecution and discrimination after the Reformation, and had difficulties in surviving. Although its organization was restored and the worst suspicions abated by 1850, reservations about it still continued in some quarters.

Today Catholicism is widely practised throughout Britain and enjoys complete religious freedom, except for the fact that no Catholic can become monarch. There are seven Roman Catholic provinces in Great Britain (four in England, two in Scotland and one in Wales), each under the supervision of an archbishop; 29 dioceses, each under the control of a bishop; and over 3,000 parishes. The head of the church in England is the Cardinal Archbishop of Westminster, and the senior lay Catholic is the Duke of Norfolk. In Northern Ireland, there is one province with six dioceses, some of which overlap with dioceses in the Irish Republic.

It is estimated that there may be some 5 million nominal members of the Roman Catholic faith in Britain today, although the number of active participants is about 1.9 million. This figure makes it the largest Christian church in Britain in terms of observance. Its membership is centred on the urban working class, settlers of Irish descent, a few prominent upper-class families and some middle-class people.

The church continues to emphasize the important role of education for its children, and requires its members to try to raise their children in the Catholic faith. There are many voluntary schools specifically for Catholic pupils, which are sometimes staffed by members of religious orders, like the Jesuits and Marists.

PLATE 11.2 At prayer: Catholic mass *(Judy Harrison/Format)*

These and other orders also carry out social work, such as nursing, hospital duties, child care and looking after the elderly.

The Free Churches

The Free Churches are composed of those Nonconformist Protestant sects which are not established like the Churches of England and Scotland. Some broke away from the Church of England after the Reformation, and others departed later. In general, they refused to accept episcopal rule or hierarchical structures, and have ordained women ministers. Their history has been one of schism and separation among themselves, which has resulted in the formation of many different sects.

Their egalitarian beliefs are reflected in the historical association between political and religious dissent, which were important in the formation of the Labour Party and the radical wing of the old Liberal Party. These churches have developed their own convictions and practices, which are often mirrored in their simple church services, worship and building. The Free Churches tend to be strongest in northern England, Wales, Northern Ireland and Scotland, and most of their membership has historically derived from the working class. The main Free Churches today are the Methodists, the Baptists, the United Reformed Church and the Salvation Army.

The *Methodist Church* is the largest of the Free Churches, with some half a million adult members and a community of 1.3 million. It was established in 1784 by John Wesley after Church of England opposition to his Evangelical views obliged him to separate and form his own organization. Further arguments and division occurred within the Methodist Church in the nineteenth century, but most of the doctrinal and administrative disputes were settled in 1932. Today the Methodist Church in Britain is based on the 1932 union of most of the separate Methodist sects. But independent Methodist churches still exist in Britain and abroad, with a worldwide membership of several million. Attempts were made in the 1960s and 1970s to unify the Methodists and the Church of England, but the proposals failed. In practice, however, some ministers of these denominations share their churches and services. The *Baptists* (formed in the seventeenth century) are today mainly grouped in associations of churches. Most of these belong to the Baptist Union of Great Britain and Ireland, which was formed in 1812 and has a total membership of some 170,000 people. There are also independent Baptist unions in Scotland, Wales and Ireland bringing the total Baptists to some 240,000), in addition to a worldwide Baptist fellowship.

The ancient Congregational Church in England and Wales had its roots in sixteenth-century Puritanism. It merged with the Presbyterian Church in England (which was associated with Scottish Presbyterians) in 1972 to form the *United Reformed Church*, which now has some 120,000 members.

The *Salvation Army*, with its emphasis upon saving souls through a very practical Christian mission, was founded in Britain by William Booth in 1865, and now has some 55,000 active members. It has spread to 89 other countries, and has a worldwide strength of about 2.5 million. The Salvation Army is a very efficient organization, and has centres nationwide to help the homeless, the abused, the poor, the sick and the needy. Its uniformed members may be frequently seen on the streets of British towns and cities, playing and singing religious music, collecting money, preaching and selling their magazine.

Other Christian churches

The number of active adherents of the large formal Christian churches above has been in decline for some time, and the total Christian membership is now some 6.7 million. But there are a considerable number of smaller Free Churches and Nonconformist denominations throughout Britain with a Christian base. The dissenting tradition has led groups in very varied directions, and they all value their independence and origins. For example, the *Religious Society of Friends* (Quakers) was founded in the seventeenth century, has no ministers and no conventionally organized services. The Quakers' pacifism and social work are influential, and their membership has increased since the early twentieth century to about 18,000 people.

There has been a significant recent increase in 'enthusiastic' Christian churches. These are usually defined as independent Christian groups, which number half a million members and are characterized by their Pentecostalist or charismatic nature. They emphasize the miraculous and spiritual side of the New Testament rather than dogma, sin and salvation. Among them are churches, such as the Assemblies of God and the Elim Pentecostal Church, which have many members of West Indian (Afro-Caribbean) descent.

Another development has been the growth of the 'house church movement', with large attendances throughout the country, and where services and prayer meetings are held in private houses. Fundamentalist Evangelical groups have also been increasing, and there are many other non-trinitarian religious sects in Britain, such as the *Jehovah's Witnesses*, the *Seventh Day Adventists*, the *Mormon Church*, the *Christian Scientists* and the *Spiritualists*.

This diversity of groups results in a very varied religious life in Britain today, but one which is an important reality for a considerable number of people. It represents a growth area in religious observance, marked by frustration with the heavy, formal and traditional style of the larger churches, and a desire to embrace a more vital and spontaneous form of Christianity. It also suggests a disenchantment with more orthodox forms of organized religion.

The non-Christian tradition

The non-Christian tradition in Britain is mainly associated with immigrants into the country over the centuries, such as the Jews and, more recently, Muslims, Sikhs and Hindus.

The Jewish community

The first groups of Jews came to Britain at the time of the Norman Conquest, and were involved in finance and commerce. The present community has been established since the middle of the seventeenth century, following the expulsion of Jews in the thirteenth century. Today it has about 300,000 members and is estimated to be the second largest Jewish population in Europe. The community is composed of the Sephardim (originally from Spain, Portugal and north Africa) and the majority Ashkenazim (from Germany and central Europe).

In religious terms, the community is divided into the majority Orthodox faith (of which the main spokesman is the Chief Rabbi) and the minority Reform and Liberal groups. The focus of Jewish religious life is the 250 local synagogues, and Jewish schools are attended by about one in three Jewish schoolchildren. The majority of Jews live in London, where the East End has traditionally been a place of initial Jewish settlement, while others live mainly in urban areas outside London.

The Jewish community has declined in the past 20 years. This is due to a disenchantment with religion; an increase in the number of civil and mixed marriages; considerable emigration by young Jews; a relatively low birth-rate; and a rapidly ageing population of active practitioners. For some British Jews, their Jewishness is simply a matter of birth, and they are tending to assimilate more with the wider society. For others, it is a matter of deep religious beliefs and practice, and this fundamentalism seems to be increasing. But the majority still have a larger global identity with Jewish history.

Other non-Christian religions

Immigration into Britain during the last 50 years has resulted in a substantial growth of other non-Christian religions, such as Islam, Sikhism and Hinduism. The number of practitioners is growing because of high birth-rates among Britons of Asian origin. There are now some 1.5 million Muslims, of whom around 1 million regularly attend mosques. Most of them originate from Pakistan and Bangladesh, but there are other groups from India, Cyprus and the Arab countries. The number of Muslims is also increasing because of conversion to Islam among young working-class non-whites and

PLATE 11.3   Regent's Park mosque, London *(Duncan Wherett/Barnaby)*

middle-class whites. The Islamic Cultural Centre and its associated Central Mosque in London are the largest Muslim institutions in the west, and there are mosques in virtually every British town with a concentration of Muslim people.

There are also large Sikh (390,000) and Hindu (300,000) religious groups in Britain. Most of these come from India, and have many temples scattered around the country in areas of Asian settlement. Various forms of Buddhism are also represented in the population.

These non-Christian religions together amount to some 1.9 million practising members, and represent a significant growth area when compared to the Christian churches. But it is important to realize that their adherents represent only a tiny proportion (some 3 per cent) of the total British population, the vast majority of which remains nominally Christian. However, they have altered the religious face of British society and have influenced employment conditions, since allowances have to be made for non-Christians to follow their own religious observances and customs. They have also become very vocal in expressing their opinions on a range of matters, such as the Muslim demand for their own schools supported by state funds; Muslim outrage against Salman Rushdie's novel *The Satanic Verses*, parts of which are considered to be blasphemous; and Muslim claims that their religion is discriminated against by British law and politicians. Blasphemy in British law applies only to Christianity.

Cooperation among the churches

The ancient intolerance and bigotry of the Christian denominations in Britain have gradually mellowed after centuries of hostility, restrictions and repression. There is now a good deal of cooperation, although ecumenism (cooperation and eventual unity between churches) stops short of unity. There have been discussions between the Roman Catholic Church and other Christian churches in Britain about closer ties, and a permanent Anglican–Roman Catholic Commission explores points of possible unity. The old enmity between Protestants and Catholics has been considerably reduced. But animosities are still present in parts of Scotland, and most demonstrably in Northern Ireland.

The new (1990) Council of Churches for Britain and Ireland is an official organization and is presided over by the Archbishop of Canterbury. It comprises representatives from the main Christian churches in Britain, and works towards common action and Christian unity. The Free Church Federal Council does a similar job for the Free Churches. The Anglican and the main Free Churches also participate in the deliberations of the World Council of Churches, which attempts to promote cooperation and the study of common problems on an international basis. The Council of Christians and Jews works for better understanding among its members in Britain, and the Council for Churches of Britain and Ireland has established a Committee for Relations with People of Other Faiths (that is, non-Christian).

These attempts at possible ecumenism and cooperation have been seen by some as positive actions, which might break down the barriers and hostility of the past and present. Others see them as signs of weakness, in that the denominations have been forced to cooperate because of declining memberships and their lack of real influence in the contemporary world. The movement towards Christian unity may also be threatened by the ordination of women priests in the Church of England, since the worldwide Anglican Communion accepts them, but the Roman Catholic Church is opposed.

Many churchmen at the grassroots level argue that the churches must adapt more to the requirements of modern life, or else decline in membership and influence. Future religious developments in Britain may be more Evangelical and ecumenical than they have been in the past, in order to reflect a diverse contemporary society. But many traditionalists wish to preserve the historical elements of religious belief and practice, and the tension between them and modernists in all religious groups is likely to continue.

Religion in schools

Non-denominational Christian religious education is legally compulsory in all state schools in England and Wales. According to law, the school day is supposed to start with an act of collective worship, and religious lessons should be provided which concentrate on Christianity but also include the other main faiths. However, if a pupil (or parent) has strong objections, the pupil need not take part in either the service or the lessons.

Custom differs in the religious lessons, particularly in areas with large ethnic communities. The lessons may take many different forms, and are not usually tied to specific Christian themes. Few secondary schools now hold daily assemblies. There have been frequent proposals that the legal compulsion in religious education should be removed, but it is still enshrined in the Conservative government's latest Education Acts. The government sees religious education and collective worship as a way to raise moral standards and encourage social values. But many schools cannot meet their legal obligations in this area and question the point of doing so. Religious services and teaching are not compulsory in Scotland.

Religious membership and observance

The continuous decline in membership of the main Christian churches since the early twentieth century has recently eased, and there has even been a slight growth. However, there has been a substantial increase in some of the Free Churches, non-Christian denominations, and the new or independent religious movements.

It is difficult to obtain precise information about membership and observance in Britain, because enquiries are not normally made about religious beliefs in censuses or other official forms, and each denomination may have its own methods of assessing membership figures. Some statistics suggest that 10 per cent of the population actually attend a Christian church, and less than 20 per cent of the total population go regularly to some form of religious service, whether Christian or non-Christian.

Yet, out of the total population which includes all faiths, it has been estimated that about 70 per cent of British people are married in a religious building, and about 90 per cent receive some form of religious burial or cremation. It seems that a small minority attend religious services regularly, others go occasionally, but the large majority enter a religious building only for baptisms, weddings and funerals.

However, these figures should not necessarily be taken as a sign of British irreligion. A distinction might be made between formal religious observance of an institutional or organized kind and the grey area of religious or moral feeling. Despite the appearance of a largely secular state, religion in its various forms is still an important factor in national life. Radio, television and the press continue to concern themselves with religious and moral topics.

Religious broadcasting on radio and television attracts surprisingly large audience figures, and recent reports suggest further demand for this type of communication.

Religion is also reflected in traditions and ceremonies, as well as being evident in national and individual morality. The various religious denominations are relatively prominent in British life, and are active in education, voluntary social work and community care. Religious leaders publicly debate doctrine, social matters, political concerns and the moral questions of the day, not always necessarily within narrow church limits.

ATTITUDES

Attitudes to religion and morality

While institutional religious observance of the traditional kind may no longer be widely popular, it does seem that there is still a degree of religious interest in the population. A MORI opinion poll in 1990 found the following levels of belief by people interviewed: in God (76 per cent); sin (69); a soul (68); heaven (60); life after death (49); the devil (37); and hell (31). These figures are somewhat inconsistent with respect to orthodox institutional beliefs, but they do indicate a considerable individual religious faith.

However, purely religious concerns seem to have been overtaken by notions of personal morality and civic responsibility. Although there may be differences of emphasis between the younger and older generations and between men and women, the British have strong views about right and wrong, although these are not necessarily tied to the teaching of any established Christian church. Opinion polls suggest that a majority of people think the following are morally wrong: hard drugs like heroin, soccer hooliganism, soft drugs such as cannabis, scenes of explicit violence on television, adultery, scientific experiments on human beings, and scientific experiments on animals. Homosexuality and cinema pornography are also frowned upon by a large minority.

Poll interviews reveal that there is still majority support for the institution of marriage in Britain, and most people apparently have traditional and somewhat conventional ideas about love, family life and their moral demands. But there is a growing support for more equality within marriage, and faithfulness, mutual respect and understanding are regarded as the most important aspects of marriage.

In terms of civic responsibility, polls suggest that attitudes to authority remain conventional, and most people consider that the law should be obeyed without exception. A majority of respondents feel that children should be taught in the home environment to respect honesty, good manners and other people. Feelings have apparently hardened towards those individuals who reject society as presently constituted, who demonstrate and protest, who break the law, and who encourage disobedience in children. A large majority would oppose any attempts by the trade unions to call a general strike in the country. Most respondents agree that schools should teach children to obey authority, and also now favour censorship of some forms of the mass media in order to preserve moral standards.

These views suggest a general return to traditional values after a period of so-called permissiveness in the 1970s and 1980s. Such poll results indicate that many British people seem now to have embraced an authoritarian posture in questions of morals and social behaviour. 'Moral traditionalism', old values and civic responsibility are supported, and there is often a greater adherence to concepts of personal and social morality than those dictated by official and legal restraints. The strong authoritarian streak in British society with respect to moral and social questions is also reflected in people's current considerable concerns about drugs, law and order, crime, violence and vandalism, and their preference for strong action to be taken in these areas.

EXERCISES

■ **Explain and examine the following terms:**

Canterbury	Henry VIII	'Low Church'	confirmation
bigotry	Iona	Free Churches	General Synod
St Patrick	episcopal	Church Settlement	John Knox
Whitby	Quakers	vicar	Salvation Army
baptism	ecumenism	denomination	Evangelism

■ **Write short essays on the following questions:**

1 What does the term 'Christianity' mean in relation to British religious history?

2 Discuss religious membership and observance in contemporary British life.

3 Critically examine the role of the Church of England.

Chapter 12

Leisure, sports and the arts

■ Leisure activities 318

■ Sports 322

■ The arts 328

■ *Attitudes to leisure, sports and the arts* 332

■ *Exercises* 334

THE DIVERSITY OF LIFE in contemporary Britain is reflected in the ways the British organize their personal, sporting, leisure and artistic lives. These features reveal a series of different cultural habits, rather than a simple and unified image. But there are some activities which are associated with, and tend to project, a national identification. In many cases, pastimes are also connected to social class and minority participation. According to the authors of *We British* (p. 124), the rich variety of leisure activities disproves the notion of the British as a country of philistines who prefer second-rate entertainment to the best.

Leisure activities

Leisure activities in earlier centuries, apart from some cultural interests exclusive to the metropolitan elite, were largely conditioned by the rural and agricultural nature of British life. Village communities were isolated and transport was either poor or nonexistent. People were consequently restricted to their villages and obliged to create their own entertainments. Some of these participatory activities were home-based, while others were enjoyed by the whole village. They might be added to by itinerant players, who travelled the countryside and provided a range of alternative spectator entertainments, such as drama performances and musical events.

Improved transportation and road conditions from the eighteenth century onwards enabled the rural population to travel to neighbouring towns where they took advantage of a variety of amusements. Spectator activities increased with the industrialization of the nineteenth century, as theatre, the music halls and sports developed and became available to more people. The establishment of railway systems and the formation of bus companies

initiated the pattern of cheap one-day trips around the country and to the seaside, which were to grow into the mass charter and package tours of contemporary Britain. The arrival of radio, films and television in the twentieth century resulted in a further huge professional entertainments industry. In all these changes, the mixture of participatory, spectator and home-based leisure activities has continued.

Many contemporary pursuits have their roots in the cultural and social behaviour of the past, such as boxing, wrestling, cricket, football and a wide range of athletic sports. Dancing, amateur theatre and musical events were essential parts of rural life for all classes, and were often associated with the changing agricultural seasons. The traditions of hunting, shooting and fishing have long been practised in British country life (not only by the aristocracy), as well as working-class blood sports, like dog and cock fighting and bear baiting. These are now illegal, although dog and cock fighting still go on clandestinely. In addition to cultural and sporting pastimes, the contemporary British enjoy a variety of other leisure activities since more diversified opportunities are now available. More people have more free time, which results from a 35–40-hour working week. Most workers have at least four weeks' holiday a year, in addition to public holidays such as Christmas, Easter and Bank Holidays. The growing number of pensioners has created an economically rewarding leisure market, while unemployment means that a further substantial group of people have more spare time. In 1992 some 15 per cent of total household expenditure was devoted to leisure goods and services.

The most common leisure pastimes are social or home-based, such as visiting or entertaining friends, trips to the pub (public house), watching television and videos, reading books and magazines, and listening to the radio, tapes, records, compact discs and cassettes. In winter, the most popular non-sporting leisure activity for the adult population as a whole is watching television (for some 26 hours a week over the whole year), and for men television viewing is apparently the single most popular pastime throughout the year.

The British now occupy some two-thirds of their spare time

using electronic equipment, and an increasingly large amount of money is spent on items such as television, radio, video recorders, computers, compact disc players, and cable and satellite television. The home has become the chief place for family and individual entertainment in these respects, and poses serious competition to other passive activities outside the home, like the cinema, sports and theatre. Some 98 per cent of households now have a television set (95 per cent being colour sets), and some 69 per cent of households have at least one video recorder.

Despite the competition from television, the cinema and other electronic media, reading is still an important leisure activity for over half of men and women in Britain. There is a large variety of books and magazines to cater for all tastes and interests. The best-selling books are romances, thrillers, modern popular novels, detective stories, and works of adventure and history. Classic literature is not widely read, although its sales can benefit from adaptations on television. The tie-in of books (of all types) with videos and television series is now a very lucrative business.

Do-it-yourself hobbies, such as house painting, decorating and gardening, are very popular, and home improvements and repairs amount to a considerable item in the total household budget. The practice of eating out has increased, and is catered for by an expanded variety of so-called 'ethnic' restaurants (particularly Indian and Chinese) and fast-food outlets.

But visiting the pub is still a very important part of British life, and more money is spent on drinking and other pub activities than on any other single form of leisure. Some seven out of ten adults visit pubs, and one-third go once or more a week. The pub, as a social institution, has changed somewhat over the years, but still caters for a wide range of different groups and tastes. The licensing hours, which apply to opening times for the sale of alcohol, have been liberalized by the government to bring England and Wales into line with Scotland. Pubs can now open from 11 a.m. to 11 p.m. on every day except Sundays, but children under 14 are not allowed in the bar. Most pubs provide food in addition to drinks, and often have restaurants attached to them. But in recent years, the establishment of wine bars, various forms

PLATE 12.1 Working men's club *(Janina Struk/Format)*

of clubs, discotheques and dance halls has meant a considerable amount of competition for the traditional pub.

Holidays and where to spend them have also become an important part of British life, and have been accompanied by more leisure time and money for the majority of the people. They represent the second major leisure cost after pub drinking. While more Britons in recent years have been taking their holidays in Britain itself, where the south-west English coastal resorts, Wales and Scotland are very popular in summer, large numbers also go abroad in both winter and summer. The number of long holidays taken away from home by the British population amounts to

321

nearly 54 million, of which some 22 million are taken abroad. Spain, France and Greece continue to be the main attractions for British holidaymakers, who buy relatively cheap package tours. But such holidays have become more expensive recently and also increasingly unattractive for a variety of reasons (such as inadequate facilities and violence). There has been a drop in demand for overseas holidays, and the number taken in Britain has increased. But the British nevertheless seem to have become more adventurous, and are now travelling widely outside Europe on a variety of holidays.

Many other people prefer to organize their own holidays and make use of the good air and sea communications between Britain and the continent. In Britain itself, different forms of holiday exist, from the traditional 'bed and breakfast' at a seaside boarding house, to hotels, caravan sites and camping. Increased car ownership has allowed greater travel possibilities. Today, more than three-fifths of households have the use of at least one car, and 16 per cent have two or more.

Sports

There is a wide variety of sports in Britain today, which cater for large numbers of spectators and participators. Some of these are minority or class-based sports, while others appeal to majority tastes. The number of people participating in sports has increased, and sporting facilities and leisure centres in both the public and private sectors have expanded. This has coincided with a greater awareness of health needs and the importance of exercise. Some one-third of the adult population participates in outdoor sports and a quarter in indoor sports. Expenditure on playing and watching sports and buying sports equipment, amounts to a considerable part of the household budget.

The most popular participatory sporting activity for both men and women is walking. Billiards, snooker and darts are the next most popular for men, followed by swimming and football. Swimming is the next most popular sport for women, followed by

PLATE 12.2   Crowd of people at football match *(Jacky Chapman/Format)*

keep-fit classes. Fishing is apparently the most popular country sport.

Amateur and professional football (soccer) is played throughout most of the year, and also at international level. It is by far the most watched sport, and today transcends its working-class origins. The professional game has developed into a large, family-oriented organization, but has suffered from hooliganism, declining attendances and financial crises. However, enforced changes in recent years such as all-seater stadiums, greater security, improved facilities and lucrative tie-ins with television coverage have greatly improved this situation.

PLATE 12.3 Football match: Derby County vs. Queen's Park Rangers *(Joanne O'Brien/Format)*

Rugby football is a popular winter pastime and is widely watched and played. It is divided into two codes. Rugby Union is confined to amateur clubs and was once an exclusively middle-class and public school-influenced game. Rugby League is played by professional teams, mainly in the north of England, and still tends to be a working-class sport. Both types of rugby are also played internationally.

Cricket is a summer sport in Britain, but the England team also plays in the winter months in Commonwealth countries. It is both an amateur and professional sport. The senior game is now professional and is largely confined to 17 English and one Welsh county sides which play in the county championships. Attendance at cricket matches continues to decline, and the contemporary game has lost much of its attractiveness as it has moved in overly professional and money-dominated directions.

There are many other sports which reflect the diversity of interests in British life. Among these are golf, horse-racing, hunting, riding, fishing, shooting, tennis, hockey, bowls, darts, snooker, athletics, swimming, sailing, mountaineering, ice sports, motor-car and motorcycle racing, and rally driving. American football and basketball are increasingly popular as a result of television exposure. These sports may be either amateur or professional, and spectator- or participator-based, with car and motor cycle, greyhound and horse racing being the most watched.

The professional sporting industry is now very lucrative, and is closely associated with sponsorship schemes and television coverage. Gambling or betting on sporting and other events has always been a popular, if somewhat disreputable, pastime in Britain, which is now much more in the open and acceptable. Most gambling (through betting shops or bookmakers) is associated with horse and greyhound racing, but can involve other sports. Weekly

PLATE 12.4   Cricket in the city, Kennington estate, London *(Cleland Brims/Barnaby)*

PLATE 12.5 Cricket in the country, Kent *(Alexander Brims/Barnaby)*

football pools (betting on match results) are very popular and can result in huge financial wins. The new-found acceptability of gambling in Britain was reflected in the establishment of a National Lottery in 1994. It is similar to lotteries in other European countries, and considerable amounts of money can be won.

It is interesting that many of these sports have contributed to institutionalized features of British life, and provide a certain degree of national identity. For example, Wimbledon is tennis; the Wembley Cup Final is football in England; St Andrews is golf in Scotland; Twickenham in England, Murrayfield in Scotland, and Cardiff Arms Park in Wales are Rugby Union; Lord's Cricket Ground in London is cricket; the Derby is flat horse-racing; the Grand National in Liverpool is steeplechasing; Henley Regatta is rowing; Cowes Week off the Isle of Wight is yachting; Ascot is horse-racing; and the British Grand Prix is Formula One motor racing. Some of these sports may appeal only to certain sections of the population, while others may still be equated more with wealth and social position.

Some people feel that the professionalization and commercialization of sport in Britain has tended to weaken the traditional sporting image of the amateur, and the old emphasis upon playing the game for its own sake. But these values still exist to some degree, in spite of greater financial rewards for professional sport, the influences of sponsorship and advertising, and increasing cases of unethical behaviour in all sports.

British governments have only recently taken an active political interest in sport. They are now more concerned to promote sport at all levels and there is a Minister of Sport, who is supposed to coordinate sporting activities throughout the country. However, the national provisions for sport in Britain are not as adequate as they might be, and there is a lack of professional coaches, capital investment and sporting facilities compared with other countries. The government has privatized some local authority sports and leisure centres, particularly in inner-city areas, in an attempt to raise sporting standards and to provide more facilities. But critics fear that this policy will not succeed in attracting people.

The sporting notion of 'a healthy mind in a healthy body' has long been a principle of British education. All schools are supposed to provide physical recreation, and a reasonable range of sports is usually available for schoolchildren. Schools may play soccer, rugby, hockey or netball during the winter months, and cricket, tennis, swimming and athletics during the summer. Some schools may be better provided with sporting facilities than others, and offer a wider range of activities.

However, there have been recent complaints from parents that team games and competitive sports are declining in state schools. School reorganization and the creation of large comprehensives have reduced the amount of inter-school competition, which used to be a feature of education; some left-wing councils are apparently opposed to competitive activities; there is a shortage of playing fields; and a lack of adequate equipment. The position is particularly acute in the inner-city areas, and is of concern to those parents who feel that their children are being prevented from expressing their normal physical natures. They maintain that the state school system is failing to provide sporting provision for children, and some parents turn to the independent sector, which is usually well provided with sports facilities. But the Conservative government now says that it is determined to improve the availability and standard of school sports.

The arts

The 'arts' once had a somewhat precious and exclusive image associated with notions of high culture, which were usually the province of the urban and metropolitan middle and upper classes. This attitude has lessened to some degree since the Second World War under the impetus of increased educational opportunities and the gradual relaxation of social barriers. The growth of mass and popular culture has increased the potential audience for a wider range of cultural activities, and the availability and scope of the arts has spread to greater numbers of people. These activities may be amateur or professional, and continue the mixture of participatory, spectator and home-based entertainment.

Some critics argue that the genuine vitality and innovation of the British arts are to be found in the millions of people across the country who are engaged in amateur music, art and theatre, rather than in the professional and commercial world. Virtually every town, suburb and village has an amateur group, whether it be a choir, music group, orchestra, string quartet, pipe band, brass band, choral group, opera group or dramatic club. In addition, there are hundreds of cultural festivals held each year throughout Britain, many of which are of a very high standard.

The funding of the mainstream arts in Britain is precarious and involves the private and public sectors. The public sector is divided between local authorities and the Arts Council of Great Britain. Local authorities raise money from the council tax to fund artistic activities in their areas, but the amounts spent can vary considerably between different areas of the country, and local authorities are attacked for either spending too much or too little on cultural activities.

Members of the Arts Council, who now operate on a regional

rather than centralized level, are appointed by the Heritage Minister. They are responsible for dividing up an annual government grant to the arts, and the finance has to be shared among theatres, orchestras, opera and ballet companies, art galleries and museums, and a variety of other cultural organizations. The division of limited funds has inevitably attracted much criticism. It means that many artistic institutions are often dependent upon the private sector to supply donations and funding, in addition to their state and local government money, in order to survive and provide a service.

British theatre can be lively and innovative, and has a deserved international reputation. There are some 300 commercial or professional theatres, in addition to a large number of amateur dramatic clubs, fringe and pub theatres throughout the country. London and its suburbs have about 100 theatres, but the dominant influence is London's 'West End'. The majority of the West End theatres are commercial, in that they are organized for profit and receive no public funds. They provide a range of light-entertainment offerings from musicals to plays and comedies.

However, some of the other London theatres are subsidized from grants supplied by the Arts Council, such as the National Theatre, the Royal Shakespeare Company and the English Stage Company. These cater for a variety of plays from the classics to modern drama. The subsidized theatres in both London and the regions constantly plead for more state financial aid, which the government is loath to give. The government subsidy is considerably less than that given to most comparable theatres in continental Europe. But there is a feeling in some quarters that these theatres should be more competitive and commercially minded like the West End, although Arts Council grants have been recently increased.

Many of the theatres in the regions outside London are repertory theatres, which means that they provide a number of plays in a given season and have a resident theatre company and organization. The repertory companies have traditionally been the training ground for British actors and actresses. They present a specific number of classical and innovative plays and a variety of other artistic offerings in a season.

Most theatres in London and elsewhere have had difficult times in recent years in attracting audiences and in remaining solvent. They have had to cope with increased competition from alternative and new entertainment activities. New commercial theatres in some cities are proving popular, and are taking audiences away from the established repertory companies. These commercial theatres provide a wide range of popular entertainment, shows and drama, as well as plays performed prior to a London run. There are now signs that audience figures for all types of theatres are picking up again.

Opera in Britain occupies a similar position to that of the theatres, and is divided into subsidized, commercial and amateur companies. The Royal Opera House in London provides for the Royal Opera, which supplies London seasons and occasional regional tours. The English National Opera Company provides a similar service from its base in London, and there is a range of other opera companies, both in London and the regions, such as the English Opera Group, the Welsh National Opera and the Scottish Opera Company. There are also several light opera groups, and ballet companies such as the Ballet Rambert, the London Festival Ballet, the Scottish Theatre Ballet and the Royal Ballet, which operates in London and Birmingham. A number of contemporary dance companies have also been formed in recent years.

Britain has many quality orchestras, although most of them are based in London, such as the London Philharmonic, the Royal Philharmonic and the BBC Symphony Orchestra. There are regional symphony orchestras, such as the Halle in Manchester, and a number of chamber groups in London and the regions. Most of the opera, ballet and orchestra activities have their greatest appeal in London, and still cater only for a minority of the people. But more popular forms, such as brass bands, choral singing and light music, have a large following. The more exclusive entertainments are heavily dependent upon Arts Council subsidies, local government grants and private donations.

Britain's operatic, dance and classical music offerings can compete against international rivals. But British popular music had led the world since the 1960s. However, in recent years, there has been a staleness in the popular field which has affected mainstream, avant-garde and 'ethnic' music alike. Some critics attribute this to commercial manipulation, and others to a lack of substantial and consistent talent. Whatever the reason, British popular music today seems to have lost its international leadership.

There is a wide range of museums and art galleries in Britain, which provide for a variety of tastes. Most of them are financed and controlled by local authorities, although some are commercial ventures and others, such as national institutions like the British Museum and the National Gallery in London, are the province of the Heritage Minister. In the past, entry to most of the public museums and art galleries was free, but in recent years entrance fees have been charged for some institutions. This development has led to protests from those people who regard such facilities as part of the national educational and cultural heritage, which should be available to all without charge. But museums and art galleries are also finding it difficult to operate on limited funds, and are dependent upon local government grants and Arts Council subsidies.

The history of the cinema in Britain has shown a considerable decline since its early days as a very popular form of mass entertainment, and from 1946 when annual visits reached a total of 1.6 billion. The domestic British film industry has virtually ceased to exist because of a lack of investment and government help. But British films with British actors continue to be made abroad and in Britain with foreign financial backing.

Many cinemas have now either gone out of business completely, or have changed to other activities such as dancing and bingo. In 1960 there were over 3,000 cinemas in Britain. Today there are 1,854 cinema screens which are situated either in single buildings or in multi-screen cinemas. Annual audience figures dropped from some 501 million in 1960 to 193 million in 1970. This decline was hastened by the arrival of television, and has continued as new forms of home entertainment, such as videos, have increased. However, although admissions sank to 55 million by 1984, there was an increase to 113 million in 1993. This improvement in audience figures has been encouraged by cheaper tickets, a wider range of films, responses to competition and the provision of an alternative leisure activity within more modern surroundings, such as multi-screen cinemas. But apparently more than 30 per cent of the population never go to the cinema, and 47 per cent of those aged over 35 never go.

As in sport, certain arts activities and their associated buildings have become virtual institutions, such as the West End, repertory companies, the Last Night of the Proms, the Royal Opera House in Covent Garden, the Albert Hall, the Royal Festival Hall, the National Theatre, the Tate and National Galleries, and the Shakespeare Memorial Theatre at Stratford-upon-Avon.

ATTITUDES

Attitudes to leisure, sports and the arts

MORI public opinion polls in 1990 showed that Britain's cultural life was thriving, and that a large number of people participate in a variety of available pastimes, sometimes with surprising priorities. One poll asked interviewees 'which, if any, of these have you been to in the past twelve month?', with the following results: library (49 per cent), cinema (32), museum (27), theatre (25), art exhibition (17), football match (14), pantomime (13), orchestral concert (10), pop concert (10), modern dance (8), opera (3) and classical ballet (2).

A second poll asked interviewees 'which of these things have you done in the past month?', with the following results: watched television or a video (89 per cent), read a book (64), had friends round to your home for a meal or a drink (51), been to a restaurant (49), been to pubs (46), general exercise and keep fit (42), gardening (40), do-it-yourself (39), been away for a weekend (23), been to a sports club (20), been to a cinema (16), competitive sport (16), been to a nightclub or disco (15), been to the theatre (15), been

to a social or working men's club (15), been away on holiday (13), and been to a wine bar (12). The interesting point
in this list is the popularity and second place of reading.

The authors of *We British* (which includes the above
polls) concluded from their investigations that 'we can report
that the nation is in no telly-induced trance. Its tastes mix
watching and doing, "high" and "low" cultures, with a rich-
ness that contradicts the stereotypes of the British as divided
between mindless lager louts and equally money-grubbing
consumers. The mix we have found will not please every-
body. Not enough football for some, not enough opera for
others. But that is what we should expect in the culture of a
whole nation' (*We British*, p. 133).

EXERCISES

■ Explain and examine the following terms:

do-it-yourself	the pub	rugby football
package tour	wine bar	sponsorship
bear baiting	darts	'bed and breakfast'
high culture	cricket	the Arts Council
'West End'	brass bands	repertory theatres
football pools	'ethnic restaurants'	multi-screen cinemas

■ Write short essays on the following questions:

1   What do the above opinion polls reveal about the
    British people? Should one trust the polls?

2   What is your impression of the British people, in terms
    of their leisure, sporting and artistic activities?

Bibliography

Annual Abstract of Statistics, Central Statistical Office, London: HMSO.

Britain: An Official Handbook, annual, Central Office of Information, London: HMSO.

British Crime Survey, annual, Home Office, London: HMSO.

Criminal Statistics, England and Wales, annual, London: HMSO.

Education Statistics for the United Kingdom, annual, London: HMSO.

Gallup public opinion polls, occasional and annual.

Jacobs, E. and Worcester, R. (1990) *We British: Britain under the Moriscope*, London: Weidenfeld and Nicolson.

Jowell, R. and Airey, C. (1984) *British Social Attitudes: 1984*, Aldershot: Gower.

Jowell, R. and Airey, C. (1987) *British Social Attitudes: 1987*, Aldershot: Gower.

Jowell, R. and Witherspoon, S. (1985) *British Social Attitudes: 1985*, Aldershot: Gower.

Jowell, R., Witherspoon, S. and Brook, L. (1986) *British Social Attitudes: 1986*, Aldershot: Gower.

Jowell, R., Witherspoon, S. and Brook, L. (1988) *British Social Attitudes: 1988–89*, Aldershot: Gower.

Jowell, R., Brook, L. and Taylor, B. (1991) *British Social Attitudes: 1991–92*, Aldershot: Dartmouth Publishing.

Jowell, R., Brook, L., Prior, G. and Taylor, B. (1992) *British Social Attitudes: 1992–93*, Aldershot: Dartmouth Publishing.

Key Data, annual, Central Statistical Office, London: HMSO.

Macey, J.P. (1980) *Housing Act, 1980*, London: Estates Gazette.

Market and Opinion Research International (MORI), for *The Times* and *Sunday Times*, regular surveys.

Population Trends, quarterly, London: HMSO.

Regional Trends, annual, Central Statistical Office, London: HMSO.

Social Trends, annual, Central Statistical Office, London: HMSO.

Sunday Times, weekly newspaper of record, London.

The Commonwealth Year Book, annual, London: HMSO.

The Economist, weekly magazine of record, London.

The Times, daily newspaper of record, London.

The World Almanac and Book of Facts, annual publication, London: Macmillan.

UK Media Yearbook, annual, London: Zenith Media.

Whitaker's Almanack, annual publication, London: Whitaker.

Suggested further reading

Survey books on British civilization

Bromhead, P. (1992) *Life in Modern Britain*, London: Longman.

Irwin, J. (1994) *Modern Britain: An Introduction*, London: Routledge.

McDowall, D. (1993) *Britain in Close-up*, London: Longman.

Sevaldsen, J. and Vadmand, O. (1993) *Contemporary British Society*, Copenhagen: Akademisk Forlag.

History

Calvocoressi, P. (1978) *The British Experience 1945–75*, London: Bodley Head.

Haigh, C. (1990) *The Cambridge Historical Encyclopaedia of Great Britain and Ireland*, Cambridge: Cambridge University Press.

Isaacs, A. and Monk, J. (1986) *The Cambridge Illustrated Dictionary of British Heritage*, Cambridge: Cambridge University Press.

SUGGESTED FURTHER READING

Kearney, H. (1990) *The British Isles: A History of Four Nations*, Cambridge: Cambridge University Press.

Marwick, A. (1987) *British Society since 1945*, London: Pelican.

Marwick, A. (1991) *Culture in Britain since 1945*, Oxford: Blackwell.

Morgan, K.O. (1986) *The Oxford Illustrated History of Britain*, Oxford: Oxford University Press.

Pounds, N.J.G. (1994) *The Culture of the English People*, Cambridge: Cambridge University Press.

Roebuck, J. (1982) *The Making of Modern English Society from 1850*, London: Routledge and Kegan Paul.

Society

Abercrombie, N. and Wardle, A. (1988) *Contemporary British Society: A New Introduction to Sociology*, London: Polity Press.

Fothergill, S. and Vincent, J. (1985) *The State of the Nation: An Atlas of Britain in the Eighties*, London: Pan Books.

Goldthorpe, J.H. (1989) *Social Mobility and Class Structure*, Oxford: Oxford University Press.

Halsey, A., Heath, A.F. and Ridge, J.M. (1980) *Origins and Destinations: Family, Class and Education*, Oxford: Oxford University Press.

Hamnett, C., McDowell, L. and Sarre, P. (1989) *The Changing Social Structure*, London: SAGE/Open University.

Sampson, A. (1983) *The Changing Anatomy of Britain*, London: Hodder and Stoughton.

Sampson, A. (1992) *The Essential Anatomy of Britain*, London: Hodder and Stoughton.

Smith, D. (1994) *North and South*, London: Penguin.

Politics and economics

Blondel, J. (1981) *Voters, Parties and Leaders*, London: Pelican.

Coxall, B. and Robins, L. (1989) *Contemporary British Politics: An Introduction*, London: Macmillan.

Donaldson, P. and Farquhar, J. (1988) *Understanding the British Economy*, London: Penguin.

Gamble, A. (1985) *Britain in Decline: Economic Policy, Political Strategy and the British State*, London: Macmillan.

Gamble, A. (1988) *The Free Economy and the Strong State: The Politics of Thatcherism*, London: Macmillan.

Johnson, P. (1994) *Twentieth-Century Britain: Economic, Social and Cultural Change*, London: Longman.

Jones, B. and Kavanagh, D. (1991) *British Politics Today*, Manchester: Manchester University Press.

Leys, C. (1989) *Politics in Britain: From Labourism to Thatcherism*, London: Verso.

May, T. (1987) *An Economic and Social History of Britain 1760–1970*, London: Longman.

Michie, J. (1992) *The Economic Legacy 1979–1992*, London: Academic Press.

Moran, M. (1989) *Politics and Society in Britain: An Introduction*, London: Macmillan.

Pearce, M. and Stewart, G. (1992) *British Political History 1867–1990: Democracy and Decline*, London: Routledge.

Robbins, K. (1983) *The Eclipse of a Great Power: Modern Britain 1870–1975*, London: Longman.

Savage, S.P. and Robins, L. (1990) *Public Policy under Thatcher*, London: Macmillan.

Scott, J. (1992) *Who Rules Britain?*, London: Polity Press.

Sked, A. and Cook, C. (1986) *Post-War Britain: A Political History*, London: Pelican.

Wiener, M.J. (1985) *English Culture and the Decline of the Industrial Spirit*, London: Pelican.

European union

Freestone, D.A.C. and Davidson, J.S. (1988) *The Institutional Framework of the European Communities*, London: Croom Helm.

George, S. (1991) *Britain and European Integration since 1945*, Oxford: Blackwell.

George, S. (1992) *An Awkward Partner: Britain in the European Community*, Oxford: Oxford University Press.

Nugent, N. (1991) *The Government and Politics of the European Community*, London: Macmillan.

Northern Ireland and Eire

Boyle, K. and Hadden, T. (1985) *Ireland: A Positive Proposal*, London: Penguin.

Darby, J. (1983) *Northern Ireland: The Background to the Conflict*, Belfast: The Appletree Press.

Kee, R. (1982) *Ireland: A History*, London: Abacus.

Law and civil liberties

Ewing, K.D. and Gearty, C.A. (1990) *Freedom under Thatcher: Civil Liberties in Modern Britain*, Oxford: Clarendon Press.

Michael, J. (1982) *The Politics of Secrecy*, London: Pelican.

Robertson, G. (1989) *Freedom, the Individual and the Law*, London: Pelican.

Spencer, J.R. (1989) *Jackson's Machinery of Justice*, Cambridge: Cambridge University Press.

Local government

Butcher, H., Law, I.G., Leach, R. and Mullard, M. (1990) *Local Government and Thatcherism*, London: Routledge.

Byrne, T. (1986) *Local Government in Britain*, London: Pelican.

Elcock, H. (1994) *Local Government: Policy and Management in Local Authorities*, London: Routledge.

Redcliffe-Maud, Lord and Wood, B. (1974) *English Local Government Reformed*, Oxford: Oxford University Press.

Stoker, G. (1991) *The Politics of Local Government*, London: Macmillan.

The media

Curran, J. and Seaton, J. (1991) *Power without Responsibility: The Press and Broadcasting in Britain*, London: Routledge.

McNair, B. (1994) *News and Journalism in the UK*, London: Routledge.

Negrine, R. (1994) *Politics and the Mass Media in Britain*, London: Routledge.

Multiracial Britain

Gilroy, P. (1992) *There Ain't No Black in the Union Jack*, London: Routledge.

Hiro, D. (1992) *Black British: White British*, London: Paladin.

Holmes, C. (1991) *A Tolerant Country? Immigrants, Refugees and Minorities in Britain*, London: Faber and Faber.

Layton-Henry, Z. (1992) *The Politics of Immigration*, Oxford: Blackwell.

Solomos, J. (1989) *Race and Racism in Contemporary Britain*, London: Macmillan.

Walvin, J. (1984) *Passage to Britain*, London: Pelican.

Walvin, J. (1993) *Black Ivory: A History of British Slavery*, London: Fontana.

Welfare state

Davidson, N. and Townsend, P. (1982) *Inequalities in Health*, London: Penguin.

Harrison, S. (1990) *The Dynamics of British Health Policy*, London: Routledge.

Hay, J.R. (1978) *The Development of the British Welfare State 1800–1975*, London: Edward Arnold.

Hill, M. (1993) *The Welfare State in Britain: A Political History since 1945*, Guildford: Edward Elgar.

Johnson, N. (1990) *Reconstructing the Welfare State*, London: Harvester Wheatsheaf.

Townsend, P. (1979) *Poverty in the United Kingdom*, London: Penguin.

Vaizey, J. (1984) *National Health*, Oxford: Martin Robertson.

Environment

Rose, C. (1991) *The Dirty Man of Europe*, London: Simon and Schuster.

Index

adult education 260
Advisory, Conciliation and
  Arbitration Service
  (ACAS) 207
agricultural revolutions 45
agriculture 23
archbishops (Church of
  England) 81, 301
arts (the) 328
Arts Council 328
aviation, civil 34; military
  130

back-bencher 93
bail 163
balance of payments 186
Bank of England (the) 198
banks 199
Baptists (the) 307
barristers 174
BBC (the) 278, 280
Beveridge Report (the)
  217, 223
bills (parliamentary) 97
bishops (Church of
  England) 81, 301

boroughs 112; London
  115
Britain 12
Britishness 58
British Telecom 35
broadcasting media (the)
  278
building societies 232
by-election 81

Cabinet (the) 101
cable television 284
Chancellor of the
  Exchequer 101
Channel 4 283
Channel Islands 12
Channel Tunnel 4, 33
Christianity 299
Church of England 299
Church of Scotland 303
cinema 331
Citizens' Charter 209
City (of London) 115
civil courts 159
civil defence 131
civil law 148

civil law appeals 161
civil law procedure 161
Civil List 78
civil servants 102
Civil War 68
class structure 190
climate 21
coal 28, 29
Common Agricultural Policy 25
common law 151
Commonwealth (the) 133
communications 35
comprehensive schools 245
Confederation of British Industry
    (CBI) 206
Conservative Party 90
constituencies 85
constitution (the) 73
consumer protection 208
council housing 122
councillors (local government) 119
council tax (local government) 122
counties 112
county councils 113, 115
county courts 159
crime and punishment 168
criminal courts 153
criminal law 148; appeals 158
criminal procedure 162
crown courts 156

defence policy 128
deindustrialization 187
delegated legislation 98
deregulation 183
devolution 60, 119
Director of Public Prosecutions
    (DPP) 162
district councils 116
divorce 218
doctors 224, 227

economic history 180
economic performance 186, 189
economic policies 182, 189
economic structure 184
education (English school history)
    240

education, further and adult 260;
    higher 255; schools 246
Eire 12, 140
elections (parliamentary) 85
electricity 29
emigration 54
employers' organizations 206
employment 193
energy sources 28
England (geography) 18
environment (the) 36
European Union (EU) 4, 135

family credit 221
family structure 217
financial institutions 197
fisheries 26
Fleet Street 271
foreign policy 128
forestry 27
Free Churches (the) 306

GCE A levels 255
GCSE 254
Glorious Revolution (the) 69
government (the) 100
government departments 102
grammar schools 240, 243
grants, government 122; student
    258
Great Britain 12, 47
Greater London Council (GLC) 115

hereditary peers 81
High-Church (Church of England)
    298, 301
High Court 159, 161
Hindus 310
holidays 321
hospitals 223, 227
House of Commons 84
House of Lords 81
housing 231

immigration 45
income support 221
Independent Broadcasting
    Authority (IBA) 279

independent schools 249
Independent Television
  Commission (ITC) 282
industrial and commercial
  institutions 202
industrial relations 206
industrial revolutions 48, 180
Inns of Court 174
institutions 1
IRA 142
Irish Republic (Eire) 12, 140
Isle of Man 12
ITV 282

Jewish community 308
judges 175
Judicial Committee of the Privy
  Council 80
jury 166
Justices of the Peace 150, 153

Labour Party 89
Law Lords 81
Law Society 173
law sources (England) 150
Leader of the Opposition 93
legal aid 168
legal history (English) 149
legal profession 173
legislation (parliamentary) 95
leisure activities 318
Liberal and Social Democrats, the 91
life peers 81
Lloyd's 200
local elections 119
Local Education Authorities
  (LEAs) 243, 245
local government: functions 119;
  history (England) 111; reorganization 113
Lord Chancellor 175
Lords Spiritual 81
Lords Temporal 81
Low-Church (Church of England)
  297, 301

magistrates 153
magistrates' courts 153

Magna Carta 67
marriage 218
media 266; freedom of expression
  286; ownership 286
Members of Parliament (MPs) 84
Methodists 306
ministerial responsibility 102
ministers (government) 100
mixed economy 184
monarchy (the) 76
mortgage 232
museums 331
Muslims 309

National Curriculum 254
National Health Service (NHS)
  223
national identity 58
national insurance 217, 221
nationalization 183
NATO 129
newspapers 266, 267
Northern Ireland 140; geography
  20
nuclear deterrent 130
nuclear power 29

Open University 259

parishes 112, 301
Parliament 80
parliamentary control of government 104
parliamentary electoral system 85;
  legislation 97; procedure 95
party political system 89
periodicals and magazines 277
physical features (Britain) 13
Plaid Cymru 91, 123
police 171
political history (English) 66
Poor Law (Elizabethan) 215
Poor Law Amendment Act 216
population 56
ports and shipping 33
Post Office (the) 35
preparatory schools 251
primary schools 247

Prime Minister (the) 100
private member's bill 97
private sector 184
privatization 183
Privy Council 79
public houses (pubs) 320
public schools 250
public sector 184
punishment and law enforcement
    168

Queen's Counsel 175
Question Time 104

race relations 52
radio 281, 283
Radio Authority (the) 283
railways 32
rainfall 21
ratings (media) 285
referendum 136
Reform Acts 71
regions and regionalism 12, 30
religion (history) 294
religion (schools) 312
roads 31
Roman Catholic Church 304
Royal Assent 98
Royal Ulster constabulary 142,
    171

Salvation Army 307
satellite television 284
school examinations 251
school history (English) 240
school organization 251
Scotland (geography) 19
Scottish National Party 60, 123
select committees 105
service sector 188, 194

shadow cabinet 93
social security 221
social services 230
social welfare (history) 215
solicitors 173
Speaker (the) 96
sports 322
state schools 246
statute law 151
stipendiary magistrates 156
Stock Exchange 199
strikes 204
sunshine 22

television 285
temperature 21
Thatcherism 5
theatre 329
trade unions 202
Trades Union Congress (TUC) 203
transport 31
Trident missiles 130
two-party system 69, 89

unemployment 195
Unionists 142
United Kingdom 12
universities 256

video recorders 284, 320
voluntary schools 243
voluntary services 230

Wales (geography) 18
Whips 95
workforce (the) 193
workhouses 216

Youth Courts 155
Youth Training 196